I would like to think that in my
journey through life I have helped
make a difference.

EUGENE O'CALLAGHAN

'Oliver, Oliver! Never before has this boy asked for more!'

Eugene O'Callaghan

Busmen in the firing line

ULSTER HISTORICAL FOUNDATION

It should never be forgotten that it was Eugene
O'Callaghan who got us up off our knees and gave
us respect and credibility when it mattered most.

LIAM HUGHES

FRONT COVER IMAGE: Bloody Friday, Oxford Street Bus Station.
Courtesy © British Pathé Ltd

BACK COVER IMAGE: TGWU, Transport House, Belfast.
Courtesy Arnaud Roger, Belfast, https://flickr.com/ar271

FRONTISPIECE IMAGE: Drawing of Eugene O'Callaghan and Werner Heubeck
presented to Eugene as a gift by a fellow busman.
PRIVATE COLLECTION

The recounted memories and views expressed in this book are those of the
author and not necessarily those of the Ulster Historical Foundation.
While every effort was made to verify his account, due to the passage of
time this was not always possible.

Published 2019
by Ulster Historical Foundation
www.booksireland.org.uk
www.ancestryireland.com

© The estate of Eugene O'Callaghan

ISBN 978-1-909556-68-3

Printed by Gutenberg Press Ltd
Design by Dunbar Design

Contents

I would like to emphasise that this memoir is my view of the events with which I was involved during my working life and since retirement, and the comments, where made, are very much my own views as I saw them. I have made efforts to verify the facts where I can, as far as possible from my own records and recollection, from public records, freedom of information requests and also from speaking with former colleagues who were involved.

In telling my story I have sought to keep the 'cause' – social justice for working men and women – as the focus, and not to level criticism at individuals unduly, though on occasion for narrative purposes some individuals are referred to by name. However, where possible, I have sought to omit personal names.

I offer an apology in advance to anyone who might feel offended at my account of events. I would freely acknowledge that this book is not intended to be definitive and that each of those involved will have their own perspective. This is my – Eugene O'Callaghan's – story. It is not history, but one man's view of history, and the troubled period my colleagues and I lived and worked through.

EUGENE O'CALLAGHAN

Preface

As word got out among family, friends and former colleagues that I have been writing this book of battles, buses, recollections and reflections, I am often asked 'why am I doing this, and why now?'

The answer is summed up in two words: 'Unfinished business'. All my working life I have been heavily involved in fighting for justice for working men and women and that is what this book is primarily about. It is the thread which runs through and connects this collection of memories; it is where my story opens and where I finish it as best I can.

Everything I have lived through shows beyond any doubt that working people only ever get anything approaching a decent standard of living and economic justice when they organise themselves and stand up for themselves – or in the words of Jim Larkin[1] – 'The great are only great because we are on our knees. Let us arise!'

Unfortunately, the moment working people forget this truth they start to lose out again. And working people are now being pushed back because they have forgotten the need to stand together and to stand up for each other. Look now at the millions on zero hours contracts, the millions dependent on benefits. Let us not forget the many being victimised by austerity and the wholesale dismantling of the welfare state. Look at the growing inequality and the trade union movement declining in numbers and too often losing the skills and determination to fight for justice. The list could go on.

But the final straw, compelling me to write this book, was an injustice that needs to be righted. I refer to the discrepancy between the pensions busmen who retired

Statue of James Larkin on Donegall Street Place, Lower Donegall Street, Belfast
WILLIAM ROULSTON

before 2002 received and the significantly larger pensions they would have received if their employer had fully and faithfully honoured the legally binding agreement it had with the unions on the contributions that the workers and the employer were to make towards funding pensions. It is the last battle I became involved in. A victory was won; a moral victory certainly and it is there on the record. A financial victory was also won but it was only a poor shadow of what it should have been.

The busmen did not obtain the full and conclusive victory to which they were entitled. The men – and now too sadly it is often their widows – did not receive the economic justice to which all men and women in a free society are entitled. Perhaps even worse, they did not succeed in holding to public account those who wilfully or incompetently deprived them of their just entitlements. It is not that they lost a battle: it is that they could never obtain a proper hearing of their case. Indifference to the fate of working men and women is the most powerful driver of injustice in our society today.

So I, writing this towards the end of my ninth decade, am dedicating this book to my colleagues who manned the buses during the Troubles; risking their lives on a daily basis; many of whom indeed paid a high price for doing so – and many, despite injury, trauma and grief at the murder of colleagues, were to be cheated on their pensions when it was all over. I am writing it in the hope that it will inspire others to continue this battle for justice for the heroic busmen of Northern Ireland.

Eugene as a bus driver, 1956

Most of my working life was shaped and dominated by the transport industry in which I initially worked as a bus driver. Later I became a full-time official of the Amalgamated Transport and General Workers' Union (ATGWU). But it nearly did not happen. That it happened at all was due to an overheard conversation in a bar.

How I obtained a job on the buses is in itself a snapshot of what life was like in the Northern Ireland of the 1950s – its bad side and its quixotically humorous, but only semi-redeeming features.

I was encouraged by my brother-in-law, Paddy Clerkin, who owned the Ulster Vaults at the corner of Memel Street, to apply for a job on the buses. After submitting my application I was granted an interview with a Mr Young, the personnel manager, in Utility Street. The interview lasted approximately two minutes; I was turned down for the job.

I made my way back to my brother-in-law's pub and in the course of informing him that they had turned me down was overheard by a Mr Eddie Rossbottom who was a regular customer who worked across the road in Wilson Supplies.

Mr Rossbottom, butting into our conversation, asked who had interviewed me. When I told him that it was a Mr F. Young he asked if I minded if he spoke with him. He went on to say that Mr Young was a member of his lodge and that he, Eddie Rossbottom, was the Worshipful Master. I laughed and told him to please himself.

Mr Rossbottom went to make his phone call. In the empty bar I could not help overhearing parts of the conversation. It included things along the lines of: 'Don't mind his Free State accent – he's one of ours; his people were from down south but they were put out'. When he rejoined us he told me to go and see Mr Young again. After being assured that this was not a joke I did what he asked. Mr Young gave me a letter and directed me to take it to Dr Stitt, the company doctor. Following a medical examination I was told to report back to Mr Young.

On my return Mr Young advised that I had passed my medical examination. He gave me a note and told me to be at Utility Street on the following Monday morning. A driving instructor would pick me up and I would begin training as a trolley bus driver. I went back to thank Mr Rossbottom who asked me to bring him back – the next time I was in the countryside – 'two good sized cock chickens'.

In this strange way began my career as both a bus driver and as a trade union activist and an advocate of the worth and dignity of my fellow workers. There were dark and difficult times ahead which few if any foresaw in 1956. But you need to have a belief in what you are doing and one of the greatest things in my lifetime was that I was started on a path through which I found a job I liked doing and I got somebody to pay me to do it. And that was wonderful.

Introduction

'Politically, the trade union movement in the six
counties is a study in paradox', wrote Andrew Boyd,
a veteran critic of the trade union leadership in
Northern Ireland.[1]

As Eugene O'Callaghan illustrates, the paradox is not confined to politics.
It extends to industrial relations, internal democracy, and the key issues
of equality and discrimination. We have in Northern Ireland a trade
unionism which is largely British-based, but within the remit of the
Dublin-based Irish Congress of Trade Unions (ICTU), largely Protestant,
historically, and ostensibly anti-Unionist, mainly Unionist and notionally
socialist, impeccably anti-sectarian in theory and slow to tackle the
problem in practice, and a model of cross-community solidarity but so
often spancelled by the brittle unity of Catholics and Protestants.[2] The
contradictions in the movement are easily criticised, but have they been
an operational necessity for a cross-community and secular movement
functioning where the sectarian divisions in Northern Ireland run deepest?

The unlikely story of how O'Callaghan got a job on the buses is a good
place to start. From its origins in the linen trades, Ulster had one,
Protestant owned, industrial economy in which Catholics were a subaltern
caste. One economy meant one workforce and created a dynamic for one
trade union movement. As Protestants predominated in most trades, they
predominated too in the trade unions, which, up to the 1890s, were
almost entirely confined to skilled men. The process of unionisation was
overlain in the late nineteenth century by the extension of British-based
unions – or 'amalgamateds' as they are known euphemistically, as so
many were originally styled 'Amalgamated Society of ...' – to Ireland.
The amalgamateds easily absorbed or marginalised the small, local trade
societies, and sidelined too the competing forces of Unionism and
nationalism, within the unions at least. As British unions were the most
powerful in the world, and as Ireland was undergoing extensive

Belfast Corporation
Daimler Fleetline
No. 703 on the
Ballygomartin Road
en route to its
terminus, a short way
on at Ardoyne. This
bus was new in 1964

HOWARD CUNNINGHAM

1

anglicisation in the decades after the Great Famine, it was relatively easy for them to bring to Ireland not just their organisation, but their views on the appropriate relationship between Labour and society, politics, and religion. That Ireland was a part of the United Kingdom (UK), and governed by the same labour legislation, made it seem all the more natural that workers should adopt, rather than adapt, the British model. So despite the intensity of political and religious divisions in Ulster, the acute problem of de-industrialisation in the south, and the weakness of socialism throughout the island, Ireland borrowed a form of trade unionism developed by a highly industrialised country, and one that was secular, and non-ideological but leaning to the Liberals and, later, the Labour Party. By 1900, about three-quarters of the trade unionists in Ireland were in the amalgamateds, but out of some 900,000 waged workers, only 70,000 were unionised.[3]

It was not long before Irish circumstances began to compel modifications of the British model. In 1894, union officials unhappy at their irrelevance within the mighty British Trades Union Congress (TUC), and anxious to address the issue of re-building the southern economy, formed the breakaway Irish Trades Union Congress (ITUC). It was a decision the amalgamateds and the TUC gradually, and reluctantly, learned to live with. The most serious breach with Britain was initiated by Jim Larkin, Ireland's best-known Labour leader and clearly a hero to O'Callaghan. Coincidentally, 'Big Jim' claimed to have been born with his mother's people in Tamnaharry, south Down, not far from O'Callaghan's Crossmaglen.[4] Larkin was sent to Ireland in 1907 to promote the Liverpool-based National Union of Dock Labourers. Less than two years later he broke with Liverpool and launched the Irish Transport and General Workers' Union (ITGWU), arguing that only Irish unions would tackle the problems of Irish workers. The spectacular growth of the ITGWU – it mushroomed from 5,000 to 120,000 members between 1917 and 1920 – meant that when the Free State was founded, some three-quarters of its trade unionists were in Irish unions, the amalgamateds retaining strongholds among dockers and in the craft sector. By contrast, the ITGWU had made little headway in Ulster. Both Catholics and Protestants were wary of its brash militancy and republicanism.

There were grounds for a partition of industrial Labour in 1921, as political Labour would split in 1924 with the formation of the Northern

Ireland Labour Party (NILP). Dublin-based unions had a tiny presence, and the ITUC was scarcely active in the North. But relations between Unionists and trade unionists were poor. The former regarded Labour as anti-partition, which indeed it was. In 1918 the Unionist Party launched the Ulster Unionist Labour Association and James Turkington promoted the Ulster Workers' Trade Union as an alternative to the ITGWU. The great bulk of workers saw Turkington's union as a sectarian intrusion onto the shopfloor, too close to employers, and 'yellow'. The amalgamateds served as the default option. Their politics might be obnoxious to most Protestant workers, and their affiliation to the NILP resented, but as long as they could deliver on wages and conditions, they were acceptable. Similarly, unions and trades councils on both sides of the new border continued to affiliate to the ITUC. The amalgamateds had no wish to jeopardise their membership in the Free State by seeking the extension of the British Trades Union Congress to Northern Ireland and they feared an 'Ulster TUC' would be prey to a loyalist take-over.

The growing leverage of trade unions during the Second World War and criticism of its silence on the six-county affairs led the ITUC to appoint a Northern Ireland Committee (NIC) in 1944. While the NIC evolved into a de facto congress, there remained a concern to keep it under wraps. Motions at its annual conferences were devised by the Committee itself, and had to be ratified by the ITUC executive. A key aim of the NIC was to secure recognition from state agencies. After some initial uncertainty, the government decided in 1950 that it would have no truck with the NIC on the grounds that it was headquartered in a foreign country. Stormont urged the creation of 'Ulster' alternatives instead. Remarkably, the NIC won solid backing from its affiliates in a selective boycott of the administration. This was all the more unusual in the heightened atmosphere of the time. The ITUC had split in 1945 when unions demanding the exclusion of the amalgamateds from Ireland decamped to form the Congress of Irish Unions, and the NILP split over the national question in 1949. Both congresses re-united as the ICTU in 1959. Fortunately for the NIC, the 1960s was a decade when tripartite consultation between government, employers, and unions was deemed to be essential for economic development. Under pressure from the business community and Protestant churches, and fearful of what might be demanded of it by a Labour Prime Minister in Westminster, Stormont caved in and recognised the ICTU's NIC in 1964.

Partition nearly coincided with the foundation of O'Callaghan's union, the Transport and General Workers (or T&G as it was usually called) in 1922, from a merger of 14 societies. It would remain the biggest union in the UK throughout the twentieth century, and a powerful influence within the British Labour Party.[5] In Ireland, its region 11, it operated on both sides of the border and was known as the Amalgamated Transport and General Workers' Union (ATGWU), following legal action by the ITGWU over its title. No love was lost between the two. O'Callaghan spent most of his days as a busman and union official in the golden age of trade unionism in Northern Ireland.

Largely confined to craftsmen up to the Second World War, unions acquired a mass base when the war brought near full employment. Membership continued to rise after 1945, reaching about 200,000 by 1953 and 263,000 by 1970, when 54 per cent of employees were unionised, compared with 52 per cent in the Republic and 49 per cent in Britain. Unions had a very traditional profile, dominated by the 'three Ms' – male, manual, and manufacturing. Density, the proportion of employees in unions, was high for men (66 per cent), low for women (36 per cent), and membership was still predominantly male (74 per cent) and blue-collar (69 per cent). Though the proportion of female and white-collar trade unionists was increasing, O'Callaghan noted of the early 1970s, 'women bus drivers hadn't been heard of in Belfast in those days'. Women feature in the narrative as wives waiting anxiously for their husbands' return from late night shifts in trouble-torn streets, or widows surviving precariously on a busman's pension.

As Northern Ireland was a cross-section of the British movement, there were many unions of various types, with membership divided between 77 craft, industrial, and general societies. The ATGWU was by far the largest, with 83,200 members. The next biggest was the Amalgamated Engineering Union, with 27,300 members.[6] Unions reflected the religious composition of employment. A survey of 53 unions in 1959 found that of 379 branch secretaries, 80 per cent were Protestant. Catholics accounted for 46 per cent of branch secretaries in the mainly unskilled ATGWU and 12 per cent in the Amalgamated Engineering Union.[7]

Before the outbreak of the Troubles, the union agenda was relatively straightforward, if not easy. Wages strategy was simply to track cross-channel rates. Parity was largely attained in the public sector, where, for most, pay was negotiated on a UK basis, at regional level where employees came under the NIO, or under agreements providing for parity with analogous groups in Britain. In consequence, public sector wages were only slightly below British norms. Private sector wage bargaining also become more integrated with UK machinery, but local wage determination still applied to a large minority and, on average, wages in Northern Ireland were the lowest of any UK region. In 1999, weekly earnings for men in Northern Ireland amounted to £344.90, compared with a UK average of £398.70; for women, the respective figures were £295.10 and £325.60.[8] The high degree of aggregation of the workforce made the task of organisation much easier and less expensive. Two sectors loomed large. As late as the 1950s, almost half of employed men were in shipbuilding and engineering, and over 80 per cent of employed women were in textiles and clothing. The abiding problem was the continuing decline of these industries. An influx of external investment had underpinned economic growth in the 1960s. Government strategy was to continue the North's traditional specialisation in the UK economy, and it focused especially on synthetic fibres, which it regarded as an appropriate replacement for the withering textile and clothing sectors. By 1970, one quarter of the UK synthetic fibre industry was located in the North, in a small number of big plants, such as British Enkalon in Antrim town. With union recognition, and good pay and conditions, Enkalon was a prize for the ATGWU.[9]

The Troubles coincided with major changes in the economy and employment, and added to the difficulty of attracting inward investment. Competition from superior American products began to affect European synthetic fibres in 1971, and the energy-intensive industry was further hit by the oil crises of 1973 and 1979. Shipbuilding also suffered severely in the 1970s, and employment in Harland and Wolff had sunk to 7,400 by 1980. The problems of synthetics and shipbuilding reflected more general weaknesses arising from dependence on a sluggish British economy for investments and markets, and a relatively high reliance on oil for energy. Difficulties intensified in the early 1980s when Mrs Thatcher's government kept sterling strong to combat inflation. The year 1986 was a nadir. Manufacturing had fallen from 172,000 in 1974 to 105,000, unemployment reached a peak of 18 per cent, and Northern Ireland was commonly characterised as having a 'work-house economy', in which almost everyone was subsidised by the government, many private businesses being dependent on government grants or contracts. It was not

Eugene with John Freeman and Dickie Atwell, late 1970s

all bad news for the unions. The decline was offset by expansion of public services, so that between 1971 and 1986 the fall in total employment was slight, from 555,000 to 549,000.[10] Seeing unemployment as a source of paramilitarism, both Labour and Conservative governments treated Northern Ireland as a special case. Roy Mason especially, Secretary of State from 1977 to 1979, thought reducing unemployment was the way to drain support from the Provisionals. Despite, or possibly because of, their similarities, O'Callaghan was sceptical about Mason. Mason had trodden a path well-worn in the British Labour movement, but not available in Ireland. A miner in south Yorkshire at fourteen years of age, he became a branch official of the National Union of Mineworkers, went to university on a TUC scholarship – O'Callaghan would surely approve of this union investment in education – and was elected Labour MP for Barnsley. He had too an arrogant and opinionated manner, as O'Callaghan discovered, and his cavalier attitude to human rights in the suppression of republicans alienated even trenchant opponents of the Provisionals, such as Gerry Fitt, former leader of the Social Democratic and Labour Party (SDLP). Mason presided over a big expansion of the public sector, an area of high union density, and employment in the sector grew to a peak of 43 per cent of the labour force in 1986. He was also willing to subvent ailing enterprises like Enkalon. By 1983, union membership had peaked at 283,000, a density of 61 per cent, compared with a UK average of 54 per cent.[11] Mrs Thatcher was not so sympathetic to so-called 'lame ducks'. The refusal of her government to grant-aid Enkalon persuaded its German owners to close the plant in 1985, with the loss of 2,400 jobs. It was a blow to the ATGWU.

Relations between trade unions and the state are a salient theme in O'Callaghan's memoir. The enemy of my enemy being my friend, Stormont took a kindlier view of unions after the outbreak of the Troubles. A state subsidy of £10,000 per annum was awarded to the NIC in 1970.[12] Opportunities for unions to influence public policy improved further with the introduction of Direct Rule in 1972. The Stormont parliament was prorogued and its government replaced with the Northern Ireland Office (NIO), which comprised a Secretary of State and up to six junior ministers. Paradoxically, Direct Rule entailed a more regional approach to governance. Since 1921, the Unionist cabinets had pursued a policy of 'step by step', enacting nearly all Westminster legislation, even where Unionist MPs disagreed with it, to keep the law on both sides of the Irish Sea as similar as possible. Now that Northern Ireland was run by ministers who could come from anywhere in the UK but Northern Ireland, the NIO created a profusion of public bodies to advise and to offset the perceived 'democratic deficit'.

Colloquially and disparagingly known as quangos, an acronym for quasi-autonomous non-governmental organisations, they were criticised on all sides for the cronyism that was believed to be endemic in the appointments system. As the NIO was reluctant to engage those not known to be sympathetic to the regime – and this was an exceptionally large segment of the population in the 1970s and 1980s – it could not avoid fishing in a rockpool. By 2000, the NIC had representation on 40 of Northern Ireland's 144 quangos, dealing with human rights, industrial relations, the economy and society, education and training, and health and personal social services. A well-connected official of an important union could expect multiple appointments, lucrative additions to his salary, opportunities for travel, and the possibility of making further career-enhancing contacts. Inevitably, the system and the growing sense of entitlement at the top, generated resentment on the shopfloor.

O'Callaghan notes that seats on quangos were 'much sought after', that, in practice, they had to be endorsed by the NIC, creating a mutual interest between the NIO and the NIC, that they went to senior officials rather than rank and filers, and that they led to the union leadership becoming 'co-opted into the system'.

Under the Labour administrations of Harold Wilson and Jim Callaghan, NIC officials enjoyed 'free and easy' access to NIO ministers, and lobbied successfully for the extension of labour legislation to Northern Ireland, notably provisions of the Trade Union and Labour Relations Act (1974), the Employment Protection Act (1975), and the Trade Union and Labour Relations (Amendment) Act (1976). The T&G was a major financial supporter of the Labour Party, and the relationship did not exclude Belfast. The acclaimed political correspondent Peter Kellner wrote in the *New Statesman*: 'When the history of the British Labour Party in the 1980s comes to be written, the name of John Freeman, the left-wing Secretary of the T&GWU in Ireland, will figure very prominently because of the influence he wields within the Transport Union'.[13] Freeman was directly involved with the Labour Party, and co-ordinated Tony Benn's bid for the party's deputy leadership in 1981.

Some questioned the relevance of this to Northern Ireland, where unions had lost their traditional political home. To avoid disruption in its very mixed membership, the ATGWU had disaffiliated from the NILP after the party adopted a pro-Union line in 1949. Close, informal connections at leadership level persisted until the early 1970s when the polarisation of Belfast, a feeble response to escalating state repression, and the emergence of alternatives, eviscerated the NILP.[14] On all sides, it lost support: Catholics to the SDLP, Protestants to the Democratic Unionist Party, and liberals to the Alliance Party. Conflicting signals from London did not help, as the British Labour Party dithered over whether to tighten or loosen ties with a party hailed as fraternal by some, and derided as crypto-Unionist by others.

In 1969 Sir Harry Nicholas, Labour's General Secretary and a former Assistant General Secretary of the T&G, made the surprising suggestion that the NILP become a regional affiliate; the British Labour Party had always feared this implicitly pro-Union move would cost it a slice of the Irish vote. With about 200 delegates present at a special conference in the ATGWU's Transport House, a motion for affiliation was carried on the card vote of 20,000 trade unionists. Anti-partitionist members were outraged. At the same time, pro-Union comrades blamed the NILP's decline on the perception of Wilson as a united Irelander, and his party ignored the affiliation request. Internment, arguably, sealed the NILP's fate. As happened in the wake of the 1949 split, it contracted to areas like Woodvale, Victoria, and Newtownabbey, but unlike the 1950s these districts were experiencing an upsurge of loyalism which washed over the gunwales and turned it into an esoteric socialist sect. Jim Callaghan had his party sever its ties with the NILP in 1974.[15]

Eugene O'Callaghan thought donations to the British Labour Party were a waste of money. But when the Conservatives returned to power under Mrs Thatcher, the employers' body, the Confederation of British Industry, Northern Ireland (CBI-NI), did not forgive or forget its days of being less favoured by the NIO. Whether the NIC might have made more of its bargaining chips in fighting the Tories is a moot point. As the propaganda war for the representation of the North as a normal society plagued by a few terrorists persisted, so too did the NIO continue to cite unions as evidence of 'normality'. Among others, NIO under-secretary Chris Patten praised them as 'a civilizing influence in this community throughout the last fifteen years'. The annual subvention to the NIC grew fatter and fatter, reaching £76,000 in 1984.[16]

Conservative industrial relations Acts were extended to Northern Ireland tardily and with some mitigation. The NIC claimed credit, but it was standard practice for routine Westminster legislation to be applied selectively to the North after a two-year process of consultation with interested parties and quangos, and CBI-NI opinion usually carried more weight. The Employment Act (1980) was extended in 1982, though without the provision repealing union rights to seek assistance from the Labour Relations Agency (LRA) in recognition disputes. Norman Tebbit's contentious Employment Act (1982), outlawing secondary strike action, prompted the LRA to suggest that as an alternative to having the Act introduced to the North, the LRA, CBI-NI, and NIC form a Standing Conference which would distance the North from industrial disputes in Britain. The idea was obviously intended to be a step towards social partnership, and away from the inherited British system of free collective bargaining.

Though UK strikes rarely involved the North, and the Standing Conference concept was commended by the ICTU and the TUC, NIC affiliates rejected the proposal. It was another assertion of their ideological commitment to the mother-country and the British way of doing things. Ironically, unions in Britain would plead for social partnership when the Blair government showed no intention of reversing the Tories' anti-union legislation. 'Tebbit's law' was extended to the North in 1987. A third Industrial Relations (Northern Ireland) Order followed in 1992, applying the Employment Acts of 1988, 1989, and 1990. Arguably, the delays in bringing in the 1987 and 1992 orders stemmed from the need to secure union support for the Fair Employment Act (1989).[17] Despite the delays, strike activity fell more rapidly in Northern Ireland than in the UK as a whole in the 1980s. Over the 1977–80 period, an annual average of 664 working days per 1,000 employees were lost in Northern Ireland, compared with an average of 587 in the UK. In the period 1987–90, the respective figures were 111 and 149.[18] Some aspects of the pro-trade union tinge to NIO policy persisted into the 1990s, and the Industrial Development Board continued to take a broadly supportive position on union recognition in dealing with incoming companies.[19]

O'Callaghan's memoir is particularly valuable for its treatment of the taboo topic of sectarianism within the trade unions. For union officials, the Troubles generated an overriding concern with organisational unity and a more contingent interest in how to respond to questions of human rights. The contrast in their response to these issues became apparent in August 1969 when the unions' sluggish response to the civil rights campaign yielded to vigorous action on unity. The immediate objective was to ensure that this round of conflict did not lead to expulsions, as had happened in crises between 1864 and 1939. The shipyard was the obvious place to start. On 15 August 1969, shop stewards and churchmen, led by senior shop steward Sandy Scott, spoke to a meeting of 8,000 workers at Harland and Wolff to warn of the economic consequences of violence for a faltering industry. A similar appeal was made later at Shorts aircraft factory.[20]

O'Callaghan suggests that Scott's example would continue to impact on busmen over the succeeding decades. Officially, shopfloor sectarianism was nipped in the bud. The NIO would come to extol unions as havens of normality in a manner all the more curious for the vilification of militants across the water: 'Members with all types of religious affiliation, as well as atheists and communists have played a full part in the development of trade unionism … with hardly an exception, sectarianism stops at the factory gates'.[21] Reality was more chequered. Groups of

Catholics were evicted from the shipyard on four occasions between 1970 and 1972, reducing their numbers from 400 to 100 in the 10,000 strong workforce. Catholics were also run out of textile factories on Belfast's Donegall Road.[22] There were innumerable lesser incidents of intimidation, and a 'chill factor' took root to deter both Catholics and Protestants from working in areas they deemed unfriendly.

In August 1969 the NIC rushed out 30,000 copies of its *Programme for Peace and Progress in Northern Ireland*; the first of a series of manifestoes calling for the restoration of good order through stability, incremental reform, and economic improvement. The *Programme* also emphasised that the status of Northern Ireland within the UK could not be changed legally without the consent of the majority. On 9 September the NIC and Prime Minister James Chichester-Clark issued a joint communiqué affirming the government's commitment to reform.[23]

In 1972 the ICTU – with the backing of all affiliates – published its first statement of political policy on Northern Ireland. It began with an acknowledgement that 'political resolutions which went outside the scope of the Constitution of Congress' were routinely removed from its agenda; affirmed that it would not be 'appropriate' for the ICTU to comment on the constitutional status of Northern Ireland – though it would repeatedly endorse the status quo and later commend the 'peace process'; and suggested three bases for political dialogue: rejection of violence, acceptance of 'the principle of non-discrimination', and acceptance of the right to advocate peaceful political change.[24] While balanced and liberal in values, the unspoken rationale of Congress manifestoes on the North was to discourage Labour Unionism in general and shopfloor loyalism in particular. Aside from minor trouble in Derry in late 1968 and during the 1981 Hunger Strike, nationalist workers were quiescent. Loyalists had a tradition.

That tradition obviously haunted the ATGWU, and O'Callaghan conflates it with the story of the Ulster Transport and Allied Operatives' Union. Formed in 1942 by busmen in dissent with the ATGWU, the Ulster Transport was one of the very few 'Ulster' unions to meet with success, and that had much to do with the fact that it was the product of genuine shopfloor grievances as much as loyalism. Led by Hugh Minnis, it grew to a peak of 8,500 members, and became the largest Northern Ireland-based union. Though recognised by the Ulster Transport Authority, established under the Transport Act (1948) to run road and rail services, other unions treated it as a pariah, ostensibly for poaching, but primarily because it posed the threat of a sectarian divide in the entire movement. After 1952 the Ulster Transport and Allied Operatives' Union sank into terminal decline, and Minnis vainly sought employment with the ATGWU. In 1963, he persuaded the remaining members to vote for a merger with the National Union of General and Municipal Workers, later known as the GMB.[25] His reward was a job as an official. O'Callaghan suggests the General and Municipal Workers was playing the 'Orange card', and one must ask why it employed an official of a failed and fading union? Loyalist paramilitary mobilisation on the shopfloor would not be so easy to contain.

Loyalist workers organised soon after August 1969, with the formation of the Workers' Committee for the Defence of the Constitution by Billy Hull, a convenor of engineering shop stewards in Harland and Wolff. In 1971 the Committee became the Loyalist Association of Workers (LAW). The LAW led a march of 4,000 shipyardmen in February 1971 to demand internment, protested against the prorogation of Stormont in 1972, and ran a two-day strike in 1973 against the internment of loyalists. Hull hoped to turn the LAW into a working class Protestant party, but was opposed by Bill Craig, leader of the Vanguard Unionist Progressive Party. Hull plumped for Vanguard instead, the LAW disintegrated, and most members backed the Ulster Workers' Council (UWC) on its establishment in 1973 and argued for industrial political action. The UWC included various trade union activists, notably Harry Murray, a shipyard shop steward, and Glen Barr, an Engineering Union branch president, but amounted to no more than a committee. Its strength lay in its connections with the Ulster Defence Association (UDA) and workers in the power-stations. On 15 May 1974 it called a 'constitutional stoppage' to destroy the power-sharing executive and the Council of Ireland set up under the Sunningdale Agreement. The strike was poorly planned and ignored by 90 per cent of employees until the barricades of the Ulster Defence Association started a snowball of genuine enthusiasm. Unwilling to fight a war on two fronts, the British army did little to stop the intimidation. Power cuts were the UWC's trump card, and the power-stations were not brought under military control. As welfare offices closed, civil servants suggested that the loss of benefits might put pressure on the UWC. Paddy Devlin, the SDLP Minister of Health and Social Services, insisted they post out the welfare giros. In another act of self-defeating ideological correctness, the Labour government and the unions baulked at saying the stoppage was not a bona fide strike.

Unions called for business as usual, and on 18 May a meeting of 400 cadres of the Confederation of Shipbuilding and Engineering Unions and the Joint Industrial Council for the Electricity Supply Industry decided to organise two 'back to work marches', to the shipyard and to Castlereagh industrial estate. To counter jibes that unions answered to a 'foreign Congress', the Belfast march would be led by the TUC general secretary, Len Murray. The NIO thought the marches might be a turning point. Billy Blease, the ICTU's Northern Ireland officer, claimed subsequently that he knew it was hopeless, but felt the NIC had to be seen to be giving a lead.[26] No attempt was made to mobilise the rank and file, and it all looked awfully perfunctory. On 21 May, about 200 turned up for the march in Belfast – many of them peace activists – and 19 in Castlereagh. On 25 May, Wilson broadcast to the nation, denouncing 'people who spend their lives sponging on Westminster' and signing off: 'We intend to see it through …'. In reality, when anti-Sunningdale Unionists won eleven of the twelve Northern Ireland seats in the February 1974 Westminster election, the incoming Labour government concluded that Sunningdale was dead in the water. After the UWC called a 'total strike' on 27 May, threatening a complete power blackout and the disabling of sewage pumps, the pro-Sunningdale Unionists pulled the plug on the power-sharing executive. Normal service resumed on the shopfloor. No attempt was made to challenge the unions. Union membership actually increased as workers sought to recoup money lost during the strike. Talk about an 'Ulster TUC' came to nothing.

The threat of further industrial political action prompted the NIC to escalate its response from programmes to campaigns involving public rallies against 'violence, sectarianism, intimidation, and discrimination' and for decent jobs, houses, education, and social security. Its first and best-known campaign, *A Better Life for All*, was launched in 1976, and was followed by *Peace, Work, and Progress* in 1986. The purpose of marching to rallies to pass pious resolutions that left everyone's politics intact caused bemusement about the point of it all. The point was the unions rather than the workers. In other words, the real objective was not to mobilise workers for change, but to convince unions that the NIC had the bottle to fight shopfloor loyalism. Loyalists could still pack a punch. The United Unionist Action Council, a successor to the UWC and

Buses halted until after funeral

ULSTER'S busmen this afternoon unanimously voted to stay out until after the funeral of the bus driver murdered yesterday.

The funeral of Mr. Harry Bradshaw is expected to take place on Friday and the busmen will hold a meeting immediately afterwards, said Mr. Eugene O'Callaghan, their convenor.

More than 700 busmen made the decision at the end of a one-and-a-half hour mass meeting at Transport House — headquarters of the Transport and General Workers Union.

Earlier, union leaders rejected an offer from Ulster Secretary Mr. Roy Mason for armed guards to be ..

Headline in the Belfast Telegraph *following the murder of bus driver Harry Bradshaw during the Workers' Strike. A deputation of union representatives led by Eugene O'Callaghan call on Secretary of State Roy Mason at Stormont Castle to discuss security for bus staff*

led by Ian Paisley, called another strike on 3 May 1977. O'Callaghan became a full-time official of the ATGWU on 10 May. As he says himself, he had 'a baptism of fire', tragically so in having to deal with the murder of a colleague, Harry Bradshaw.

The strike never commanded the same degree of support as the UWC stoppage. The demands – tougher measures against the Provisionals and the implementation of the report of the 1975 Constitutional Convention – were unrealistic. Unionists may have had a veto, but were never in a position to tell Downing Street what to do. The public misgivings of mainstream Unionists and a failure to secure power cuts rendered the strike less than effective. Its opponents were prepared. Mason relished the opportunity to show his mettle. The trade union response was firm and, ironically, its confidence was most evident in O'Callaghan's ability to get the busmen back to work after the suspension of bus services in protest at the murder of driver Bradshaw. Next day, the strike was called off.

Whereas the quest for unity against loyalist disruption was perceived as synonymous with moderation, defence, and common sense, human rights were seen as nationalist grievances and political, and they generated both internal dissent and international pressure. Under General Secretary Michael Mullen, the ITGWU was the most feisty. The union collected 'very substantial' donations for Northern relief after August 1969 – almost £6,500 by December 1969 – Mullen toured the North, and his general officers lobbied the TUC for a Bill of Rights.[27] The ITGWU's annual conference in June 1971 called for the release of 'political prisoners' in Britain and Northern Ireland, and Liberty Hall was targeted by one of two loyalist bombs in Dublin in December 1972.[28]

In 1975 the ITGWU called on the ICTU to demand the repeal of the Republic's Offences Against the State Acts and deplore Section 31 of the Broadcasting Act.[29] Amalgamateds were more inclined to tender motions against violence, and those with no members in the Republic were most uncomfortable about dealing with civil liberties. The NIC's role was to discourage action and formulate balanced policy documents. Internment drew condemnation from the ITGWU and led the Irish National Teachers' Organisation to convene an anti-internment conference in Belfast. International federations and the Transport Workers of America protested to the British government. The NIC issued a non-committal statement on 10 August 1971 and said nothing further until its 1972 programme, *Peace, Employment, and Reconstruction*, slipped an end to internment into a list of demands which also included repeal of the Special Powers Act, a Bill of Rights, the return of troops to barracks, an end of the nationalist boycott of Stormont and inter-party talks, more jobs, and 200,000 houses.[30]

Trade union aphasia reached its nadir in the aftermath of Bloody Sunday. Two days later, a joint ICTU-TUC conference opened in Belfast to launch *Peace, Employment, and Reconstruction*. The only conference reference to Bloody Sunday was a remark by TUC General Secretary Vic Feather, deploring the 'condition of society which invited tragedies such as that at Derry'. Next day, Feather and Blease met Derry trade unionists to enlist their opposition to the blacking of British cargoes by American longshoremen. Derry trades council merely passed a vote of sympathy to relatives of the dead and hoped 'that those injured would soon be restored to health'.[31] The Northern response also illustrated how effectively the border had compartmentalised unions. Southern workers downed tools and marched en masse on the Republic's day of mourning on 2 February. Worried about a backlash against the amalgamateds, Matt Merrigan, the senior ATGWU official in the Republic, telegrammed a sharp denunciation of British policy in the North to his general secretary, Jack Jones, and circularised his members with a mendacious apologia for British Labour.[32] Privately, Merrigan could be scathing about his UK brothers, and Jones, christened James Larkin Jones, had had a shadowy liaison with Irish republicans before joining the International Brigades in the Spanish Civil War. Jones was too, widely admired as a Labour leader. The Northern ATGWU stuck to its moderately pro-Union outlook just the same.

Unions gradually found a consensual voice on rights. The establishment of quangos like the Standing Advisory Commission on Human Rights, the Office of Ombudsman, the Police Authority, and the Fair Employment Agency, encouraged the formulation of policies, and created acceptable outlets for policy implementation. It was too dilatory for some. The NIC was able to marginalise ginger groups like the west Belfast-based Trade Union Campaign Against Repression. International trade union pressure could not be ignored so easily, and it persuaded the NIC to adopt a Memorandum on the Protection of Human Rights in Northern Ireland in 1978.[33]

Fair employment became a particularly thorny issue. Four trade union and four employer representatives were nominated to the Van Straubenzee committee in 1973, which laid the basis of the first legislation, the Fair Employment (Northern Ireland) Act (1976), and established the Fair Employment Agency. Union satisfaction with the Act, despite an unemployment rate for Catholic men of over 35 per cent, compared with under 15 per cent for Protestant men, seemed to critics to be another example of foot-dragging.[34] Moreover, it was whispered that unions themselves engaged in discrimination and the Fair Employment Agency corroborated the allegation against one NIC affiliate, the GMB.[35] It was the first trade union to be prosecuted under the Act, as O'Callaghan notes. His testimony on other instances of discrimination is valuable in exposing a little more of the extent of a practice cloaked in secrecy. The launch of the MacBride Principles, which called inter alia for affirmative action for equality, by the Washington DC-based Irish National Caucus in 1984, transformed the debate.

The British government was highly sensitive to its image in the United States, and the NIO countered with a fierce propaganda war. Aghast at the willingness of Northern colleagues, including Freeman, to be enlisted in the campaign, some senior officials in the Republic formed Trade Unionists for Irish Unity and Independence and canvassed for ICTU endorsement of the MacBride Principles.[36] To prevent a division of leading personalities into rivalling camps led by the NIO and the republican-backed MacBride Principles campaign, the NIC's 1985 conference adopted a stronger commitment to equality, and in 1986 the NIC appointed a permanent equality committee, adopted a Charter for Equal Opportunities, and launched a new campaign, *Peace, Work, and Progress*, to publicise its position. Thinking along similar lines, the government decided to outflank the MacBride Principles with the more effective Fair Employment Act (1989).[37] It was indicative of a greater confidence in addressing sectarianism that in 1990 the NIC appointed an anti-intimidation officer and launched an anti-intimidation programme, 'Counteract'.[38]

A principal theme in the memoir is pensions. The concern could not be more pertinent. Pensions are a source of nagging anxiety for an ever-increasing number of workers, and remind us that under capitalism, one is never secure. On a more positive note, O'Callaghan is silent on the question of fair employment beyond his personal experience, a tribute, one hopes, to its insignificance in the garages. He himself was adamant that sectarianism, or any concessions to politics, would not be tolerated in the operation of the buses, a view shared by Werner Heubeck, his sparring partner on the management side. This was all the more remarkable as bus crews faced uniquely acute threats to maintaining a modus operandi between men and women from different communities. Confronting those threats required a daily commitment to the principles which governed O'Callaghan's work as a busman and union official. Those with any doubts about the courage required should read Michael Collins's excellent *Buses Under Fire*, which features an interview with O'Callaghan.[39] Perhaps the ultimate tribute to the value of Ulsterbus and Citybus in not only serving a divided community, but in helping to hold that community together, is the fact that it was never privatised. And, not surprisingly, O'Callaghan has something revealing to say on that. To understand the measure of the bus crews' achievement, read this memoir.

EMMET O'CONNOR
SENIOR LECTURER
ULSTER UNIVERSITY

JAMES CALLAGHAN m 1

1890 **Owen (O) Callaghan** m 1890 Rose Anne Caffrey
1864[?]–DATE NOT KNOWN   1869[?]–DATE NOT KNOWN

OWEN JOSEPH (EUGENE) m 1955 Nora Patricia Hughes
O'CALLAGHAN   1932–
1929–2018

Peter John
O'Callaghan
[no dates]

Owen
O'Callaghan
d. 1927

Eileen Marti
née O'Callagh
d. 1963

Patrick Joseph
O'Callaghan
1956–

Nora Patricia
O'Callaghan
1957–

Eugene Peter
O'Callaghan
1959–

Margaret Mary Bridget
Stephens (née O'Callaghan)
1960–

Kevin Damian
O'Callaghan
1961–

Sean O'Callaghan
1989–
Katie O'Callaghan
1992–
Kelly O'Callaghan
1995–

Oisin O'Callaghan
1998–
Eoghan O'Callaghan
2000–
Dara O'Callaghan
2002–
Aodhan O'Callaghan
2004–

Ciara Patricia Stephens
1991–
Grainne Stephens
1993–
Orla Stephens
1995–

Teresa Bridget McCou
1987– (née O'Callagha
Bronagh O'Dwyer
(née O'Callaghan)
1989–
Karen O'Callaghan
1992–
Christopher O'Callagh
1997–

Eugene with
Patricia, baby
Eugene and Pat,
c. 1960

Catherine O'Callaghan[?] (née Gregory)
DATES NOT KNOWN

Patrick James O'Callaghan m 1918 Bridget O'Callaghan (née McNulty)
1892–1971   1892–1983

Patrick	Kevin	Nan Lennon	Bridget Larkin	Rose McNamee
O'Callaghan	O'Callaghan	(née O'Callaghan)	(née O'Callaghan)	(née O'Callaghan)
d. 1986	1926–2005	1931–2000	1927–	d. 1990

Eileen Martina	Anne Therese	Joseph Martin	Geraldine Sarah	Ciaran Gerard
O'Callaghan	Fearon (née O'Callaghan)	O'Callaghan	Brady (née O'Callaghan)	O'Callaghan
1963	1963–	1965–	1970–	1973

Sean Pearse	Conor Patrick Fearon	Emma O'Callaghan	John Luke Brady	Cara O'Callaghan
O'Callaghan	1985–	1985–	1992–	1991–
2000–	Caoimhe Anne Fearon	Sarah O'Callaghan	Liam Brady	Shona O'Callaghan
	1987–	1987–	2001–	2001–
		Micheal O'Callaghan		
		1997–		
		Lauren O'Callaghan		
		1999–		

The O'Callaghan family gathered for Eugene and Patsy's fiftieth wedding anniversary, 2005

The O'Callaghan family in 1936
BACK ROW FROM LEFT: Rose, Bridget (mother), Kevin
FRONT ROW FROM LEFT: Nan, Bridie, Eileen and Eugene
Patsy is missing from the photograph

1
Crossmaglen

Eugene O'Callaghan, as I am known, was born
in Crossmaglen on 2 March 1929.

The town of Crossmaglen stands mainly on the townland of the same
name and partly on the townlands of Rathkeelan and Monog. It lies about
eight miles northwest of Dundalk and 14 miles southwest of Newry. It is
set in the southwest corner of County Armagh. The land
boundary with the Republic of Ireland lies less than two miles
away in both a southerly (County Louth) and westerly (County
Monaghan) direction.

I was the youngest son of nine children born to Patrick and
Bridget O'Callaghan. Throughout my entire life I was known
as Gene or Eugene and it was not until I applied for a PSV
Public Service Licence that I became aware that my real name
was Owen Joseph. Despite the fact that I am now 89 years of
age the name I still identify with is Eugene. A possible
explanation for the anomaly in my name is that one of my
brothers was named Owen Joseph. He was killed in a cart
accident before I was born.

I grew up as a child of the thirties now known as 'the hungry
thirties'. Poverty among the working class was rife. Outdoor
relief was administered by the Poor Law Guardians who were
not known for their generosity. Riots were taking place in
Belfast and Jim Larkin was organising the workers' strikes in the Irish
Free State. Striking workers were being baton charged and
demonstrations broken up by the police.

In 1939, the Unemployment Assistance (Emergency Powers) Act was
introduced to extend the Unemployment Assistance Board's activities to
meet whenever need arose from the war-time situation. By 1940 the Board

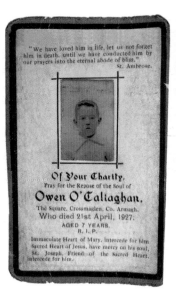

" We have loved him in life, let us not forget
him in death, until we have conducted him by
our prayers into the eternal abode of bliss."
St. Ambrose.

Of Your Charity,
Pray for the Repose of the Soul of
Owen O'Callaghan,
The Square, Crossmaglen, Co. Armagh.
Who died 21st April, 1927,
AGED 7 YEARS.
R. I. P.
Immaculate Heart of Mary, intercede for him
Sacred Heart of Jesus, have mercy on his soul,
St. Joseph, Friend of the Sacred Heart,
intercede for him.

A memoriam card for
Owen Joseph who
sadly died in 1927

had received a new title as the 'Assistance Board' with the responsibility of supplementing the entire range of benefits. Further legislation, just after the war, for all practical purposes ended the life of the 'Poor Law' and ushered in the era in which the Health Services Act (Northern Ireland) 1948 and the National Assistance Act (Northern Ireland) 1948 well and truly ended the humiliating misery of the poor laws and inaugurated the Welfare State in this part of the world. Social security and its benefits and also free healthcare became the entitlement of every citizen in Northern Ireland. Progress indeed.

But even in the very recent past in some parts of the country including south Armagh the hiring fairs had operated. The nearest to Crossmaglen was in Newtownhamilton. Young people, boys and girls, would attend with their parents and line up for inspection by the prospective hirer. The large farmers and business folk would walk up and down the line choosing who they wished to hire and then haggle about the price. This would normally be a set amount for six months. There would be no stipulation about hours of work per day as this would be determined by the hirer. Those hired would be driven away to reside and work for the period so hired. Many would endure severe hardship, long hours, inadequate food and poor conditions. In many cases the living quarters was a bed in the loft over the stable with no heating. In the absolute degree of control the employer had over the hapless child for the duration of the contract it would not, I believe, be unreasonable to draw a comparison to the situation of black slaves in the southern United States. Those times are a blight on our history and should never be erased or forgotten.

My early school years were spent at the Crossmaglen Public Elementary School. Teachers were harsh and in some cases brutal. Corporal punishment was administered at will for minor infractions. One teacher in particular would stand behind his desk with a bamboo cane concealed behind his coat up his back. He would then walk behind pupils shouting 'NTF is my rule, no tom foolery'. The unfortunate pupils would have to hold out their hand whilst he administered six strokes of the cane. There was no point in complaining as there was little your parents could do. The school was run by the parish priest whose word was law. Keep your child off school and you could be prosecuted and fined – something parents could ill afford. If a parent took his anger out on the school teacher they ran the risk of imprisonment. It is hard for people nowadays to believe that those things could have happened; let alone that they were accepted and even approved of. Child protection has come a long way since then and teachers like that would be prosecuted and possibly jailed. Teachers then – or 'Masters' as they were known – would administer various punishments such as lifting pupils and shaking them, twisting their ears and using a half-closed fist to strike from behind.

It was there that I gained my first experience of collective action. One of the older boys organised a walk-out against the teacher's behaviour. The entire class walked out cheering as they moved down the Carron Road. Unfortunately, it achieved nothing, a one-day wonder, as we returned the next day to even worse punishment. The lesson I learned was: if you are going to embark on a course of action your first priority is to assess the probability of success; pick the terrain on which you are going to fight; make sure it is at a time of your choosing; know your enemy's weakness and where they are most vulnerable. What I learned from that experience would stand me in good stead later in life.

Like all other families in Crossmaglen at that time we were poor, though perhaps a little better off than others. Our house was on the corner of 'the Square', a vast expanse of open ground which was ideal for the monthly fair.

My father as an eight-year-old boy was recorded in the 1901 census where he and his younger sister Bridget were referred to as 'visitors' living with my great-aunt and and great-uncle Anne and Thomas McNamee. Curiously, they were recorded under the name of Callaghan and not O'Callaghan. Their father had died in England so they were fortunate in having a wider family circle to take them in. Their aunt, to our everlasting good fortune, had the foresight to ensure that Patrick was apprenticed and learned a trade. As a result my father was a carpenter by trade whose chance of finding work was a little better than most. So we were 'the rich of the poor' as they said.

The O'Callaghan house and shop on the corner of the square. The valuation revision books (PRONI) record Eugene's grandmother Rose Anne O'Callaghan taking over the rental in 1913 for £8 per annum. His parents subsequently purchased the property. The new Crossmaglen Credit Union building now occupies the site

Bridget O'Callaghan with her brother and Eugene's father, Patrick James

When he was not employed he had a small workshop where he made and sold furniture all of which was made from solid wood. I always marvelled at the way he dovetailed the joints all by hand. The making of farm carts for farmers required expertise in blacksmithing, a skill which he had. The centre of the wheel, known as the knare, had to be precise. The spokes were then shaped and made to fit into the small grooves which had been carved in the knare. The fellows were then made. This was the outside rim which also had to be perfect as the spokes from the knare would be connected to slot perfectly into position making a circle. The final piece was to shoe the wheel with an iron casing to hold everything in place in addition to meeting the road. This is where the blacksmith's forge would come into play, and my father would fix and hammer the iron into shape. As children we loved to pump the bellows which made the fire burn while my father hammered and shaped the iron until it was a perfect fit. The iron was then taken out with large tongs and while still hot was hammered into place. All of this was done without drawings or the use of specialist tools. They do not make tradesmen like that anymore, more's the pity.

My mother ran a small shop from the front of the house and also took in lodgers. On fair days she would prepare and sell meals to the traders and farmers; she was also skilled at making Carrickmacross lace and used this skill to supplement our income. Twice a year she would take the train from Cullaville to Dublin and sell her lace to Roches Stores. Afterwards, with the money she made, she would shop for whatever new clothes we needed. We had a small holding and kept a cow for milk – which was often shared with the neighbours. What was left over was churned and made into butter and the buttermilk was used to make bread. Every year we would plant a half acre of potatoes, cabbages, turnips and carrots with a small plot for lettuce and scallions. Again any

24

Bridget O'Callaghan, Eugene's mother

surplus was given to our less well off neighbours. All the children had their chores and my parents instilled in us a work ethic and a responsibility for those less fortunate.

The people of Crossmaglen were like a large family; what we had was shared. And while we may have had our differences among ourselves, pity the outsider who interfered with any of us as we would close ranks against any opposition. When you understand the bonds that held the people of Crossmaglen together you can begin to understand why, decades later, they made life hell for the army which was imposed upon them. 'Cross people' have been demonised in the media and by politicians who refer to their part of the world as 'bandit country'. But this in no way describes the Crossmaglen in which I grew up where everyone helped their neighbour, doors were unlocked at night and what you left outside would still be there the next day. When help was needed it did not need to be asked for but was given.

Eugene's sisters Nan and Bridie

On fair days in Crossmaglen farmers and dealers came from far and near to trade. Throw in the odd circus show or other entertainment and it was always a memorable day. You could always be sure of four or five fist fights when disputes were settled by forming a circle while the combatants did battle.

As a very young boy I always wanted a dog. At home we had a number of sheds which were rented out to farmers to use as stalls for their horse and cart at a cost of sixpence per day; a not inconsiderable sum of money to rural working families in those times. One man I remember well was Thomas Murphy whose son I believe is the man commonly known as 'Slab' Murphy. Tom, as he was known, owned a pedigree Irish Terrier and he promised me a pup if I made sure his horse was well looked after. True to his word on his return he told me to come and collect the pup from his farm. As a very small boy I walked the four or five miles to collect my pup. At first I was disappointed as I was looking forward to a pure-bred but, alas, the bitch had been crossed by a stray resulting in cross-bred pups. I did however pick a dog pup and was I proud when I

The young Eugene who went to find work in London

arrived home. I could not say the same for my parents! Nevertheless, Toby as I called him, remained my constant companion who went everywhere with me. Of all the dogs I have ever owned – and many were champions – he was the most intelligent. My father used to say if that dog could talk he would tell you the time.

We both grew older together, he quicker than me. After I left for England he used to travel rather slowly and visit all the places to which we would have gone together. My mother told me he died of a broken heart though we will never know for sure.

Crossmaglen when I lived there was neglected by the powers that be. There were no factories or sustained work. Those seeking employment travelled to Dundalk or Dublin. Few travelled in the other direction. Belfast in those days seemed like a million miles away. A bus journey of over an hour to Newry was required. You then hung about waiting for a connection for a further two-hour bus journey to Belfast whereas you could ride a bicycle to Dundalk, Castleblaney or Carrickmacross or catch the train at Cullaville to Dublin. That is not to say there was much work in the south either.

The alternative was the boat to England – a journey I made just before my eighteenth birthday. I got a job in Wall's meat factory boning pigs. When I received my first pay it was way below the level of others doing the same job. I went to the office to ask why and was given the explanation that I was under age and therefore they were not allowed to pay me more. I upped and as they say 'jacked the job'. There was nothing else for it, the landlady charged full board and the train to work was full fare.

The loneliest place in the world is a city of millions with no one for company. Having left my first employment, I travelled with some of the other lodgers to work on building sites. Many of the buildings which were being demolished contained asbestos but no protective equipment was provided as at that time it was not known how dangerous it was. My lungs still show the evidence of asbestos damage. The work was hard and you earned every penny you got. There was no such thing as holiday pay or any other fringe benefits which became the norm later on. I soon fell

into the pattern where you chased the money – moving to wherever the best paid job was.

Patrick O'Callaghan, October 1964

It was working on the building sites that I acquired the brogue that led more than one person over the years to refer to me as a 'Free State man'. It was not the accent I spoke with when I left Crossmaglen but strange to tell, one I acquired in England. And the reason I was forced to acquire it was so as to be understood by the men from the west of Ireland with whom I was working.

I missed Crossmaglen, the ceilidhe houses where people gathered and where stories were told and retold. Many of the older generation would relate their experiences of the hiring fairs and relay stories told by their parents of the famine, eviction from small-holdings, whole families dying of starvation, white wakes and death. The custom in Ireland is that when

a person died they would hold a wake, neighbours would gather to pay their respects. The white wake was different – when a person was emigrating to America or Australia neighbours would gather to see them off as it was often the last time they would see them. Even if they survived the hardships of the journey and arrived at their destination it was unlikely they would ever return. I learned more about history from the old folk than you would ever find in a book. Unlike reading books, these characters brought the stories to life, naming people and all the different aspects of what went on.

After a few years working in England I came home on a visit, went to a dance in Camlough and met my wife to be, Patsy Hughes. We were married over 63 years ago, moved to Belfast and I got the job on the buses, which is when this story really begins.

Patsy and Eugene's wedding, 1955

2
The bus driver

And so it began. I started off as a trolley bus driver in 1955 operating out of the Haymarket depot in Turnley Street.

Twin-axeled trolleybus Belfast Corporation Sunbeam F4A, No. 246, the last trolleybus bought new by the Corporation, turns from Oxford Street to East Bridge Street. It is being followed by a Daimler Fleetline bus and a Guy Arab bus. Trolleybuses ran in Belfast from 1938 to 1968

HOWARD CUNNINGHAM

During my involvement with the industry – which has now spanned more than half a century – it went through several organisational changes. When I signed on there were two dominant bus undertakings in Northern Ireland both of which were publicly owned. Within the County Borough of Belfast and slightly beyond there were the 'red buses' owned and operated by the City Council or Belfast Corporation as it was then known. This meant that the workers were all municipal employees – a point which will become more important later in the story. But outside Belfast there were the 'green buses' and the services were operated by the UTA (Ulster Transport Authority) which was a government-owned body which operated Northern Ireland's trains and the country bus services.

In time this would change. In 1967 Stormont passed the Transport Act (Northern Ireland) which became law on 14 December of that year. Section 47 of the Act established the Northern Ireland Transport Holding Company.[1] Ownership of the UTA was vested in this new holding company. From this Ulsterbus was born. With the re-organisation of local government in 1973 the buses in Belfast ceased to be a local authority function and the responsibility for Belfast's buses passed to Citybus. Sometime later – in 1973 if my memory serves me correctly – Citybus and Ulsterbus were merged with the new company retaining the name Ulsterbus. Subsequently Northern Ireland Railways and Ulsterbus were both put under the authority of Translink which more or less recreated and expanded the old UTA with a new title.

When I 'passed out' as a driver I was what was then known as a 'spare man' – in other words a dogsbody after which you were appointed to 'Letter duties'. These were duties made up by covering one of the regular driver's shifts when he – women bus drivers had not been heard of in Belfast in those days – was having his rest day. This invariably was a late shift and in essence meant always working late nights.

Holiday allocation was also based on the principle of seniority; those with the longest service got first choice e.g. first: the two weeks of the 'twaalth' of July; next: the two weeks before; next: two weeks after and so on. This meant that junior employees got their summer allocation

A Guy Arab bus, No. 310, runs into the yard of Mountpottinger depot down a narrow roadway beside the Picturedrome cinema. Note the tram rails in situ in the square setts. The last trams ran in Belfast in 1954

HOWARD CUNNINGHAM

Sunbeam F4A trolleybus No. 246 turning from Castle Street into Queen Street in 1968. It was new in 1958 and only served for 10 years due to the closure of what remained of the electric route network

HOWARD CUNNINGHAM

either before or after everyone else's holiday with the end result of having summer holidays in March or at the end of October.

There was always plenty of overtime due to the sizeable turnover of staff. However, the distribution of overtime was a bone of contention. This was due largely to the fact that it was distributed at the sole discretion of the inspectors who operated from 123 Royal Avenue. Their blue-eyed boys – as they were known – were first in line to be allocated and given first choice of shifts. The remainder got the late or Saturday shifts that no one else wanted.

Challenging the lack of fairness in these arrangements forced me to recognise that the union and its full-time officials were frequently indifferent to, complicit in or just impotent in the face of the conditions management imposed on the workers. I made repeated attempts through the union to have the system changed but to no avail. I was always given the stock answer, 'Well, everybody had to accept it; that is the way it was when we started'.

Trolley buses were phased out in 1968 but long before that happened I had been transferred to omnibuses operating at first out of Mountpottinger depot which has now been re-developed for housing. When the Mount, as it was called, closed I transferred to Short Strand where I remained for the rest of my employment with Belfast Corporation.

The time spent with Belfast Corporation was, you could say, uneventful. But these years were also an education. As well as earning my living as a bus driver I learned a lot about the shortcomings of the trade union movement, about its potential to improve wages and conditions and the reasons why it often missed opportunities to do so. Although I did not know it at the time, what I was learning would later be put to good use when I became a full-time official of the Transport Workers' Union.

The reason that I refer to this period as 'uneventful' is, of course because the Troubles had not started. With the exception of industrial disputes – usually over excessive disciplinary action against individuals – there was little of note. Wages were negotiated nationally as were other employment issues of any importance.

This suited the trade union officials of the time who were, in my opinion, weak. As things were negotiated at a national level they could blame others for a lack of progress. But, despite the peaceful times and the growing sense of prosperity in the 'you've never had it so good' Britain of Harold Macmillan, sectarianism in Belfast was never far away. Tensions were quietly simmering beneath the surface.

In the early sixties a Mr A. Bell and a Mr H. Minnis were the leading members of a local – i.e. Northern Ireland-based – union founded in 1942, known as the Ulster Transport and Allied Operatives' Trade Union (UTAO). The idea behind its formation was to have a 'Protestant union for Protestant workers'. For reasons best known to themselves the Ulster Transport Authority agreed to grant them recognition for the purposes of negotiating wages and conditions. Until this time my union – the Amalgamated Transport and General Workers' Union (ATGWU) as the Transport and General Workers' Union was for legal reasons known in Northern Ireland and the Irish Republic – had held the sole negotiating rights. The failure of the ATGWU to challenge the company on this issue had allowed the UTAO to gain a foothold. The UTAO established an office in Donegall Square West next to the City Hall. Alfie Best was appointed as a full-time officer with Hugh Minnis as Chairman, Bertie West went to inspecting duties in Smithfield.

Bertie Minnis, who was a brother of Hugh Minnis, was appointed as a tours operations manager. Tour operators were the highest paid drivers: guaranteed 11 hours pay per day. At the end of the tour tips were given by the passengers and these could run into hundreds of pounds which went straight into the driver's pocket and were not to my knowledge declared for income tax. The drivers were also allowed to claim reasonable expenses which could also be substantial.

In fact over time it became evident to anyone who bothered to think about it that the lack of management oversight in this area of the company's business activities was building up to a crisis waiting to happen. And years later it did when I was a full-time officer.

The tours operations manager, Ian Millar, booked a tour for members of his church. It came to light that the driver had submitted a claim for hotel expenses for which the company billed the church. The church queried the bill as they had already paid the driver's hotel bill and so they were being asked to pay twice. Ian Millar was enraged and instigated an investigation. What he discovered was that this was in fact common practice. Cases came to light which showed that in some cases drivers had obtained blank receipts from hotels, filled them in and claimed the money despite never having stayed at the hotel. All hell broke loose and Werner Heubeck himself (Ulsterbus MD, 1965–88) became involved, resulting in a full audit and paper chase. For once the company did not know how to

The red hand logo of the Ulster Transport Authority (UTA) used from 1947 up until the late 1950s when it was replaced with a new crest. The red hand roundel probably survived in use for much longer as it was not replaced overnight

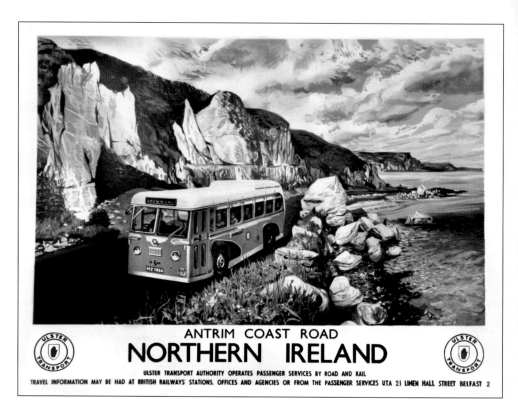

ANTRIM COAST ROAD
NORTHERN IRELAND

ULSTER TRANSPORT AUTHORITY OPERATES PASSENGER SERVICES BY ROAD AND RAIL

TRAVEL INFORMATION MAY BE HAD AT BRITISH RAILWAYS' STATIONS, OFFICES AND AGENCIES OR FROM THE PASSENGER SERVICES UTA 21 LINEN HALL STREET BELFAST 2

A depiction of a Leyland Royal Tiger, bodied in-house by the Ulster Transport Authority. Oddly, the Authority had no luxury coaches, yet operated coach holidays from its hotels, and others, also for cross-channel operators from whom it had to hire in coaches

deal with it. Ordinary service drivers who were aware that the penalty for ticket fraud for even a small amount was instant dismissal were demanding the same penalty for tour drivers. Shop stewards were crying out for blood.

There is no doubt that what had happened was due to sheer greed and deliberate fraud. Nevertheless, these tour drivers were union members and were appealing to me for help in saving their jobs. The company was in a bind because if they sacked them all tour operations would collapse as it took some time to train the operatives. This would result in the cancellation of tours, which in turn would lead to the cancellation of hotel bookings. This in turn could lead to claims against the company. Heubeck sought my advice on how to deal with the situation. Whilst he wanted to dismiss the men and be consistent in the way he dealt with fraud he was only too well aware of the possible cost to the company and the damage to its reputation.

I advised him and indeed pressed the point that what had happened could be directly attributed to his tour manager's negligence in failing to make any meaningful checks over the years of expenses claims. While I had little sympathy for those involved I was nevertheless duty bound to

34

represent them in the same way that a member of the legal profession is required to defend a client in court.

After much toing and froing Heubeck and I agreed to set aside a full day for a hearing into the affair. No other managers would be in attendance as participants, only Heubeck and his trusted staff officer, Sam Thompson, to take the minutes. I would also be on my own to represent the drivers who would be called individually to give evidence. Throughout the hearing I continued to demand that the tour manager be called to give evidence – something which Heubeck would not concede.

The hearings started at 9:30 in the morning and finished at 7:00pm that night with a short break for lunch. Each driver interviewed was given the opportunity of explaining his case. When we finished for the evening, physically and mentally exhausted, we had reached agreement on all cases but one. That individual did not want me to represent him but preferred to be represented by the General Municipal Workers Union of which he was a member. At the end of the session Heubeck rose from the table with a look of relief on his face. Turning to me he said, 'I know what I'm going to do, go home for a soak in the bath, what are you going to do?' 'Well', I said, 'I am going to get a drink for I think I need it.' I proceeded to Richardson's Social Club which was beside Transport House, a place where busmen often congregated. I was standing at the bar having ordered a small whiskey and a chaser when Heubeck appeared behind me and said to the barman, 'I think you better double that; he deserves it'. I turned and asked, 'What are you doing here?' Heubeck smiled and said, 'Did you think I wouldn't face the bear in his den?' He then touched his hat and said 'if you ever need a job there will always be one available', whereupon he left just as quickly as he came in – having of course nobly paid for the drink.

The story did not finish there. The one driver who had been represented by the General Municipal Workers Union remained sacked. All of those I had represented were reinstated. The General Municipal Workers Union took their member's case to an Industrial Tribunal and lost based on the decision in Burchell v The British Home Stores [1978 IRLR 379]. We never posted or gave details of how the other cases were resolved.

As I was explaining – before I got diverted into the story of the tour drivers – at the time of the emergence and growth of the UTAO some Unionist Party politicians had been urging Protestant workers to form Protestant unions. In their opinion the Dublin-based Irish Congress of

Trade Unions' (ICTU) sympathies were too much in support of a united Ireland. But despite this external political support and in spite of all their huffing and puffing the UTAO union was unable to get a foothold in any other industry. They were frozen out by the big engineering unions. It may be hard to believe now but at that time before you could get a job in Shorts or Harland and Wolff you had to produce an 11/30 Transport Union card. If you could not produce the card then you were not granted an interview. The closed shop was rigorously enforced and because of this the UTAO could not achieve financial viability. Its membership had peaked at just over 8,000 but it was in sharp decline by the late fifties. It had not the financial strength to fund strike pay and so could not really afford to be militant but made do with disputes around scheduling bus services; a petty way of throwing your weight around which did more to disrupt services – and so annoy the public – than to advance the interests of the workers.

So eventually the UTAO approached the ATGWU to see if we would take them in. As part of the deal they wanted an official's job for Hugh Minnis. The then Regional Secretary Norman Kennedy refused point blank; UTAO members would be welcome but there would be no job for Minnis.

Kennedy's approach was right. The UTAO should have been left to wither on the vine – it had no part in post-war trade unionism. But the UTAO then approached the National Union of General Municipal Workers (GMB) which as a major British trade union, which incidentally likes to claim Karl Marx's daughter Eleanor among its founder members, should have known better. But spotting a chance to expand into another industry the GMB agreed to the UTAO's terms which included installing Minnis as a full-time official for the passenger transport industry. This gave the GMB a foothold in the road passenger industry where it inherited the UTAO's predeliction for irritating the public with scheduling disputes but contributed no creative thinking or muscle to enhancing the status, pay and conditions of the workers in the industry; the burden for this as we shall see fell entirely on the ATGWU.[2]

Minnis had now achieved financial backing with which he was able to establish himself and at the same time increase his membership through playing the Orange card and working hard, but also capitalising on the weakness of the ATGWU.

The ATGWU seemed to hold all its meetings in Belfast. The branch committee was made up of Belfast men, giving the impression that the union was not functioning throughout the rest of the province. When I became a shop steward in 1956 I collected the union contributions as there was no such thing as payroll deductions. In some cases contributions were collected outside the depot gates. Management appointments and promotions were made by the City Council and as the council was Unionist controlled I believe it is unnecessary to go into the makeup of management.

Reports were demanded and expected for the most frivolous matters. Failure to submit a report on something that came to management's attention at a later date would result in a charge being issued and placed on your record along with any punishment that was deemed appropriate. All reports had to begin 'I beg leave to report ...'. The reports went to managers of the most limited ability who had obtained their appointments through City Hall connections.

While I, as a shop steward and branch officer, made every effort to improve the working conditions, what could be achieved was limited due to weak trade union leadership, apathy and a 'there's nothing we can do' attitude. I can recall numerous occasions when spontaneous industrial action was taken only to be classed as 'unofficial action' because the officials did not want to be seen to be involved.

Post-war, Belfast Corporation was still running its electric trams, but the infrastructure was deteriorating. Diesel buses, rather than electric trolleybuses, were the preferred replacement. Guy Arab III No. 346 was new in 1951 and is now in its forty-fifth year in preservation having been withdrawn by Citybus in 1975
PAUL SAVAGE

37

3
Moving sideways

Leyland Leopard No. 1327, one of the first such vehicles ordered by the newly-created Ulsterbus, preparing to depart Kilkeel for Newry. It served for 16 years from 1969 to 1985

While still in the employment of the Corporation I applied for a job with the Ulster Transport Authority. For family reasons my wife, Patricia, and I had thoughts of moving back to the country and away from Belfast.

But I was turned down on the grounds that there was an agreement with the Corporation to the effect that neither company would poach each other's drivers while they were still in employment with their counterpart.

Sometime later I left the Corporation. An English brewery was hoping to develop its sales into Northern Ireland, the money was better and I worked as a lorry driver but the work did not last. I got another job as a fitter but that did not last either and I became unemployed.

The UTA was again advertising for workers and I responded to an advertisement in the press. As I was now unemployed I had no reason to suspect that the 'no poaching drivers' justification previously used for refusing me would still apply. I was, of course, wrong. I was turned down again – and given no explanation. Perhaps I should mention that during my time as a Belfast Corporation bus driver that whatever management might have thought of my trade union activities they could make no criticism of my employment record nor of my competence as a driver as I never had an accident.

So I asked my brother Patsy, who worked for the UTA and was active in the union, if he could explain why a well-qualified applicant with an unblemished and accident-free employment record as a bus driver was being denied the job. He in turn asked the relevant officers in the UTA with the result that I was offered a job subject to a medical. On this occasion 'two good sized cock chickens from the countryside' were not required to complete the transaction.

I took up employment with the UTA in 1964, working out of the old Smithfield depot. A man called Jack Campbell was the head inspector. I got on very well with Jack who was a decent sort. However, after a few months I was transferred to the UTA's Oxford Street depot. Jack Campbell later became depot manager at Oxford Street and re-appears later in this story in more tragic times. The conditions at Oxford Street were, to say the least, very poor. There was no proper canteen and the buses were old and poorly maintained.

Patsy O'Callaghan (conductor) with Frank Fegan (driver)

Very soon I started to campaign for improvements. I went to all the union meetings and agitated for change gaining some support. This did not make me very popular with either the company – which was perhaps understandable – or with the trade union officials – which was somewhat more baffling.

One particular incident that stands out in my mind was the occasion when a major issue was up for discussion and it was well known that I would oppose the union's recommendations. On the day of the meeting some of the so-called 'hard men' were waiting for me near Transport House. As I recollect, one of them was out to pick a fight with me even before I went into the meeting. After he threw the first punch I simply flattened him – I had done some amateur boxing in my youth. To my surprise he took out a summons against me. To my even greater surprise his action was backed by the union.

On the day of the hearing a witness in the case, a Martin Hopkins, whose father I believe had some connection with the judiciary, was asked what he had seen. He stated: 'Mr McC had punched O'Callaghan after which O'Callaghan punched him back knocking him down.' When asked if he was sure it was a punch he said: 'If it was not a punch it was a very hard push.'

The magistrate asked me if I had hit him. I said, 'Yes, I retaliated.' He said, 'Did you have to hit him so hard?' I replied, 'Well now if you look at the size of him compared to me I was afraid that if I didn't hit him hard he would probably half kill me.'

The magistrate looked at McC and said, 'I believe you were the architect of your own misfortune; what did you expect this man to do after you struck him? He had every right to defend himself; I am therefore dismissing your case'. I believe the plan of the union organisers was to get me convicted and dismissed from my employment but – if that was their plan – fortunately it did not work.

Remarkably, I had two further encounters with 'Brother' McC. The first was over a decade later in 1977 when I had been appointed as a full-time trade union official. Mr McC was in charge of recruiting members and collecting union subscriptions. Collectors were appointed by branch officials due to the fact that they were accountable for all money collected for and on behalf of the union.

Mr McC came to see me during my first week in the job, handed me his collection book and outstanding subscriptions. I asked what this was for, to which he replied, 'You will hardly want me in now after what happened between us.' I knew that apart from being a good organiser and being now retired from full-time employment he needed the money – 10 per cent of all subscriptions were allocated to the collector. I handed him back the book and said, 'What is in the past is best left in the past. I have no problem with you as long as you play straight with me.' He thanked me and left and proved himself to be a loyal and trustworthy colleague.

The second occasion was some years later after he had stepped down from his union duties when he came to my office looking rather dishevelled. When I asked what was wrong he said that he had bought this old coat in War on Want: 'I have nothing, can you help me?' We had a discussion from which I learned that money would not be the answer. I rang my chairman and got his approval for what I intended. I took McC to Gowdy's on the Beersbridge Road and rigged him out with a new outfit including shoes and socks and gave him the money to buy a meal. He could not get over it, apologising for the past, how wrong he had been and how he had misjudged me. But that is to digress.

In 1965 Werner Heubeck became managing director of the UTA where I had been working since 1964. The UTA had been losing substantial amounts of money to which the politicians' answer was to move it into a new company to be known as Ulsterbus and to retain Heubeck as managing director. Werner Heubeck was a German and I have introduced him prematurely but fully in character in my digression earlier in the previous chapter about the sins of the tour operators. However, on the subject of Werner Heubeck there is more – much more – to come.

Negotiations of a sort were held with the trade unions about the new company and an agreement was cobbled together and recommended for acceptance by the union's negotiators. But the deal recommended by the union fell far short of the deal which could and should have been made. No consideration was given to the substantial differences in wages between the Belfast Corporation busmen and those carried forward from the UTA into the newly established company. Conditions fell below standard. The employees were offered £2 per week extra to accept.

Werner Heubeck, an illustration by Ruth Graham in *The Busworker*, May 2002

I opposed the agreement. Although relatively new to the UTA, I was again by this stage a shop steward. I totally opposed the deal but had little support in my opposition. In articulating my position I argued that we were not being told that there would be a 25 per cent reduction in duties with, as a consequence, less employment. Despite my vehement opposition to the deal it was recommended by the union's bus branch negotiators and voted through by the members.

Crucially, what was not known to the members at the time was that most of the negotiators, including the chairman of the union branch who had succeeded my brother Patsy in that role, and others whom I knew and could name if challenged (though publicly shaming them 50 years after the event would be a small-minded and petty way of dealing with the past), had been promised well-paid jobs within the new company as depot managers and senior inspectors.

The crux of my criticism of the deal was that no serious effort had been made to address the wage differential with the Belfast Corporation Transport Department's terms and conditions. The way in which work rosters were organised was re-arranged more or less unilaterally by management which meant that the workload had increased. And in return for a significant deterioration in our terms and conditions all we secured was a miserly additional £2 per week. Unfortunately, with the backing of the full-time official and the negotiators, the deal was put through.

The company was now re-structured into four areas: Central, Northern, Southern and Western. For administrative purposes these areas would contain four area managers and 22 depot managers. Twelve of the depot managers were ex-shop stewards: that is to say members of the negotiating committee. What you might call 'an interesting coincidence'. The erstwhile union chairman took up his position at the old Smithfield depot.

When the union members came to realise the full effect of what they had been hoodwinked into accepting the remainder of the union reps came in for a hard time. New elections had to be called and I put my name forward for branch chairman and Bus Council. I was elected to both positions. I have already mentioned that I was a shop steward at the time of the negotiations but that had clearly not been a very influential position.

When elections were held for the Regional Committee I also ran and took the position in subsequent elections and retained it until I was appointed a full-time official in 1977. The Regional Committee was the governing body of the entire union for the whole of Ireland. It consisted of 23 elected lay members.

4
A bird's eye view of the union

My Regional Committee colleagues then elected me to
the Sub-Committee which acted as a sort of
permanent executive committee overseeing the
workings of the region between Regional Committee
meetings, carrying out investigations on behalf of the
region and reporting back on its findings. This gave
me a bird's eye view of the union.

Nothing, however, highlighted the deficiencies of the union as much as
the investigations that the Sub-Committee had to carry out. These of
course turned the spotlight on exceptional and usually disturbing aspects
of union life rather than the good work that was done by many dedicated
shop stewards, branch officials and full-time officers of the union. The
only redeeming feature of these investigations was the degree of farce and
entertainment which they sometimes afforded in recalling them
afterwards. One investigation particularly stands out in my mind.

There were ongoing problems at the British Enkalon factory between
the senior shop steward, the full-time union officer and the members. On
the direction of the Regional Committee, the Sub-Committee consisting
of Andy Holmes, Chairman, Mick Blair and myself conducted an
investigation which took place at a hotel in Antrim.

On the morning of the hearing Cecil Vance, the Northern Ireland
Secretary – a full-time officer of the union and the second in line to the
Regional Secretary – came in and sat down at the table with the
investigating committee. I asked him what he was doing as the panel was
there to conduct an investigation into the Branch. His reply was, 'I am to
sit in on the investigation as Northern Ireland Secretary.' I made it quite
clear that he would have to wait outside as he had no role or function to
play unless he was required to give evidence or if it emerged that he – as

the officer responsible – had failed to oversee and ensure that officials performed their duties in a manner consistent with, and within, the terms of their appointment.

Mr Vance then asked for clarification from the Chairman who confirmed that my interpretation of the rules of procedure was correct and that he would have to wait outside and make himself available if required to give evidence. This was a shock to him; no one had ever spoken to him like that before. In my view he was full of his own importance. He later became chairman of the Ulster Unionist Labour Association.

The investigation was in itself quite straightforward. Members came in individually and gave their evidence and they were questioned as to how they thought things could be improved. Over 90 per cent of those who attended were very critical of the full-time official, his handling of complaints, poor representation and his failures of leadership. One thing they all had in common was a claim that the official was trying to get rid of the senior steward who stood up for the members.

When it came to the official's time to give evidence it was quite amusing. He came in smoking a large cigar and wearing a polka dot bow tie. He looked like someone from a stage show. His evidence was equally hilarious. It is sad to say he was a disaster and it was beyond my comprehension how he ever came to be an official.

Picking up on the evidence, I asked him if it was true that he had gone to members' houses at night asking them to sign a petition against the senior shop steward. He admitted that this was true. After I had put a number of more damaging questions to him the Regional Secretary, Norman Kennedy – who had up to now been a silent witness of these proceedings – at this stage lost his cool and told the official that he would be advised to shut his mouth as he had already done himself enough harm.

At the conclusion of the investigation it was agreed that the Regional Secretary would arrange for his secretary to draw up the report which would then be posted out to us. If we agreed with the content we would sign and return it. When I read the report I thought that it bore no resemblance to the evidence. I contacted the two other members of the Sub-Committee who agreed with me.

There followed a meeting of the Sub-Committee with the Regional Secretary. This meeting became very heated. The Regional Secretary threw the papers at me and said, 'You draw up the report.' I immediately took him up on his offer. I drafted and submitted a report and sent the draft to Andy Holmes, Mick Blair and the Regional Secretary. A further meeting was arranged to consider the report and with a few minor amendments the report was agreed.

What happened then was pure pantomime. The Regional Secretary called for his secretary to come in but there was no response. He jumped up in a fit of rage shouting, 'Where the hell is she now?' It turned out that the secretary, who was known to be fond of the drink, was in Mooneys quenching her thirst. When she finally arrived the Regional Secretary 'let rip' whereupon – being slightly inebriated – she tickled him under the chin and said, 'Norman, Norman temper, temper; think of your bad heart.'

Norman Kennedy could not get us out of there quickly enough saying, 'I'll get this typed up'. This version of the report, which upheld the members' complaints, was presented to the Regional Committee and adopted despite the fact that it was an indictment of how the official had been carrying out his duties.

Needless to say this did not make me very popular with the full-time officials. The story then took a remarkable turn. Mr Dempster – such was the name of the official in question – ceased to be an official. Did he fall on his sword or was he pushed by those in authority in the union? When the job was subsequently advertised the senior shop steward whom Dempster had tried to get sacked was appointed. His tenure of office coincided with an increase in membership, terms and conditions improved and the union was seen in a new light.

George Craig, for that was his name, performed his duties with distinction in the Antrim area and later in Coleraine and Derry before resigning the position on a point of principle. George had been sent for by the then Regional Secretary, John Freeman, who had succeeded Norman Kennedy. Freeman encouraged him to apply for the Northern Ireland Secretary's job advising him he had been earmarked for the position. This post would require him to move to Belfast. What John Freeman failed to tell George was that he had promised the same job to at least seven other officials. Craig himself was a man of principle and could never get over this deception by the man who was his boss. When he retired he went to live on the north coast but I still see him occasionally and receive a card from him at Christmas. In contrast, in my view, Freeman could be relied on to always put his own interests before everything else.

As a member of both the Regional Committee and the Sub-Committee I also had a say on various other matters. Officials had to submit a quarterly report which was scrutinised and debated. These reports would contain information on the workings of the branch for which they were responsible, list what meetings had been held, what improvements had been made in respect of terms and conditions and recruitment among other things. I recall one occasion when we received a report from an officer which highlighted what he claimed were improvements in the terms and conditions of the members he represented. On closer examination it was obvious that the trade-offs conceded far outweighed the benefits. I proposed that the report be rejected and returned with instructions that the proposals be renegotiated. The proposal was seconded and passed which once again did not go down well with the full-time officers.

The full-time officers realised that if they did not do their job they might be next in line. I was instrumental in having another directive sent to all branches which would ensure that a general meeting of members would be held at least monthly and that any changes to terms and conditions must be put to the members for approval or rejection. In other words the branches had not only to be democratic in their structure but also had to be run democratically.

Even the Regional Secretary, Norman Kennedy[1] found himself at the wrong end of the Regional Committee's decisions when he was appointed to a government quango[2] that had been established after the prorogation of the Northern Ireland Parliament in 1972 by Willie Whitelaw, the Secretary of State for Northern Ireland. The Regional Committee, by a unanimous decision, instructed him not to accept the appointment. He said that the committee did not have the authority to overrule him as he was the Irish Regional Secretary. He was advised by the Chairman that clarification had been obtained from Head Office which had confirmed the chair's ruling and that he must comply with the Regional Committee decision. I will have more tales of quangos later.

During this time I was still nevertheless earning my living as a bus driver though more and more of my time was taken up with union activities. But for ten years, prior to becoming a full-time official in 1977, I was heavily involved in the affairs of the union right across Ireland but particularly in Northern Ireland where most of the union's members were. As the anecdotes I have just recounted illustrate, this vantage point at the top of the union gave me plenty of opportunity to see who among my colleagues were working effectively for their members, which of them were only going through the motions and who were just timeservers working for themselves.

Being at the heart of the union regionally reinforced the instinct that I had had as a schoolboy walking down the Carron Road when my school mates and I went 'on strike' against a tyrannical school master – though he was probably no worse than many and typical of his times. Without the ability to combine in a union the individual worker was in as hopeless a case as those hapless children on that road a lifetime ago.

I immersed myself in the union and came to appreciate that it was also important that it was bigger than just Belfast; that it needed to have influence also where power lay and where laws were made. Over time I got to know many of the leading spirits in the union, in Northern Ireland across the island of Ireland – because Region 11 covers the whole of Ireland – and throughout the rest of the United Kingdom. In time I would serve as a full-time official under several General Secretaries and I came to see quite clearly that while the number of members that the union had was the source of its strength, the effectiveness of that strength depended greatly on the character, integrity and intelligence with which it was used.

Jack Jones as a young man wearing a beret, recently returned from Spain

JACK JONES ARCHIVE MODERN RECORDS CENTRE, UNIVERSITY OF WARWICK (625/17/428)

Beyond a doubt numbers and unity mattered; but what was equally vital was how individuals in key positions used the strength that numbers and unity potentially gave them.

The General Secretary set the tone and the standard for the entire union. During this period I served four different General Secretaries; Jack Jones, Moss Evans, Ron Todd and Bill Morris. Bill was the first and so far only member of an ethnic minority to become General Secretary.

Jack Jones

As stated elsewhere in this book Jack Jones was in my opinion the best, not only for his leadership and how he built up the union, but how he improved the working conditions of working class people. Jack never forgot his roots or the background from which he came. Even in retirement he did not cease in his efforts to improve the lives of the less well off.

I remember an occasion shortly after I had been appointed as an official. A bus driver attended the office of the ATGWU finance department after he had been prosecuted for some minor traffic offence. Under the rules he would qualify for legal representation provided he had 39 weeks paid-up membership. Even though he was a member in good standing the finance officer turned him down on the grounds that the incident for which he was prosecuted occurred prior to completing the 39 weeks. He then came to my office to see if I could assist him. I went downstairs to the finance office and instructed that he be given the necessary approval to see a solicitor. The finance officer refused whereupon I went upstairs to see the Regional Secretary, John Freeman, and requested that he instruct the finance officer to comply with my instruction, which he did.

Not to be outdone, the finance officer then rang Jack Jones the General Secretary. Jack asked who the official was. The officer informed him that it was a new official called Eugene O'Callaghan. Jack replied, 'Well he is going to be a good official, this union is not about bureaucracy or red tape, I hope you understand that.' Needless to say I never had any more problems in that area. That was Jack, the members always came first.

All trade union officials including myself come in for criticism at one time or another. In all my years I have never heard anyone have a bad word to say about Jack Jones. Trade union officers, in particular senior officials, tend when they retire to walk away and make no further contribution, not Jack. Having set up the Retired Members' Association he travelled up and down the country organising meetings, seminars and education classes for pensioners, lobbying parliament on behalf of the poor and underprivileged right up to his death at 96 years of age. At the end of his sessions Jack would get up and give a rendition of Harry Lauder's famous song:

> Keep right on to the end of the road,
> Keep right on to the end ...
> Tho' you're tired and weary
> Still journey on till you come to your happy abode.

Moss Evans

I never got to know or have the same relationship with Moss Evans. I did meet him on a number of occasions when he visited the region or at biannual delegate conferences. Moss was more low-key than Jack. In my view it was just a job to him. When he did visit Northern Ireland he was described by those who came into contact with him as having short arms and long pockets. I do not think I need interpret that further.

Ron Todd

Ron was an ex-paratrooper and a decent enough sort of fellow. He was the only General Secretary who stood down within months of being elected. This all came about as a result of allegations of ballot rigging in the first election when Ron Todd was opposed by George Wright. George was the Welsh Regional Secretary and the darling of the Tory press, who portrayed him as the saviour of the union and favourite to take the position. What the press and George Wright did not understand was that by associating himself with right wingers he was putting himself in a no-win situation. The ballot of members was held and when the count took place Ron Todd was a convincing winner. The right wing press then called foul and made allegations of ballot rigging. These allegations were not confined to Great Britain but spread to Ireland. The bus branches in Ireland came under scrutiny despite the fact that every depot had a ballot box where members could vote.

Ballot boxes were manned by scrutinisers elected by the branch. A few individuals claimed they could not get a vote and these allegations were made to a *Daily Express* reporter. From what I was told I believe they were made in McAreavy's pub after plenty of alcohol was supplied. Needless to say, on investigation it was found that there was no substance to the claim.

Meanwhile when George Wright arrived from Wales displaying two large suitcases which he claimed contained evidence of ballot irregularities he was met at the railway station by a posse of reporters. Once again the evidence did not stack up which meant Ron Todd was eligible to assume the office of General Secretary. To everyone's surprise Ron promptly resigned and called for a re-election stating that he would not accept official duties while any doubt remained about the ballot.

Todd makes new attack on reforms

LABOUR 88

SHOCK-WAVES from Mr Ron Todd's denunciation of Labour's policy reforms continued to reverberate around the party's conference yesterday.

The party leadership tried to minimise the damage and divisions Mr Todd has caused but already they were steeling themselves for further turmoil today as right and left clash once again over nuclear weapons.

Labour leader Mr Neil Kinnock had to listen grim-faced on the conference platform to the Transport and General Workers' Union general secretary renew his warning that the Aims and Values statement, written by Mr Kinnock and his deputy Mr Roy Hattersley, had to take second place to democratic decisions of the conference.

Mr Todd, speaking in support of a motion calling for Conservative union legislation to be repealed, said if it was approved by the conference it would become party policy.

"We will insist on that as we will that statement, does not and cannot supersede democratic decisions of the conference," he said.

Mr Todd also told delegates, to loud applause while Mr Kinnock sat in stony silence: "Yes, I do have a Filofax, I do have a car, I have a word processor, a computer — but I'll tell you something else I have: I have a belief in the union's policies that we have carried out over the years."

Then, to Mr Kinnock's dismay, Mr Tony Benn used a debate on energy to attack the idea that Labour should operate a mixed economy, while the miners' leader, Mr

ON ATTACK: union chief Ron Todd angers Kinnock faithful

from decisions which helped to boost his authority over the party.

Delegates narrowly resolved that constituency votes in leadership elections should be decided in future on the b

The ballot was re-run with Ron being re-elected with a massive majority. George Wright returned to Wales with as the saying goes 'his tail between his legs'. Ron was an easy-going fellow and not a great orator. He was not the type to inspire an audience. However he did provide the backup required when Northern Ireland bus services were under threat of privatisation.

Bill Morris – now Lord Morris of Handsworth

Lord Morris of Handsworth by Chris McAndrew

Bill Morris is a West Indian. Born in Jamaica, he came to England as a teenager with his mother after the death of his father. He was appointed first as a district officer and later the National Officer for the road transport industry. In other words he had overall responsibility for the road passenger industry throughout the UK including Northern Ireland. He was responsible for negotiating terms and conditions through the National Joint Industrial Council (NJIC) which covered the municipal bus workers and the rural bus workers. For the purposes of negotiation these were separate operations.

As for Northern Ireland – he never became involved. When asked about this on a number of occasions he would say, 'The man I have there is more than capable of doing the job without any help from me.'

It was during his term as National Officer that I got to know him. I was impressed at how he prepared and submitted his application for improved terms and conditions; the amount of detail was phenomenal so I made it my business to travel over to London to meet him. The meeting took place during a delegate conference called to discuss the workings of the bus industry.

I took the liberty of inviting him to Belfast, an invitation which he accepted. As I had prepared the groundwork he was given a resounding welcome.

Bill was elected three times. The first was to the position of Deputy General Secretary under Ron Todd. Bill saw off no fewer than eight other challengers for this position. Ron Todd retired as General Secretary in 1991 and Bill Morris was elected, beating the Welsh Regional Secretary, George Wright. Historically the General Secretary once elected remained in post until retirement. Legislation was changed by the Tories and re-election had to be sought every five years. Bill would have been obliged to seek re-election in 1996. He chose to bring forward the date of the election to 1995.

Bill's opponent this time was Jack Dromey who was a senior official of the union. Dromey's campaign was backed by the modernising 'New Labour' wing of the Labour Party of which Dromey's MP wife, Harriet Harman, was a leading member.

All the big guns in the union were lined up in Dromey's favour. From memory apart from the invariably robust and reliable Eddie Sheridan – my successor as the busmen's full-time officer – mine was the only dissenting voice. I was retired but I still had some sway among the busmen and I teamed up with Eddie to support Bill Morris.

We did this in the face of opposition from within the Irish region. Our Irish secretary, John Freeman, did everything in his power to stop Bill getting any branch nominations in Ireland. Our branches defied instructions and nominated him anyway. This brought us into conflict with Freeman. We then went further and invited Bill Morris to address a number of meetings which we organised. This did not sit well with Freeman. We were summoned to his office and told that we did not have the authority to invite Morris without his permission. The meetings went ahead and took place in Transport House.

Bill Morris was duly nominated by our branches and subsequently re-elected General Secretary. This he achieved against all the odds including the stoked up racial prejudices of the time. One English newspaper, apparently had a front page headline, 'Irish man runs for top job against Trinidadian'. This was wrong as regards the origins of the two contestants – Bill was from the West Indies but not Trinidad and while Jack was of Irish descent he was born and grew up in England.

It is a sad reflection on society that the colour of one's skin or the place in which they worship is used against them even if their ability to do the job far outweighs the ability of their opponents.

Judging by my working knowledge of the author over many years, the pages of this book speak to his commitment to public transport in delivering social and economic justice to all sections of the community without fear or favour.

BILL MORRIS, LORD MORRIS OF HANDSWORTH
TGWU General Secretary, 1992–2003

5
Meanwhile back on the buses

During my ten years on the union's Regional Committee there were further changes to the bus industry: in the way it delivered its services and in the pay and conditions of its workforce.

Workers are entitled to pay and conditions which enable them to maintain a decent standard of living for themselves and their families. In their retirement they deserve a pension that recognises their years of service to the community and protects them from ending their days in poverty.

However, the work of rationalising – or cost cutting – in the industry continued relentlessly. In 1969, while I was still employed as an Ulsterbus driver, one-man buses were introduced to Belfast. The Corporation reached an agreement with the union for an enhanced payment for operating these vehicles – 17.5 per cent for single-deck buses and 25 per cent for double-decker buses. When double-decker buses were phased out in 1992 a common rate of 22 per cent was agreed for the single deckers. These were now much larger carrying up to 78 seated and 22 standing passengers. The introduction of the one-man buses of course meant that conductors who could not be retrained as drivers were made redundant. Some, of a certain age who had the required length of service, were able to avail of the pension scheme.

Drivers now had to issue tickets as well as drive buses. If tickets were issued as they had been by bus conductors this would have slowed down journeys considerably. To overcome this problem machines which accepted tokens were fitted to buses. These tokens could be purchased in advance at different outlets at a small discount to the normal fare. Tickets, however, could still be purchased from drivers.

In the drive to eliminate bus conductors bus tokens were introduced on 20 February 1970

The scheme was badly thought out and may have cost the company millions in lost revenue – I have never seen a convincing calculation of the total cost. Many scams were used to cheat the system. The major one was that counterfeit tokens were being turned out at engineering works and sold on to shops who in turn sold them to the public. Shops were raided by the police and prosecutions made. These events made front page headlines resulting in the scheme being abolished.

The token fiasco was followed by the eight-journey ticket. Again this ticket could be purchased either from the driver or from various outlets. In order to speed up passenger flow 'cancellators' were fitted, one of which was half way down the bus. This system enabled passengers to cancel their own tickets after boarding the bus. As the system depended on the honesty of the passengers it too was open to abuse and it should have been no surprise that fare evasion took place on a massive scale with substantial loss of revenue. This in turn led to increased fares for the honest passenger and to the public picking up the cost in subsides. Eventually this system also had to go.

The eight-journey ticket

Next we saw the introduction of the wayfarer register which could print out tickets and which has been modified and upgraded and which, at the time of writing, is still in use. In summary, a lack of vision and poor management had to be paid for in one way or another out of the public purse. So who knows if abolishing bus conductors actually saved money?

6
The inferno:
years of mayhem and murder

Bristol LHs Nos 1108 and 1109 burn in the aftermath of Bloody Friday at Great Victoria Street depot on 21 July 1972. Transport targets that day included the bus depots at Great Victoria Street, Oxford Street and Smithfield

© BRITISH PATHÉ LTD

In 1969, following the creation of the Civil Rights movement, demonstrations were organised and marches held to demand 'One Man One Vote' and for housing to be allocated on the principles of equality and need.

Opposition to the Civil Rights movement was organised by the Rev. Ian Paisley with counter demonstrations leading to wide-scale rioting. Public transport was now coming under sustained attack; buses were burned and used as road blocks on numerous occasions.

With the introduction of internment in 1971 the situation deteriorated further. Violence increased dramatically with gun attacks and bombings taking place on a scale never before experienced. Bus drivers were no longer safe from being attacked and also robbed. Whole streets were burned down. Both sides now seemed hell bent on destroying public transport.

On 21 July 1972, Bloody Friday brought a heightened reign of terror. A total of 26 bombs were planted by the Provisional Irish Republican Army (IRA) and, in the resulting explosions, 11 people were killed and a further 130 civilians injured.

At 2:48pm[1] a car bomb exploded outside the Ulsterbus depot on Oxford Street, the busiest bus station in Northern Ireland. An Austin 1100 saloon car loaded with explosives had been driven to the rear of the depot. The explosions resulted in the greatest loss of life and the greatest number of civilian casualties up to that date. At Oxford Street some of the victims' bodies were torn to pieces by the blast, which led the authorities to give an initial estimate of 11 deaths. The area was being cleared but was still crowded when the bomb exploded.

Two British soldiers, Stephen Cooper (19)[2] and Philip Price (27),[3] were near the bomb when it detonated and were killed outright. Three Protestant civilians who worked for Ulsterbus were killed: a young parcel boy, William Crothers (15),[4] Thomas Killops (39)[5] and Jackie Gibson (45).[6] One other Protestant Ulsterbus employee, who was a member of the Ulster Defence Association, was also killed in the blast: William Irvine (18).[7] Crothers, Killops and Irvine had been in the vicinity of the car bomb helping to search for the device at the moment it exploded, killing the three men instantly. Bus driver Jackie Gibson was killed after having completed his bus route just minutes before the blast. Almost 40 people suffered injuries. These were not just cold statistics to me but flesh and blood people whom I encountered daily in my working life – now just callously blasted to smithereens leaving behind a long trail of pain and grief.

Jack Campbell, previously encountered in the story as the head inspector when I started with the UTA in Smithfield, and who was now the Oxford Street depot manager, was blown on to a flat roof and badly injured but thankfully survived.

I had been on a day's holiday when I heard on the car radio about the bombs. When I arrived at the depot I found utter chaos and panic. Dickie

GLENOWEN PATRICIA, BALMORAL,19

Tommy Killops, a former bus conductor from Portadown, and I shared an interest in showing dogs, an interest I had taken up a few years earlier. Coming up to my birthday one year, my wife Patricia had been wondering what to buy me and we were down in Murphy's shop in Gresham Street. He was asking £5 for an Irish Terrier bitch pup but she beat him down to £4.50. A couple of years later nothing would please Tommy but to have one of her pups. But poor Tommy never had any money so I said, 'I'll tell you what – you do me a painting of my dog and I'll give you the pup.' Tommy was a great painter and painted the banners for Orange lodges and so forth. But this pup was more trouble in the house than his wife could put up with so he asked me if I would take it back, which I did. Tommy was blown to pieces two days later.

His poor widow was naturally disconsolate and her sorrow was compounded by her anguish for making Tommy give the pup back. So she asked me for it back. When I went to see her about the claim for compensation because of Tommy's death she was sitting weeping in her chair and nursing the pup. Tommy's painting of my terrier 'Glenowen Patricia' still hangs on our landing.

Atwell and John Hinds were collecting the remains of those killed. I joined in and eventually a sort of deadly calm was restored. Dickie Atwell and I visited the homes of those killed. We extended our sympathy and assured them that whatever assistance was required would be made available. We arranged for immediate access to a union solicitor, making an immediate £1,000 grant from the union available to cover urgent needs.

Dickie and I then formed a small committee of members who were anxious to help. We sawed a barrel in half; one half was placed in Oxford Street station and the other in Great Victoria Street. Smithfield station had already been bombed out of existence. We made an appeal through the media for donations towards a fund for those killed and injured. As usual the Northern Ireland public was more than generous and a substantial amount was raised. This was divided equally among the families.

It would be remiss of me not to pay tribute to Dickie Atwell who at that time and indeed throughout the Troubles up to his death was a tower of strength. We were from different sides of Northern Ireland's divide and despite that or maybe because of that he was one of the best friends I ever had. Even before Bloody Friday Dickie himself had been put to the test when his brother, William, was killed by a bomb thrown over the wall at Mackie's Engineering plant where he worked.

On the morning of the incident, 9 August 1971, Dickie was in my house. He had been on duty at the corner of Cromac Street and Ormeau Avenue directing buses away from Cromac Street due to attacks on buses in that area. I was on my way into Oxford Street driving the Belvoir Park bus. As things had quietened down I told him to jump in as there was now no need from him to be there. That was my last run of the morning

Dickie Atwell with his wife Sarah, Eugene and Patsy

part of my duties so afterwards I brought Dickie to my house to get some breakfast.

While there I received a phone call from Jack Campbell who asked if Dickie was with me. As Dickie was supposed to be on duty I said no. Jack then said: 'This is very serious. His brother has just been killed at Mackies'.[8] I looked across at Dickie and did not know what to say. After an intake of breath I asked Jack to leave it with me as I knew how to contact him. I then turned to Dickie and said, 'Take my car and go straight home; your brother has been badly injured in a bomb explosion.' I did not want to tell him he was dead.

I did not see Dickie again until the day of the funeral. When I indicated to some of my colleagues my intention of attending I was strongly advised not to. Indeed, some said I was mad to even think about it as I could be killed. The number of death notices in the paper had indicated Dickie's brother was a member of the Masonic and Orange lodges. I made it clear that as Dickie was my friend I was going. On the day of the funeral Dickie spotted me. He came over and said, 'I want you to carry the coffin as my friend.' I said, 'Are you sure? I will stick out like a sore thumb as almost everyone else is wearing a collarette'. He said, 'It makes no difference; it's what I want.'

I duly carried out his wishes. As it so happened that my 'lift' – my turn – came as we were rounding the bend where all the press were lined up taking photographs. I do not know what they made of it, a Catholic with no collarette carrying the coffin.

Over the years my relationship with Dickie Atwell and his family remained steadfast. My wife and I attended his daughters' weddings and likewise he and his wife attended weddings of members of my family. We socialised together and remained friends – our friendship undiminished by was happening around us.

Trade union solicitors were now processing compensation claims on behalf of those killed or injured on Bloody Friday. In respect of one case I was summoned to the Regional Secretary's office. 'Eugene' he said, 'you have dropped us in it. We are now going to have to pay out twice in some of these cases'. He produced a letter from a firm of solicitors acting on behalf of a Scottish woman who claimed she was the legal wife of one of those killed and was entitled to the money paid out.

I asked to see the letter. Having read it I said: 'If you read the rule book it says that benefit will be paid at the discretion of the union where deemed appropriate. As far as I am concerned the woman who got the money may not be his legal wife but she has four children with him and lived with him. So I exercised my discretion.' He told me to deal with it so I wrote to the solicitors and as a result heard nothing further.

It is interesting to note that in 2017 the Supreme Court reached a conclusion similar to mine in a pension's case which coincidentally also involved a Translink employee, Leonard McMullen. Although Mr McMullen had been a member of the pension scheme throughout his employment until his untimely death, Northern Ireland Local Government Officers Pension Scheme (NILGOS) declined to honour the pension entitlements of his surviving unmarried partner Denise Brewster who successfully brought a legal case and was eventually awarded survivor pension rights.[9]

After the funerals we were contacted by Mr Heubeck. An approach had been made to the company by Jim Kilfedder, the maverick Independent Unionist MP for North Down, about holding a memorial service for the victims in the bus station. At that time I had agreed a policy with the company that we would have no dealings with politicians from any side as they brought us nothing but trouble and were only interested in scoring points. Against my better judgement and bearing in mind that all those killed in the Oxford Street bomb were of the Protestant community I agreed. After Mr Kilfedder had completed the service I approached him and put it to him that as we were in the process of organising a collection on behalf of the victims it would be appreciated if he, in addition to making a contribution himself, would approach his fellow MPs to make a donation. After two weeks of waiting and having heard nothing from him I wrote to him reminding him of his undertaking. I received the princely sum of £2.50 as a contribution from him.

The union solicitors were organised and instructed to lodge claims on behalf of the relatives of those killed and also on behalf of those injured. I visited all of the homes and made sure that those entitled to claim did so. An approach was made to me by Inspector McGouran acting on behalf of Jack Campbell who was in hospital. When I enquired if he could tell me what he wanted he said, 'It's in connection with his claim; Jack would like to speak with you.' I visited Jack in hospital; we discussed what had happened on that awful day. He then asked me to look after his interests and prepare a claim for him. After I had pointed out that it was normal for the company solicitor to handle management cases he was still insistent that I look after his case. When I asked if he was absolutely sure he said, 'I believe I know you long enough to know that you will ensure that I get the best deal possible'.

After I had thought it through I decided not to use the services of the Union solicitors. Instead I approached Sean O'Neill who had taken over from M.J. Bready in Donegall Street. I was satisfied that he would be best suited to handle Jack's case. I went to see him and gave him a brief outline of the facts and asked would he represent Jack to which he agreed. I met with him and Jack on a number of occasions to consult on the case. Jack received a substantial out of court settlement.

I do not know for sure Jack's reason for wanting me involved. I do, however, believe that it was due to the fact that during the time he was off work his salary continued to be paid. If the company solicitors had handled his case in all probability they would have reclaimed the salary out of the settlement. I can never be sure but thankfully Jack made a good recovery and returned to work.

Jack was management and I was a trade union representative but despite operating on different sides we became good friends and often had a drink together. On numerous occasions when standing at the bar he would remove some particle of glass which had lodged in his body as a result of the bomb and had worked its way to the surface. Jack has now passed away.

Dickie became very active in the trade union and was elected on to the General Executive Council which met at least quarterly in London. The GEC as it was known operated as the governing body of the union. Dickie established himself as a first class representative earning the respect of all concerned including the General Secretary, Ron Todd. Unfortunately, Dickie died from a heart attack while attending a meeting in London. Such was the esteem in which he was held that the General Secretary cancelled all his appointments to attend the funeral. The union lost a wonderful stalwart and I lost a wonderful friend.

Meanwhile the attacks on public transport continued unabated. Buses were being destroyed at an alarming rate. The injuries to drivers kept piling up. But it was not only the buses. The violence continued to escalate and got to the stage where you were no longer safe in your own home. On 6 September 1972 I arrived home and went upstairs to wash and shave when the room was rocked by an explosion. I looked outside to see what the cause was. A bomb had been thrown into the hallway of a house

across the street; the house was occupied by Councillor James O'Kane of the Republican Labour Party.

I rushed out and went across to the house by which time a crowd had gathered. An army patrol had also arrived on the scene. The house and street were full of dust with sparks flying from what I believe was the house wiring being disconnected. Floors had collapsed due to the explosion. People were shouting that there were children in the house. I volunteered to go in but I would need a torch or a light of some kind.

A young soldier who had a torch volunteered to assist handing his rifle to one of his colleagues. We safely negotiated the broken stairs avoiding the collapsed part of the flooring. We reached the children and carried them out. To my horror instead of thanking the young soldier for his help in rescuing the children he was verbally abused in a way which made me feel very ashamed. It was only the next day that I learned that beneath the hall door which had been blown in by the force of the explosion was the body of a women, Bridget Breen,[10] who lived nearby and had gone in to use the telephone. Unknowingly, we had been walking over her body.

The children who had no clothes as they were in their pyjamas and either in bed or getting ready for bed were taken in by my wife and looked after for a number of days. She clothed them with some of our own children's clothes until they were able to be taken back by their parents.

Bristol RE 1054 bus destroyed at Stanley's Walk, Derry city, *c.* 1978. In 1969, Ulsterbus upgraded its Derry City Services fleet with 20 new Bristol RE buses, Nos 1051–70. Such was the scale of destruction, only one, No. 1058, saw a full service life, being withdrawn in 1985; the other 19 were destroyed between 1972 and 1983

PRIVATE COLLECTION

61

On another occasion arriving home from work on a bright summer's evening after alighting from my car, I observed a number of soldiers standing at the corner of Vancouver Drive and Cedar Avenue which was approximately 20 yards from my front door. They were standing with rifles at the ready; smoke was billowing from Vancouver Drive indicating a fire of some sort. I approached the soldiers and enquired what was wrong. The soldier nearest to me informed me that a car had been set on fire going on to say, 'I think it's a trap set to lure us in.' At that moment a shot rang out. I could see the sparks where the bullet had hit the ground before ricocheting upwards striking the soldier I was speaking to in the upper leg. As he fell to the ground he said, 'Please help me.' By this time the rest of the patrol had taken shelter behind garden walls or hedges. Putting my hands under his armpits I dragged him back along the entry out of the line of fire. Blood was pouring out of the wound in his leg. He reached me some kind of scarf and pleaded with me to tie it round his leg to stop the bleeding, tears were in his eyes, whether from fear or pain, I am not sure.

At times like this you do not stop to think: you simply act – not out of courage but out of an instinct that it is the right and humane thing to do. When I had secured the scarf and stemmed the flow of blood it dawned on me that it was time to get out of there. I made my way down the entry at the rear of my home as you can imagine my hands were covered in blood as were my clothes. When I tried to get in the entry door to my backyard I found the door securely locked. I knocked loudly, although I knew according to our house rules no one would open it. This meant I had to retrace my steps still covered in blood not knowing what would happen.

When I got in the front door I shouted at my wife Patsy, 'You kept me locked out. I could have been shot.' She replied, 'You always told us to keep the entry doors locked to prevent gunmen from running through the house', which was of course correct. When I told her what happened she said, 'You did the right thing, he was some mother's son. I would like to think if it was one of our sons someone would help them.' At times like that you don't think – just act.

Recently when discussing this incident with one of my daughters she reminded me of how I had changed the front door handles to work in the opposite direction. The door was always kept unlocked for the children who knew the handle worked in the opposite way but a stranger turning the handle would think the door was locked. On the only occasion when knowing this could have been a matter of life and death I had forgotten it entirely!

The early '70s were taking a toll every day and brought their own harrowing stories. Hijackings, robbery and assault continued. Soon the intention was murder. Sydney Agnew[11] was hijacked and his bus burned on the dual carriageway at the top of the Ormeau Road. The police were charging and bringing to court those they believed were responsible. Mr Agnew was summoned as a witness. When this became known this unfortunate man who had committed no crime was shot dead on his own doorstep (18 January 1972).

Paddy Crossan[12] was shot dead (2 March 1973) on his bus at Woodvale off the Shankill Road. His only 'crime' was the fact that he was a bus driver, earning an honest wage for his wife and family, a Catholic and a soft target. Nevertheless, life had to go on. Some sections of the population were growing closer together and working out ways of getting by.

When it seemed it could not get any worse, in 1974 the loyalist paramilitaries called a political strike which became known as the 'Ulster Workers' Council (UWC) strike'. Its target was the power-sharing executive whose supporters in the Unionist community had been the big losers in the 1974 Westminster elections. In the beginning this was largely ignored and people went to work as normal. Workers, however, left their cars at home for fear of having them hijacked and went to work by bus. Initially drivers were not harmed provided they carried out the rioters' instructions and drove their bus into a position to block the road whereupon the bus would be set alight. It was later claimed that these so-called vigilantes were only protecting their area. The failure of the authorities to deal with the problem encouraged the paramilitaries to step up their actions, take control of the fuel depots and escalate their campaign against public transport.

Road blocks were erected to stop people going about their lawful business; workers were threatened and assaulted with seemingly little attempt by the authorities to address the problem. I remain convinced that it was the failure of the authorities to stamp out this practice early that contributed to the instability created. Buses, which were attempting to provide a service to the public and bring children to school, were attacked and drivers assaulted. In the end people stayed at home. Finally,

Belfast Telegraph

THURSDAY, MAY 23, 1974 Price 4p

RELIABLE INFORMATION
Every Night in the
Belfast Telegraph

In the line for relief—today's scene at Belfast's main labour exchange.

EMERGENCY TALKS ON PETROL CRISIS

in the interest of safety the management decided to withdraw services. The population were living in fear with atrocities being carried out by all sides involved in the conflict. The paramilitaries appeared to be in full control despite the fact that there were 14,000 heavily armed soldiers and police.

A further problem was created as those claiming benefits were not able to obtain their giros[13] as all the benefit offices were closed. The man who came to their aid was Paddy Devlin, an MP with the Social Democratic and Labour Party (SDLP) and also the Minister responsible for Health and Social Services. Paddy was a decent man; he over-ruled the civil servants and ordered them to post out the giros. There was widespread chaos as all and sundry were claiming including those who were organising the strikes. Paddy became known as 'Paddy Giro'.[14]

At the time of the UWC strike I lived in Cedar Avenue off the Antrim Road in Belfast. I was able to get bread brought in from the country via Ulsterbus which I then shared out with the neighbours. Gas and electricity

The army operate petrol stations during the UWC strike, 1974

VICTOR PATTERSON

were being rationed out at the behest of the paramilitaries who – unhindered (as it seemed to the public) – had taken control of the power stations. One neighbour who was a builder, Seamus Feighan, had a large acetylene gas cylinder which we used for cooking. On one occasion having run out of milk someone went into town and came back with an electric milk float fully laden with milk.

The Ulster Defence Association took over the fuel and the power stations. They were allowed to influence what was appearing in news reports and had control over what was happening in some parts of the country. In Belfast, the capital city of Northern Ireland, they held total control. In order to function the paramilitaries not only asked for but demanded contributions from the business community which they claimed was to cover the cost of refreshments for the vigilantes. Woe unto the business which did not pay up. For them it was a question of who to fear most.

Over the period of the loyalist strike 44 people were killed in Northern Ireland and the Republic.[15] Three days into the UWC strike, on 17 May 1974, two Ulster Volunteer Force (UVF) teams from the Belfast and Mid-Ulster brigades detonated three 'no warning' car bombs in Dublin's city centre during the Friday evening rush hour, resulting in 26 deaths and close to 300 injuries. Ninety minutes later a fourth car bomb exploded in Monaghan killing another seven people. Nobody has ever been convicted for these attacks. Through those 19 days in May another 11 individuals died, bringing the grim count to 44 fatalities.

But the threat to buses and bus crews did not end with the ending of the Ulster Workers' strike which brought down the power-sharing executive. Matters continued to deteriorate with armed paramilitaries from both camps setting the agenda with their terror campaigns. Innocent civilians were being assassinated and murdered indiscriminately. You only had to be in the wrong place at the wrong time to suffer such a fate – a most violent death at the hands of murder gangs who roamed the streets seeking out victims. As if these killings by paramilitaries were not bad enough the work of the Historical Enquires Team has demonstrated that some members of the security forces were not only willing participants in the killing but also supplying information and identifying those marked for assassination.

In this situation it is not my intention to take sides or justify in any shape or form the actions of any particular organisation. Rather my intention is to say what it was like to be a bus driver and to highlight the courage and dedication of bus workers who through their commitment under appalling conditions brought children to school, workers to their employment and helped maintain a form of some kind of normality for the people of Northern Ireland.

Just for a moment reflect on the kind of Northern Ireland we would have if the paramilitaries had gained control of public transport. Ghettoisation would have been created on a scale unimaginable. In some areas schools would have had to be abandoned; workers would be afraid to venture out of their own area; hospitals would not have been properly staffed as nurses and other hospital workers would be unable to travel for fear of attack. In certain areas of the city the police were refusing to enter unless escorted by the army. They were all armed with the most modern equipment using armoured vehicles known popularly as 'pigs'. Yet bus drivers – without any form of protection – were providing a highly vulnerable service to the public. It was in fact so vunerable that over the course of those years the entire bus fleet in Northern Ireland was destroyed and had to be replaced.

It is difficult for people now to fully appreciate just how exposed and at risk bus drivers were. Mobile phones and the remote tracking and monitoring of individual vehicles were things of the future. In the 1970s drivers had no means of communication and no means of summoning assistance. Soldiers going into battle have comrades facing the same risks with them. Each bus driver was on his own – every time he left the depot. Even when he made it safely back to the depot the driver's problems were not yet over; he still had to get home through the dark and deserted streets where any encounter would be a legitimate cause for apprehension. And if it went badly even one single encounter with violent men could leave a driver – even if not physically injured – severely traumatised for the rest of his life. It took a special kind of dogged courage to operate in those conditions.

The drivers also had to live in the knowledge that their occupation imposed a tremendous psychological burden on their loved ones. It is easy to dismiss it now but think what it was like then. The generality of what was happening on the streets was on the television news every night. Try to imagine yourself into the fears of the wife, the children, the mother, the father watching the burning buses on the news and wondering anxiously if the driver caught up in the hideous drama was the man who had left their house a few hours earlier to play his part in keeping alive the hope that normal life in Belfast could survive.

In my opinion the media did not help by behaving in a way which heightened fears and in so doing promoted tensions. How often did we see relatives of those killed or injured having a microphone stuck in their faces with the usual loaded questions? Do you expect retaliation? Do you think there will be retaliation? What would you like to happen to those responsible?

What did the journalists hope the unfortunate wife, husband, son or daughter would say? They – the reporters – were like vultures hovering over a carcass. I often wondered were they partly disappointed when the relatives of victims appealed as they so often did for no retaliation and expressed the heroic hearfelt plea that no other family should have to suffer what they were currently suffering.

Keeping the buses on the road and moving was critically important. Above all else they maintained the connections of daily life between home and work and home and school. But how we got through those years I really do not know.

I am certainly not attempting to paint all bus drivers as angels for that was certainly not the case. Of course they were human and considering what they had to endure should it be a surprise if on the odd occasion they were to lose their cool? But you would imagine in the times when bus services were not to the level of what normally would be expected, that, before sounding off, a little understanding from members of the public of the problems should be called for. After all they were avidly watching their television screens so they knew or should have known what the situation on the ground was like. Let me give an example.

On one occasion due to a bomb scare buses were being diverted away from Chichester Street, outside Malcolm's the jewellers. People were being shepherded away from the area. One irate intending-passenger who had been waiting for a bus was giving verbal abuse to the inspector who was trying to clear the area. When the bomb went off showering the area with glass how did the intending passenger respond? 'You see. You bloody busmen, you'll get an excuse for anything!' But maybe this was just another example of that famous Belfast gallows humour that enabled people to survive and stay sane amid the inhuman madness of daily life in their city.

7
The full-time official

Perhaps it will seem strange that after I have been so
forthright in my criticisms of full-time officers that I
should in time join their ranks – and lay myself open
to all the criticisms I had made of some of them. And
as with the other steps in my life it was not a
straightforward progression from militant shop
steward to full-time official.

In 1976 a job became available for a union official to service the tobacco
factories. I decided to apply for the job and was granted an interview.
Having briefed myself in advance on all aspects of the industry, I sailed
through the interview and was the unanimous choice of the interviewing
panel.

What happened next is not formally recorded in the union's annals. I
only had it on the word of one of the members of the appointment panel
that had interviewed me. However, it perfectly explains that what
happened next, is credible and somehow fits with what I had come to
learn of the moral ambivalence of the union which was – on many
occasions – fortunately checkmated by the courage and integrity of
individual union members who fully lived up to the standards to which
the union formally subscribed but did not always honour as it should.

According to my informant, the Regional Secretary, who had sat on the
appointing panel, convinced two of the three members to change their
minds. He advised them that he was reliably informed that my
appointment would lead to several thousand members leaving the union.
The tobacco industry had a majority Protestant workforce and they
would not accept a Catholic official. This was the information which was

passed on to me by the panel member who had refused to change his mind, standing by his original decision. So I was not appointed – ironically the victim of religious discrimination by my own union. Of course this example of discrimination and favouritism did not deter me from continuing to agitate and promote the case for improvements in the terms and conditions of bus workers.

On one occasion, during the course of a strike at the Oxford Street depot, we were addressed by the Northern Ireland Secretary who was still the same Cecil Vance whom we met already in the farcical episode at Enkalon. When he was addressing the meeting Vance pulled out a gold watch from the waistcoat he was wearing. He informed the meeting he had been presented with the watch by Gallaher's Tobacco for the years of loyal service he had given. Hugh McVeigh, who was sitting next to him, snatched the watch and flung it down the concrete steps; needless to say the meeting, and the watch, broke up to the cheers of those present.

There was a deadly, dark sequel to this story which all too starkly shows the way in which the humdrum of the normal daily life of an industrial city rubbed shoulders with a much more sinister reality. Hugh McVeigh left the buses and got a job as a van driver. Big Hugh, as he was known, was a member of the loyalist paramilitary organisation, the UDA. He was later kidnapped and murdered by a rival loyalist organisation – the Ulster Volunteer Force.[1] His helper, David Douglas, was also kidnapped and murdered with him.[2] The bodies were later dug up from an unmarked grave off Gobbins Road near Whitehead. I believe the bodies were found on information supplied to the security forces by an informant.

In the latter stages of 1976 Max Reid who was the official for the 11/15 Ulsterbus Branch died from a heart attack. Sid Percy, who was the official for the 11/12 branch which represented the Citybus drivers, assumed responsibility for both branches which continued to meet separately. It was during this period that Sid Percy also died of a heart attack which left a vacancy for a full-time official for the bus industry. It was decided by the powers that be to appoint a stand-in official to cover the work pending the appointment of a permanent official. This was the prerogative of the Regional Secretary. To the surprise of many he appointed Eddie Sheridan, a Citybus driver, as the stand-in official. The general belief and expectation was that, as chairman of the Bus Council and chairman of the branch Regional Committee, I would have been appointed.

I learned later that a delegation of drivers went to the Regional Secretary's office and made their views known in no uncertain manner. Strange to say, after that I was asked by the Regional Secretary if I would share the position with Eddie Sheridan. Mindful of what former US President Lyndon B. Johnson once said, 'Better to have him inside the tent pissing out than outside pissing in', I took the offer. But who was in this tent? After a period of time I discovered that it was the company and not the union that was paying my wages. This was indeed going a step too far so I went back to the driving. When the job was eventually advertised I did not apply.

A few days after the closing date the Regional Secretary approached me saying, 'Eugene I see you have not applied for the job'. I said: 'You're right I did not.' He asked why I had not applied and I responded by reminding him of my previous experience at interview. He then asked me to come in the next day and complete an application form. I highlighted to him that the closing date for applications had passed to which he said, 'It doesn't matter. I'll take care of that.' I went in the next day, completed the application form, was subsequently interviewed, and was appointed by the unanimous decision of the panel.

My first day as an official was 10 May 1977. If ever a full-time union officer had a baptism of fire I had it that day. The United Unionist Action Council (UUAC), involving Ian Paisley and others, attempted to repeat the success of the earlier UWC strike (1974), by calling another. Within an hour of my arriving for work Transport House was swarming with angry bus drivers. Harry Bradshaw, a bus driver, had just been shot dead by a UDA gunman, Kenny McClinton.[3] Jim Rutherford had been badly wounded. Their offence? Failing to comply with the strike demands. Harry Bradshaw was a 46-year-old married man with five children, a Protestant and a driver with Citybus. On 10 May 1977 he was shot by the UDA on the Crumlin Road when he stopped the bus to pick up passengers.

The big room in Transport House was capable of holding five to six hundred people. I had the room opened and Joe Trainor set up the tannoy system; I knew it would be difficult to be heard above the shouting. The first question hurled at me was, 'What are you going to do about it?' I responded just as strongly asking, 'What do you expect me to do. Wave a magic wand and do what the army and police have failed to do, round these people up and lock them away?' I said, 'It's your decision what we do but let me assure you that whatever decision is taken I will support it. Now let us have a reasonable discussion, the enemy is not in this room, we are not here to quarrel among ourselves.'

Another driver spoke up and said, 'The man is right. We are not here to fight each other.' The meeting lasted over two hours with some very heated exchanges. I then put forward a suggestion that all services would be withdrawn until after the funeral when we would again convene and make a decision on the way forward. The suggestion was put forward as a proposal, seconded and agreed. All bus services were stopped for three days after the murder.

After the meeting I was surrounded by the media demanding answers to all sorts of questions: When would the buses be back? What is your next move? Television and newspapers all wanted statements. I learned a lot on the first day on how to handle the media. Following one question, my responses, despite the very dark and angry mood, drew a laugh. I was being pressed at the same time by both the *Irish News* and the *News Letter* for a statement. I started by asking, 'Who's first: the Voice of the Vatican or the Protestant Telegraph? I want to make sure I respond in a suitable manner for your readers.'

In the period leading up to the funeral, following a visit to Harry Bradshaw's home, I arranged to meet with Mr Heubeck. Obviously we had plenty to talk about. His first reaction was to get the buses back on the road and only withdraw them during the funeral. I made it clear that in view of the decision taken at the meeting this was a non-starter. It was not a time for belligerence if he wanted the services resumed after the funeral – and that would be the earliest – then I required a gesture from him in that there would be no loss of pay for anyone. If this was agreed then I would endeavour to get a full resumption of services the day after the funeral.

In addition, I needed a step up in security. Shop stewards should be released from normal duties and supplied with a company vehicle in order to scout the roads at night, they should be supplied with a two-way radio, and if danger was imminent they would be able to contact central control, who would then divert or withdraw buses if stoning or riots were taking place on a particular road. I also said that we should examine ways of securing the driver's cab to protect them and make it more difficult for them to be assaulted.

The next step was a meeting with the Secretary of State to be arranged by the Regional Secretary. John Freeman, as was well known in the Transport Union, made large financial donations to the Labour Party and therefore had some influence within that party. Freeman liked to think that as the Irish Regional Secretary he was a man of importance and where possible would like the public to think so as well. His contribution was to arrange a meeting with Roy Mason, the Labour MP, who was at that time the Northern Ireland Secretary of State. As my immediate boss he directed that I fulfil that engagement. When attending the meeting, which was held at Stormont Castle, I made sure I was accompanied by the senior shop stewards. Having met previous Secretaries of State, I was keenly aware how statements could be misrepresented. It would not be what you said but what 'they said that you said' which would be reported as fact.

When we arrived for the meeting, having cleared all the security checks, we were received by Don Concannon who was Mason's Minister of State. Following introductions, he advised us that as Roy Mason was unavoidably delayed he would be taking the meeting. I looked at him and before I could say anything one of the shop stewards launched into a verbal assault in what can only be described as un-parliamentary language. Concannon looked at me and raised his eyebrows.

I said: 'Let us be very clear, either you get Mason and you get him now or I'm telling you that the buses will be back alright but they will be back to blockade Stormont and I will make sure the public know the type of arse hole we have running the country. Furthermore, busmen will be putting questions to our executive committee on the question of political contributions to the Labour Party.'

Concannon asked us to wait a few minutes. After 15 minutes he returned followed by Roy Mason. Now Mason was a very small man smoking a bent pipe who put me in mind of a then popular cartoon character, Popeye the Sailor Man. Unfortunately, he did not have Popeye's magical flair for acquiring instant strength to bring about quick solutions to problems. He started by telling us that he was on top of things, everything was under control and how he was going to resolve 'the problems', as he called them. Quite frankly, he talked a lot of rubbish; as one shop steward put it, 'If that's who's in charge of Northern Ireland then God help us.' The whole exercise, as I believed it would be, was a complete waste of time.

Harry Bradshaw was buried in Carmoney cemetery; the funeral was attended by hundreds of bus drivers who were aware that I had arranged a meeting for that afternoon. They said I was mad as things could get out of hand. Nevertheless, the arrangements stood; it was time to show leadership.

Prior to the meeting I had arranged for a number of prominent speakers to be in attendance and address the bus workers. First up was Sandy Scott, a shipyard worker and shop steward. Following the riots and widespread intimidation in 1969, at an impromptu meeting of the shipyard shop stewards they decided to call a mass meeting of their workforce the following day. At the meeting, as senior shop steward, Sandy Scott appealed: 'If we act as workers irrespective of our religion we can hope for an expansion in work opportunities and a better life.' Scott commended the busmen on their courage and how despite violence, intimidation, injury and even murder they had stood together and defied the extreme elements trying to enforce the 'strike'. He went on to say how proud he was to have the opportunity of addressing the meeting and said it was one of the proudest moments of his life to be among real heroes.

Next up was Donal Nevin of the Irish Congress of Trade Unions. Donal said he would endorse everything Sandy Scott had said and that the

Harry Bradshaw was shot while driving his bus on the Crumlin Road during the loyalist strike

News Letter, 11 May 1977

73

Bus crews attending
the funeral of Harry
Bradshaw, 13 May
1977

example the bus workers had shown in their determination to demand the right to work, their refusal to be bullied and the courage they had shown were admired throughout the length and breadth of Ireland. The third speaker was Andy Holmes, a well-known trade unionist and a member of the Communist Party. Andy was a superb orator and well versed in the ability to speak at length on any subject. On this day he was at his brilliant best. Terry Carlin, the Northern Ireland Secretary of ICTU, was next to lavish his praise on the actions of the bus workers; he said that they had set the template for other workers to follow.

When it came to my turn to speak and wind up the meeting I was convinced that we would win the day and that there would be a full resumption of services the next day. I outlined what discussions had taken place and what efforts would be made to secure their safety; I said that there could be no guarantees for that would be impossible but what I could guarantee was that no-one would lose a penny in wages for the period they had been off the road. This announcement was met with applause as obviously everyone who lived from wage packet to wage packet needed the money. I then went on to say that by returning to work in an orderly fashion they would be defending the principles for which Harry had died. To have a debate or invite questions at this stage was the wrong option, it was better to make a decision while the men were in the right mood. Therefore, I recommended a return to work the next morning which was unanimously endorsed. The following morning there was a full resumption of services and 'Paisley's strike' as it was known collapsed.

Following the end of the 'strike', the commitments I had given were implemented and shop stewards who were prepared to undertake the scouting job were relieved from driving duty on full pay; a company car in the form of a black taxi which was fitted with a phone connection was made available. This facilitated contact to the radio room at Lagan Bank Road thus enabling some degree of control in diverting buses away from danger areas.

Ongoing experiments were carried out to see if a solution could be found to protect drivers from attack. This was a very difficult problem to solve because what we thought was a solution to safeguard drivers had its drawbacks in the event of petrol bomb attacks. If the driver was encased in the security cab the delay in getting out put him in even greater danger. Despite the best efforts of all involved we never did find a satisfactory solution to this problem.

Kenny McClinton, the person responsible for the murder of Harry Bradshaw, was arrested, charged and brought before the courts. He was found guilty and sent to prison. Following the killing, the UDA wrote to Harry's widow, Sheila Bradshaw, stating that they were sorry for the murder and that they had believed her husband to be a Catholic. A ten-pound note was included with the letter. However, according to Martin Dillon, the attack was ordered by James Craig.[4] Craig wanted to send out a message to other Protestant bus drivers that their failure to support the strike as they had done in 1974 was not going unnoticed.

Ian Paisley who instigated the strike which resulted in the death of an innocent bus driver was never charged with any offence. He was instead honoured, fêted and flattered by the British establishment, ending up as First Minister of Northern Ireland. Compare the treatment of that 'strike leader' with what happened to the striking coal miners in Margaret Thatcher's Britain who were striking to protect their livelihoods. They were battered off the roads and dragged before the courts.

I was hijacked four times. One time I was robbed in Ladybrook; your man robbed me and he only got about £13. He turned around and handed me a pound and said, 'Here you go driver get yourself a drink.'

One night the Falls Road depot was set on fire and 13 buses were burnt out; this was back in the day when there were no mobile phones; we had to stay in the depot all night to help out and make sure the service was up and running for the public by morning. When I got home the next day my wife was furious, she was worried sick about me, but that's the way it was.

I've had many happy years working on the buses. We had our dark days when some of our drivers were shot dead, that was hard to get over. It was a horrific time. You were going up roads and you weren't sure if you were going to come back down them.

KEVIN MAGUIRE
Started on the buses 17 July 1967
and retired 25 April 2017

75

8

Keeping the buses on the move – an improbable alliance

I had had dealings with Werner Heubeck before
I became a full-time officer of the ATGWU but as
I have recounted in the preceding chapter the tragic
events on my first day in post threw us together
more than ever to face the common foe.

I have already recounted the ad hoc way we had produced a pragmatic resolution to a very difficult industrial relations problem which had been allowed to develop in the bus tours side of the business. Our solution was not a text book answer but it served both our interests and contributed to building the confidence and trust between us, which no matter how adversarial our relationship might be on particular industrial relations issues endured throughout Heubeck's time at Ulsterbus. We were – let's face it – a most unlikely combination; you could not make it up if you tried. The 'odd couple' that had to try to keep Ulster's buses on the roads and its bus drivers safe was a team made up of a former soldier in Germany's Afrika Corps and a Catholic trade unionist from what some in the media and some politicians chose to demonise as the 'bandit country' of Crossmaglen.

We were also outsiders in a world where everyone was dripping with degrees and diplomas because we both left school with no formal qualifications. What we knew we had learned from life and hard experience. Werner Heubeck was a tough man and a brave man. He was born in Nuremberg in 1923 and at the age of 19 he was conscripted from the Hitler Youth to be a soldier and engineer in the Luftwaffe's Herman Goering division. He was posted to France, then Italy and finally North Africa. The ship in which he was being evacuated from North Africa was

sunk but he managed to swim several miles back to the North African coast where he was taken prisoner and sent to the United States. After the war, back in Germany and working as a proof reader and translator at the Nuremberg trials, he met and eventually married Monica who had worked in Bletchley Park breaking German codes during the war. He was working in Scotland when he saw the advertisement for the job of UTA managing director in 1965.

He died in 2009 and I was not at liberty before to recount his good deeds to alleviate suffering because he swore me to secrecy on the grounds – or so he said – that he never wanted to appear 'soft'. But after all these years it is only right that tribute should be paid to his decency and humanity in a period of our history when man's inhumanity to man dominated the news headlines.

He once said to me, 'Mr O'Callaghan you have a very high IQ in reading situations.' My response was, 'No, but I do have animal cunning when weighing up what was going on in another fellow's mind.' And it was this combination of 'bleeding hearts and bloody brains' that enabled us to keep the buses on the roads during those years when never a day went by without attacks on buses and assaults on drivers. We were also management and labour, normally engaged in naturally combative roles and, as will become evident before long, we had our disputes which we fought vigorously.

Werner Heubeck visiting another burnt-out bus station, 1974
VICTOR PATTERSON

I even had to take action to stop him driving buses in an emergency – he had his HGV licence but I regarded it as unacceptable to have him driving a bus for PR reasons whether designed to boost his own public standing or to put the unions in a bad light. I had no support from the union hierarchy for this uncompromising line – 'they're his bloody buses – sure he can drive them if he likes'. But my reasoning was that if we allowed Heubeck to drive buses before we knew it he would have inspectors driving buses during industrial disputes. So it could not be allowed to develop. We settled this argument, however, in a humorous way which reflected the spirit of an adversarial relationship devoid of any personal rancour. It was agreed that if Werner drove a bus the bus driver who was next on the rota and who should have been driving it would be paid as if he and not Werner had done the driving.

Clearly what we shared was a passionate concern for the industry and the men who kept it going – 17 of whom paid with their lives just for doing their job. And we were fast running out of replacement vehicles. Between 1964 and 1998 – as Michael Collins in his book *Buses Under Fire* meticulously recorded – 1,484 buses were maliciously destroyed.[1] An idea was floated and acted upon whereby large numbers of old second-hand buses were purchased in England. Shop stewards were organised to drive them to the boats which brought them to Belfast. On arrival they were initially parked in Duncrue Street and later at Sydenham Airport. Engineers set about making them fit for service which meant that if ten buses were lost the previous day we had another ten ready to roll the next morning. In that way we were able to maintain a service. The buses may not have been the most modern but they managed to do the job.

An oil tanker was also purchased as were storage tanks. The Managing Director himself would drive the lorry. As an ex-soldier who had served in Rommel's Afrika Corps Werner Heubeck had obviously learned – perhaps from that time during the desert war when the German Army ran out of fuel – of the importance of having fuel supplies secured. And with the risk, as happened during the first UWC 'strike', that the paramilitaries could take full control of fuel supplies and ration it out, Mr Heubeck was going to make sure that the buses had adequate supplies.

Again I can say that buses or no buses, fuel or no fuel, there still would have been no service if it had not been for the courage of the men who drove the buses and the women who anxiously waited each night wondering if they would return home safely. But as well as the physical battle to keep people safe there was a major physchological battle for the hearts and minds of the people. The public had to believe that they need not be driven into conflict with their fellow citizens in order to survive; they had to be persuaded that it would be possible for people to live together in a peaceful future. I believe that the Transport Union played a major role in ensuring that sectarianism was not allowed to gain a stranglehold. It was not just a matter of fine words or backbone or stiff upper lips. We had to take positive steps to retain the confidence of the workers and the public; to anticipate the changing nature of the threats that the bus industry faced and deal quickly with the unexpected.

At one stage, for example, we were facing a situation where the blue Ulsterbus vehicles were threatening that they would refuse to come into Belfast. This followed a bad incident when a Newry bus was hijacked, taken to Sandy Row and the driver kidnapped and held for a period of time. It is understandable that a driver from the country, possibly from an area where everyone knows everyone else, on being asked to come into Belfast late at night would be fearful and apprehensive. Again we were able to overcome this problem using various approaches with some confidence-building arrangements but the possible loss of employment was another consideration for drivers if they failed to carry out their allocated duties.

Buses acquired in Great Britain to replace destroyed vehicles were often put to work in their original colours. Bristol RE No. 730 was purchased in August 1987 from Cumberland Motor Services, Whitehaven, where it had been used on workers' services at the Sellafield nuclear plant. This created rumours that the buses were lead-lined. It was destroyed in 1988

PAUL SAVAGE

Another replacement bus bought in from England. This one came from Ribble Motor Services, Preston and was pressed into service without even a proper external clean. Oddly, only second-hand buses ever had the 'Citybus' fleet name affixed; new deliveries just wore the red and ivory livery of the fleet

PAUL SAVAGE

We understood that if you backed down in one place other pressures would follow and ultimately the bus service would collapse. This is where the trade union shop stewards, committee men and leaders stood tall; they never asked anyone to do what they themselves were not doing on a daily basis. Somehow we weathered the storm. It is ironic that many of those carrying out the attacks expected and indeed were provided with buses for their demonstrations and rallies; buses which were driven by the same drivers whom they were attacking on other days.

Over this period in the 1970s Werner Heubeck was making a name for himself as the man who carried bombs off buses. There is no doubt he made a significant contribution as this was good for morale though it is fair to say that the drivers – because of their experience of the situation – could nearly always tell whether the package placed on board was real or a hoax. The key to this was: if it was a hoax the bombers travelled on the bus almost to its destination but if it was real they would, after robbing the driver of his identification, travel in a car behind the bus. If the driver did not do what he was told he was left in no doubt as to what would happen to him. These instances had the effect of relieving drivers of the requirement to carry their PSV badges which was the law at the time thus making it more difficult to identify them. It has to be said though in such a small a space as Belfast most of the drivers were known anyway.

Yet, to this day I am convinced that it was the sight of buses operating which created a sense of normality. That is what the busmen achieved – but at great cost in many cases. Lives were lost, many drivers injured and hospitalised, and many had mental health breakdowns, hundreds of buses were destroyed and depots operated under a state of siege. Yet despite everything that was thrown at us buses continued to operate and life went on. We coined the phrase: 'We buried the dead, bandaged the wounded and went back to work.'

There is no doubt that the public had to endure the odd wildcat strike. These originated as a result perhaps of a driver being badly injured, beaten up or robbed. One thing that can be said though is that, irrespective of the situation, if children were taken to school in the morning, services would resume for the hour in order to get the children home.

In the midst of all that was going on there emerged the growth of the black taxis. Whatever the position is today it was widely believed that the paramilitaries had a role in their organisation and it is believed that the black taxi drivers were obliged to pay for the privilege of being allowed to operate. Operating as they did in areas where the conflict affected public transport most, it came as no surprise that at no stage were the black taxis attacked but did assist in blocking roads and participating in some demonstrations.

When the army was installed in the Citybus and Ulsterbus depots this also created problems. Additionally there was the problem of Ulster Defence Regiment (UDR) members who drove buses on a daily basis. These two issues had to be addressed but this had to be done in a very delicate manner which is what I suggested when Heubeck sounded me out. I should have known better – Heubeck was not the type of man to take the diplomatic approach. He went directly to Army Headquarters in Lisburn and told them, 'I want you lot out of the depots.' I think at first they did not believe him but after a while they got the message and moved out. He also spelled out his attitude to the UDR men driving buses; he told the army 'that the Ulster Defence Regiment and driving buses don't mix',[2] and that, 'I could not stop them joining but the army had to accept the consequences.'[3] Had

Heubeck risks life to shift bus

MR WERNER Heubeck, chief of Ulsterbus, again risked his life at the weekend when he drove away a hijacked bus which could have contained a bomb.

The bus was hijacked near Kilnasaggart on Saturday by three armed and masked men, and the driver was ordered to park it under Kilnasaggart Bridge close to the border.

Cross-border train services were disrupted for the remainder of the day.

Mr Heubeck drove the bus away from the bridge, and it was found later that there were no explosives on board.

Train services were back to normal yesterday.

News Letter, 2 August 1982

I done this I would have had every Unionist politician shouting from the roof tops for my hide. But Heubeck being Heubeck – not a cheep.

When you consider it, what he did was absolutely the right thing to do. Otherwise it was only a matter of time before a bus would be hijacked and driven into a depot with a bomb on board, parked behind the army and detonated with devastating effect. Being subject to attack as bus operatives was bad enough and we could not afford the additional heightened exposure to attack from being fully identified with the army. And looked at rationally it did not make much sense for the army to be barracked with us as there was also always the possibility of their presence giving rise to friction between those who supported the armed forces and those who did not. The good relations which had been fostered between employees could have been fractured to the detriment of those relationships with a knock-on effect on transport as a whole.

With hindsight the removal of the army was the logical hard-headed thing to do and – even if it seemed to be a retreat in the face of potential attack by the Provisionals – made political and security sense. It also demonstrated that keeping politicians at arm's length and dealing with issues, which, if unresolved, would give them the opportunity of making capital out of them, was correct.

Another difficult and sensitive issue was allocating drivers to routes in 'their own territory'. Some drivers wanted Catholic drivers for Catholic roads and Protestant drivers on Protestant roads but we strongly opposed it. While this demand may have been made out of fear and not for any ulterior motive we demonstrated by weight of argument why this was a bad idea. To do so would make it easy for the gunmen on either side to identify a target. While we remained mixed it made it more difficult for them, if one side or another murdered 'one of their own' the outcry from within their own community would be such that they would be more likely to be caught. We put it to the men that there would be no 'horses for courses'; this policy was adopted and maintained throughout the Troubles.

There were lighter moments. With the visit of Pope John Paul II to Ireland in September 1979 we had a further opportunity to develop relationships. As usual Mr Heubeck – craving the limelight – announced arrangements for the transport of thousands of people to the various locations in the Republic of Ireland which the Pope was due to visit. I rang him and asked what he was doing as he had no agreement with the union in relation to what he was proposing. Heubeck responded saying he did not need an agreement. I told him that if he wanted to move all these people he would find that he certainly did need an agreement. We then had a number of meetings without making any progress and reached a stalemate. Heubeck threatened me saying he was going to go on national television and to the press where he would accuse me of obstructing his efforts by withholding consent. I said: 'Well, you do that but you won't be able to accuse me of sectarianism so go ahead if you think it will help your cause.'

I offered him the opportunity of a further meeting provided the shop stewards were present at which I would endeavour to reach agreement provided he was prepared to make the same effort. We met in the Board Room at the Falls Road depot on a Saturday morning prior to the visit. We laid out our case on how the operation should proceed. As far as possible, buses should operate in convoys led by an experienced driver used to travelling through the Republic with those less familiar with the routes taking up the rear. The routes had to be well signposted; breakdown trucks were to be stationed in strategic locations; and arranged parking for buses on arrival and proper overnight accommodation provided with a shuttle service to and from the parking sites to the accommodation. The toughest issue to crack was the rates of pay but after considerable hassle and negotiation we reached an agreement. As I could see the relief on his face I thought I would push the boat out and said, 'Mr Heubeck, I think you should show your appreciation to these shop stewards who travelled here today by taking them out to lunch.' I got no argument, he called up his righthand man, Sam Thompson, and told him to get a bus and take them all to the Chimney Corner Hotel and order lunch for them. Turning to me he said, 'You can come along as well, that is if you want to.'

When we arrived at the Chimney Corner Hotel Mr Heubeck was there also, having travelled up in his car. There was considerable delay at the hotel as they were unaware that we were coming or how many they should cater for. I then approached him and said, 'I think you should buy these fellows a drink to try and keep them happy while we are waiting.' Again there was a positive response, he asked for an empty till with a blank tape in it and told the staff to let everyone have a drink. Obviously he was unaware of the Irish way, as when there is a free for all, extra drinks are ordered and hidden behind curtains, seats and wherever.

Worse was to follow … somebody wanted to buy cigarettes! When he was told by the barman he was not allowed to take money there was a run on cigarettes and cigars. Nothing more was heard of it until six months later at a meeting in Omagh. I threw away a chance remark, 'Mr Heubeck, it's a long time since you bought a drink', he put his hand in his pocket, pulled out the till roll from the Chimney Corner thrust it at me and said, 'No, No, No, I know what you Irishmen are like at a free bar, you hide the drink and stock up for later, on that I don't mind but cigarettes and tobacco £250, no.' What the busmen did not know was that every time they ordered cigarettes or cigars there was an asterisk on the cash register roll. I sure as hell walked into that one!

Credit where credit is due, every aspect of the agreement reached at the Falls Road depot was put into operation with military precision, even to the extent that arrangements had been entered into with Ireland's national public transport provider, Córas Iompair Éireann (CIÉ), where replacement buses could be provided if necessary. Heubeck certainly loved the praise he received for his organisational skills and our members enjoyed the rates of pay negotiated so everybody benefitted.

Of course as management and unions we had our battles and these are recorded in other chapters. And perhaps I even, if inadvertently, saved his life on one occasion: at least I would like to think that I did. It happened when we both arrived at a place where a bomb had allegedly been placed in a hijacked bus. He was going to move the bus or carry off the parcel but I engaged him in conversation; while we were talking the bomb exploded.

At a personal level we rubbed along, coming over time to recognise and respect each other's strengths, commitment and integrity. But we were not on Christian name terms – except once. I declined an invitation to his leaving party when he retired as Northern Ireland's transport supremo. My refusal clearly hurt him because he said to me something along the lines of 'Eugene, why won't you come – between us we have done so much for the bus industry in Northern Ireland and I would like people to recognise that.' I gave him my reason. The hotel he had chosen for his 'big splash' had a non-unionised work force. So, fair play to Werner, he moved it to a hotel where the staff were unionised.

He was kind to me personally – he came to see me when I was recovering from illness. On one occasion he could not come at the last minute so he sent his driver with a bottle of whiskey. Now his driver was a real character and probably the only over-indulged employee of Ulsterbus. He was better fitted to drink the whiskey than I was so as one wee dram led to another before a couple of hours had passed Heubeck's whiskey was all drunk and his chauffeur was in no fit state to drive his boss's car back to base. Fortunately, I had a son in the motor trade and so the driver was packed off home and the limousine safely parked where it should have been – though its official driver phoned up the next day wondering what had happened to his boss's car. But that was another escapade he survived.

Yes, however improbable it was, we became an effective partnership and I think what we did together demonstrates how in times of trouble the most unlikely alliances of people can come together and work for the common good. It is a pity our politicians still seem so slow to learn that lesson.

However, there is one question I would give a lot to be able to ask him now. If I had asked it 30 years ago it would have saved a lot of pain and hurt for a lot of people and righted, in good time, a wrong that was waiting to burst into the light of day. It concerned pensions and it will be considered in the final chapters of this book.

I could not have asked this question 30 years ago because I did not at that time know about the covert injustice which was being practised on the busmen. But it seems to have started on Werner's watch and I would so like to have said to him, 'What the hell do you think you are doing? For goodness sake put this right before it is too late.'

But Werner retired in 1988 and died in Scotland in 2009 and neither I nor anyone else will ever be able to ask that question. Knowing and respecting him as I did and acknowledging the genuine concern he had for the well-being of his workforce, I believe that he did not fully realise the significance of what might have seemed like a minor administrative adjustment. Alerted to its full significance in time I have no doubt he would have put it right.

Queen Street, Belfast, Saturday, 31 January 2004 and driver Mickey Clarke has charge of bus No. 2548. This was the last journey worked with a Bristol RE bus, a type in service since 1976

PAUL SAVAGE

9

Union priorities – forays and excursions

I thought that there was a lengthy agenda of major priorities which the union should plan to achieve for its members who worked in the bus industry in addition to continuously seeking opportunities to improve the living and working conditions of present and past members of the industry.

As will be seen, these concerns have been the major preoccupation of my life both as shop steward and as an officer of the union and indeed subsequently have given me plenty to do in my retirement.

Two major concerns were:

- to ensure fully parity of terms and conditions between the Citybus and Ulsterbus,

- and to ensure that all employees on retirement would enjoy the pensions they were entitled to and to whose funding they had contributed.

But first I wanted to put the union's own house in order starting with myself. In the week prior to taking up my appointment I went into Transport House and, with the help of Joe Trainor, who was the caretaker, cleared out the office I was to occupy. I intended to start with a clean slate and would rise or fall by my own standards. Given the amount of physical and psychological trauma so many union members suffered during the Troubles there were an abnormally large number of claims always being processed. Both justice and union morale necessitated that members should have confidence that their claims were being speedily and competently followed up and monitored, as a day seldom went by without attacks on buses and assaults on drivers. It made my workload as a union officer very different from that of a typical official in Great Britain who would never have had to deal with the volume of claims for injury that passed across my desk.

In some ways it was like running a casualty station. We had a team of solicitors constantly processing claims. Throughout the period that I was a full-time official I kept detailed records of each individual's case. Indeed through the 15 years I worked in Transport House I kept meticulous records of events. Legal documents were filed under each solicitor's name and these files contained the records, names and dates of every case they handled including the final outcome. The minutes of all meetings held with the company were filed and logged in chronological order year after year. All correspondence was logged to and from the company as was correspondence with government. In fact everything was logged and retained. Unfortunately when I left these records were shredded when the offices were transferred from Transport House to Amicus House on the Antrim Road in 2008.

What was not appreciated then was that what the shredders were destroying was a treasure-trove of information which can never be replaced – the history of what bus work was like during the Troubles. One of the best solicitors we used was Ken Young of Greene and Gribbon with whom I had a very close working relationship. Ken was not just a paid solicitor but someone deeply committed to the labour and trade union movement. In 1970 he had stood as a Northern Ireland Labour Party candidate in North Down against the sitting Unionist MP, Jim Kilfedder. Ken never really had a chance of winning in that middle class constituency but he polled a very commendable 14,246 votes. Our working relationship later developed into a friendship and when we both retired we would occasionally meet up, as we still do, to reminisce over old times.

Ken would always give priority to bus workers and would keep me updated on the progress of each individual's case. Because of this, when a member contacted me I had an up-to-date record and could inform the individual of the stage his case was at.

TGWU Transport House, Belfast
ARNAUD ROGER, BELFAST

7

I wanted the membership to present a united front to the employer, to be well-trained, self-confident and disciplined. The death of Harry Bradshaw reinforced my belief that there was a need to unite the bus workers into one cohesive organisation – if only to strengthen our bargaining ability. I was aware that this would not be easy due to the differences in terms and conditions between Citybus and Ulsterbus. At the time that I assumed the role of full-time officer, the wages for a Citybus driver were about £15 per week higher than Ulsterbus. I decided that if progress was going to be made I would have to organise, educate the members and also try to eradicate the wages differential. But I faced a difficulty. I knew that Citybus drivers would ask the inevitable question, 'If our Ulsterbus colleagues are getting more, what are we getting?' The wages gap placed management in a strong position to exploit their power to 'divide and rule' by playing off one set of employees against the other. Sorting this one out would be no easy task. I decided to start with the structures and procedures of the union itself.

As I mentioned previously, the former Corporation Transport employees and the UTA employees had been in separate branches and this had persisted as Citybus replaced the Corporation buses and everything merged into Ulsterbus. But relations between the Ulsterbus 11/15 branch and former Belfast Corporation 11/12 branch had not been good and past attempts by the Corporation to extend the boundaries and allow their red buses to expand their catchment area had been a bone of contention. The crews of the blue buses, as the Ulsterbus buses were known – having by degrees mutated from the green of their UTA era – saw this as an incursion into the areas they serviced and, rightly or wrongly, they feared consequent job losses. As a result, the branches spent more time quarrelling among themselves than they spent on dialogue with management on issues of importance such as terms and conditions. So my strategy was first of all to end the causes of divison and the potential for conflicts of interest and create a united and cohesive trade union in the bus industry.

The Bus Council had to be restructured. I divided the province into 12 areas; each would elect a Bus Council representative. Due to its size Derry would have two council members. One would represent the city and the other the county, i.e. Claudy, Donemana, Dungiven, Limavady and Strabane. Another area example included Coleraine, Ballycastle, Ballymoney, Bushmills, Garvagh, Kilrea and Portrush. The Council met monthly in Belfast or at another location if so decided by council members. Members were paid for attending the meeting; minutes were recorded and posted to shop stewards. Council members held meetings in their local areas in order to ensure that the union members they represented were kept fully informed.

Once the Bus Council members were elected they could then elect a sub-committee which would be known as the negotiation committee. In order to comply with the general rule they would also form the branch committee. When all the structures were in place they were put before the general membership for endorsement; a similar endorsement was given by the Irish Regional Committee and the General Executive Committee of the Transport and General Workers' Union. After making these changes the members in Derry, Coleraine, Omagh, Armagh or wherever had the same say in running the branch as those in Belfast.

I personally visited almost, if not, all depots and outlined how I proposed to organise, educate and make sure every member was fully versed on the role they could play in improving conditions. I set about organising educational classes on the basis of one day per week for ten weeks with a maximum of 12 per class. Top tutors were engaged to lecture on legislation and on the various aspects of employment law. Among those who acted as tutors were J.B. McCartney, a senior law lecturer at Queen's University Belfast, and Richard Steele and Phyllis Bateson, also law lecturers from Queen's University. The Chairman of the Industrial Tribunal and representatives from the Labour Relations Agency also participated. In relation to benefits, we had lectures from representatives from the Law Centre and Social Security offices. None of the lecturers requested or received payment. A tribute must also be paid to Sean Morrissey, the TGWU's Education Officer, who prepared the agenda, organised the classes and made sure everything ran smoothly. Sean's son, Mike,[1] who was an academic, also conducted a number of seminars.

What we established soon became the trend for other branches. Due to the ever-changing legislation in relation to employment law and benefit regulations I believed it was essential for the representatives to be equipped with the knowledge to deal with issues at the level of the shop floor as that is where cases or disputes arose. What happened at that level would often be used and indeed have a bearing on the outcome of some cases at tribunals or, on appeal of tribunal decisions, at the Court of Appeal.

THE QUEEN'S UNIVERSITY OF BELFAST
STUDENT CARD 1984-85
Name OCALLAGHAN, OWEN, J.
Student No. 8489602 UG [1]
Signature O JOCallaghan
Date of B/ 02/03/29
Faculty/Year: LAW 1
Ref.: 10903 PART-TIME

Eugene's student card, 1984–5, as a law student

I later availed of the offer made to me by J.B. McCartney and sat in on some of his lectures to law students at Queen's University. His colleague Richard Steele – who was to be a key member in our 'Brandeis Brief' team – encouraged me to sit the labour law paper of the degree course.[2] I joined in with the students, sat the exam and passed with flying colours, having satisfied both the internal and external examiners. I received complimentary letters from J.B. McCartney and Richard Steele both trying to persuade me to take up law as a profession. But I had to make a living and would not have had sufficient spare time to make a success of a move of that magnitude so I had to decline. And I really was not tempted to leave my colleagues in the bus industry at this crucial stage.

The education programme we had initiated proved highly successful on a number of fronts. Shop stewards were better equipped to deal with the ever changing employment legislation, Public Service Regulations, PSV, European legislation on drivers' hours, etc. Some of those who participated progressed to higher levels within the trade union's education system. Gerry Mullan, sponsored by the branch, successfully studied for and obtained a master's degree in labour law at Queen's University. When Gerry was approached by management and offered a management position he came to see me before accepting. We discussed the offer and I suggested he take it. He said he felt guilty about it as had it not been for my and union support he would not have gained the qualifications and subsequently been in a position to receive the offer. He said he felt rotten after all we had done for him. I said, 'Well don't be. There would be no future for you in the union. The "jobs for the boys" system would see to that. Take the offer but don't expect any favours from me if we come across each other on an industrial matter.' Gerry was very intelligent and would have made an excellent research officer for the union but I could not see the union members propelling this unassertive, thoughtful man into an elected leadership position. I would have done him an injury if I had urged him to seek to make a career in the union.

Following Gerry's appointment, I was subject to regular abuse as he was seen as benefitting from a trade union-sponsored education. But he was not the only successful graduate of a union education. I could name

90

many, including numerous inspectors, who were recipients of education provided by the union, who subsequently applied for positions and were promoted within the company. I think this clearly demonstrates that a strong union raising the educational standards and skill levels of its members is good not just for the union but for the whole company and the wider economy.

The education policy also increased members' interest and participation in the trade union movement. When shop stewards were about to be elected there were so many candidates that we had to organise ballot box elections which was of course a very healthy sign. It also promoted togetherness between Citybus and Ulsterbus, so much so that I thought the time was now ripe to move them even closer. I took the opportunity with all the changes that were taking place with employment legislation to push on. I was able to promote and negotiate time off for union duties and education purposes. These negotiations were more fruitful than expected as the company agreed to 300 days paid leave for Ulsterbus employees, 70 for Citybus, and days off for a full-time convenor would be agreed between the staff officer and me.

Leo Flanagan (former shop steward) with Liam Hughes (former shop steward)

Following an approach to management I was able to get agreement for wages negotiations and other matters of major importance to be conducted on a joint basis as the old way was a duplication of effort where one part of the company met in the morning and the other in the afternoon. The afternoon meeting was a repetition of the morning with the same presentations or arguments. Meetings were normally held in the board room at the Short Strand depot. Werner Heubeck was always accompanied by his Ulsterbus area managers and/or the Citybus operations manager who advised him. I was always accompanied by my chairmen and sub-committee members. By jointly dealing with the issues at hand the company benefitted by freeing up its area managers and operations manager for part of the day while I was able to follow my own agenda of

securing greater unity and doing what everyone said was impossible, namely bringing the two branches together as a unified group while at the same time allowing them to retain their autonomy.

Following the retirement of Jack Coyle, who was the official for Derry and country bus employees, the Irish Regional Secretary transferred responsibility for Derry 11/3 branch, as it was known, to me. I did not see this as a problem as they were under the umbrella of 11/15 for the purpose of wage negotiation and I had already met with their Bus Council on a number of occasions. I arranged a general meeting of the membership in that area on a 'get to know you' basis. I gave a general outline of my ideas on how to best service the membership. Leo Flanagan was the senior shop steward. Leo was a very genuine man who called a spade a spade and not an agricultural implement. We became and remained good friends even after we both retired.

The bus branches were now the most powerful in the union as far as influence was concerned. When it came to electing delegates to rules conferences, General Executive Council or any other constitutional committee, where a vote of the entire membership was required, other branches had to seek our support. For that support they would pledge in return to support the busmen's nominations.

I would travel to Derry and hold a meeting in the evening time, having already arranged a meeting for the next morning with the Derry management. The shop stewards and I would deal with any matters arising from the previous night's meeting. Their Bus Council delegate now sat in and participated in all meetings affecting terms and conditions; he would then report back to the members. Therefore, despite the distance, the workers were kept up to date during my tenure. Whilst I was looking after the Derry men we formed a strong friendship. On my retirement they arranged a dinner for me at which they presented me with a wallet full of

The Platform Staff Agreement covered conditions of employment and rates of pay for bus drivers, auxiliary staff, cleaners and miscellaneous grades

notes and my wife, who attended, received a large bouquet of flowers. Overnight accommodation was also provided for us. I have to say a more loyal bunch of men I never met; all they ever asked for was the truth even when it was unpleasant.

I continued to build up relationships between the members of the union's different regions. On matters of major importance meetings would be arranged for a Sunday as the majority of drivers would be off duty. By arrangement with the company we laid on buses to bring the members to Transport House from outlying depots. These buses were supplied free of charge and our drivers drove them without pay. We always endeavoured to have a well-informed membership.

The branches were now so active that at election time there were more candidates for shop steward and committees than there were positions. We would prepare and send out ballot boxes, the candidates themselves would nominate scrutinisers who would be present at the count. In this way everything was seen to be fair.

We no longer followed the national trend on terms and conditions but led the field. For example for sick pay we negotiated:

	FULL PAY	HALF PAY
After six months but less than a year's service	4 weeks	4 weeks
After one year but less than two years' service	9 weeks	8 weeks
After two years but less than three years' service	13 weeks	13 weeks
After three years but less than four years' service	16 weeks	16 weeks
After four years but less than six years' service	20 weeks	20 weeks
After six years	26 weeks	26 weeks

A driver having to go off work due to an assault would be paid at average pay for the period of incapacity. While these payments may appear generous it has to be remembered the conditions under which busmen worked. We had to make sure that they were protected financially.

The continuing violence, bombings, assassinations and attacks were having a knock-on effect on the everyday life of the citizens of Belfast. Fewer and fewer people ventured out at night, resulting in Belfast City centre at times resembling a ghost town. This in turn led to a reduction in evening services, after the peak period buses only operated an hourly service. We were, however, able to prevent any redundancies.

During my long service I have seen many changes. It was a good time when BC Council left the scene and Citybus and Ulsterbus came into being as semi-government companies under the direction of Werner Heubeck. I became a steward under the new Trade Union Officer, E. O'Callaghan. He was a very abrupt man who did not suffer fools gladly, either members or management. He would have fought to his last breath for the members. With his encouragement I became branch chairman where I remained all during the Troubles. They were difficult times for shop stewards as they were always on the ground trying to keep the men going as well as worrying about their own safety.

I was hijacked a few times but was able to recover my buses after they were used as roadblocks. I was exceptionally lucky as others were shot, killed and burned.

My eldest son, a teenager at the time, was always worried when he saw rioting on television. I never told my family if I would be driving difficult routes.

I was operating as branch chairman and driver encouraging others to keep going in an effort to maintain some sort of normality in Belfast. I often wonder if I was right in maybe unknowingly sending some to their death (as happened) or being killed myself.

FRANK FOX
Over 41 years' service on buses
(1954–95) BCT, Citybus, Metro,
Translink

Along with the progressive policies we were following, we also negotiated with the employer and established what is known as the 'closed shop' – employees would become and must remain members of the trade union. But in practice bus drivers in Northern Ireland could chose between us and the GMB union.

The closed shop has always been a subject of dispute. One side argues that an individual should be free to decide for him or herself if they want to join a trade union; that it is a matter of individual rights and freedoms. The other side would point out that there is usually an enormous imbalance of power between the employer and the individual worker; the only effective way of establishing an equality of bargaining power is for the workers to band together and speak with one voice. But if most workers band together and pool their resources and secure improved terms and conditions, any individual who shares all the benefits of the improvements in pay and conditions but does not contribute to the common effort is getting a free ride.

Such behaviour is seen as selfish, unfair and unethical. There is a deep-rooted public resentment towards those who do not pay their share as the current anger about the ultra rich and multinational companies who go to great lengths to avoid paying their fair share of taxes demonstrates. Not being prepared to pay your union dues is like not paying your taxes but expecting the NHS to be there for you when you are ill, or the fire brigade to turn out for you if there is a fire at your property. So I do not believe trade unionists should be in the slightest degree apologetic for seeking to establish and enforce the closed shop. The consequence of living in a society, where in so many ways we all have obligations to act collectively, is that we all have limitations on our total freedom to act, without regard to the effect on our fellow citizens or workers, whether it is to wear seat belts in our cars or the loss of freedom to smoke where it will damage the health of other people.

So I make no apology to anyone for the trade unions' desire to secure the closed shop. The power to enforce the closed shop should always be one of contributions which the trade union movement insists that a Labour government makes to the betterment of the lives of working people. The Conservatives made a fetish of removing it, proving beyond doubt its importance in the armory of working people. Any future Labour government worthy of the name should surely restore it.

But in Belfast one individual, a Mr M–, refused to sign up; the company was informed and given an ultimatum.

Max Hale was the operations manager at that time. Now Max was an Orangeman but he had an Achilles heel in that it was said that Max would go to Mass if it would avoid a strike. Max suspended M– until he got himself a trade union card. Strange as it may seem, as Mr M– was a Catholic, he brought his case to the Rev. Ian Paisley. On the morning after M– was suspended I was summoned to the Regional Secretary's office. The first thing I noticed was his state of excitement: 'Eugene', he said, 'have you a problem with a fellow called M–?' I replied, 'No, but he has a problem with me, as a result of his refusal to join the union.' Getting more excited by the minute he said, 'It's Dr Paisley on the phone, I think you'd better talk to him.' I took the phone and said, 'Mr Paisley, O'Callaghan here, what's your problem?'

He started by telling me that he represented Mr M– and what I should or should not do. I interrupted his flow of speech and asked if he still ran the four buses used to bring his people to the Martyrs Memorial Church. He replied that he did but asked what has that got to do with it? 'Well', I said, 'you give him a job; to my knowledge your drivers don't belong to a union, now stop bothering me.'

John Freeman, our Regional Secretary, was standing with his mouth open. When he got over the shock he asked, 'Do you have to be so bloody ignorant?' When walking out of his office I said, 'The next time anyone rings you about buses tell the switch board to put the call through to me, I am the officer not you.' I am sure that with the many incidents experienced over a lifetime Ian Paisley probably forgot all about it. Mr M– never did get his job back.

As a result of the policies pursued on education, members became more aware of their rights which in turn led to more disputes in particular on scheduling. EEC Law on drivers' hours was now a major issue and was something with which local managers had not yet got to grips. When disputes arose, under the procedure, the area managers and I were called in to try to resolve the issues. In the majority of cases compromises were reached and the problems solved. On the odd occasion where agreement was not possible then the issue was referred to the managing director and me. These cases proved to be very time consuming. Nevertheless, they had to be dealt with.

The depot at Larne never seemed to be able to resolve scheduling problems. For reasons I could never comprehend the GMB steward – without fail – turned down any and all proposals put to him. The full-time GMB official would support him and as disputes could not be settled without both officials being present I found myself being dragged into needless disputes which did nothing for the image of either the unions or the company.

The GMB shop steward would inevitably call an overtime ban, which in Larne had the effect of causing major disruption to the services. This only served to irritate the public. While I have no complaint about imposing overtime bans when appropriate, there was an agreed and established procedure for resolving the disputes affecting Larne. But the ban was usually put in place before full-time officials had the opportunity of addressing the issues. In some cases, where the ban had been introduced, a number of services which could not be operated were subsequently withdrawn as the dispute had exposed a lack of demand from the travelling public for these services. This resulted in the union 'shooting the members in the foot' as the drivers ended up worse off than before they started. As I pointed out to my own members, the quickest way to social justice is industrial action but it is also the quickest way to disaster. If you decide to take industrial action you decide the issues and

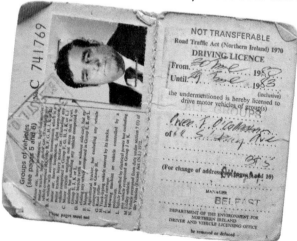

make sure they are fought on your ground.

By now the policies we in the Transport and General Workers' Union were pursuing were paying off in terms of membership numbers. We had increased our position from a minority to where we now had 90 per cent of the employees to the GMB's 10 per cent.

10
Tribunals and quangos:
in whose interest do we serve?

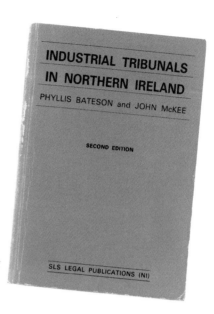

It was around that time I was invited to serve on the Supplementary Benefits Appeal Committee.

This was a committee which heard from claimants appealing against decisions of the Benefits Adjudication Officer regarding grant applications for benefits or other such matters. The position was voluntary and attracted no payment but it was, however, very rewarding as it provided an insight into what real poverty was all about and the humiliation experienced by claimants having to appear before an appeals tribunal seeking assistance. Some represented themselves, others were represented by would-be politicians who were, in the main, unqualified with little or no knowledge of the legislation.

The experience gave me a greater understanding of what life was like for the unemployed and the very poor. The case which sticks in my mind concerned two old ladies from Blythe Street which was off Sandy Row. They were a mother and daughter. The mother was 78 years old and the daughter 60 years old. They had made an application to the Department for a grant to purchase a folding bed. The application had been turned down by the benefits officer. The case was built on the fact that they lived in a small house. The mother suffered from arthritis and cardiac problems. The benefits officer's case was that they already had a folding bed. I asked the mother if this was correct. 'We have sir,' she replied 'but it's broken and we can't put it up.'

Turning to the benefits officer, I asked if this was correct. 'It is', he replied, 'but with a bit of effort it could be put up.' I asked him what age he was. 'Thirty-four', he said. I said, 'Is it not a bit rich for you to expect a 78-year-old woman with arthritis and a heart problem to be able to exert the same degree of pressure which you as a 34-year-old man could?' He then said, 'Well, we could get it fixed.' I asked how he proposed to do that. He said that we could take it to a garage and get it welded. 'How much would that cost and how do you propose bringing it there?', I asked. 'Well we could hire a van', he replied.

It was normal practice for the panel to retire after hearing all the evidence and reach a decision. However, by this time I was exasperated as it was clear that the cost of the repair would exceed the saving. The sensible thing would have been to grant the application and the case should never have been brought to the appeals committee. I said: 'I have heard enough bloody nonsense, as far as I am concerned the application will be granted.' So without further ado the appeal was upheld. As they were leaving, the daughter, who was pushing her mother in front of her, said in a very loud Belfast accent for everyone to hear: 'Ma, if it hadn't been for that wee Free State man them bastards would have give us nothing.' As I mentioned earlier, because my south Armagh accent had a strong overlay of a brogue I had acquired in my youth when working in the building trade they assumed I was from, as they called it, 'the Free State'.

To say the least, benefits legislation is among the most complicated and complex. I believe that when panel members are appointed they should be given the necessary training to ensure they are capable of understanding all the issues. When adjudicating on a case they should not only understand the legislation but ensure that decisions are arrived at in a fair and equitable manner. Too often I heard a fellow panel member say, 'Well, I don't know, I'll leave it up to the chairman who is better qualified than me.' In fact the chairman is often an establishment figure, having already formed an opinion which is, as they would put it, that 'these people are already getting too much.' I speak from experience as having been in the minority on many occasions, especially in cases where the applicant was endeavouring to represent himself.

After two years I moved to the Industrial Tribunals where for 13 years I acted not only as a lay advocate but also as a panel member. During this time I had numerous successes. In the Ulster Print Workers[1] case I represented a group of workers who had been made redundant as a result of the closure of a factory following a long dispute. The company in question had a second factory and was in fact recruiting workers to that location. I argued that before making the applicants redundant they should have been offered employment at the second location. After two days of argument the tribunal found that the workers had been unfairly selected for redundancy and therefore unfairly dismissed. They were awarded compensation.

The company sought and was granted a review of the case. They engaged Phyllis Bateson QC to represent them. As I have stated previously, Phyllis was also a lecturer at Queen's University and a person I knew very well. She had helped me with advice on previous occasions. The review was heard by the Tribunal President who later became a High Court Judge. Phyllis outlined in considerable detail the reasons why the review had been sought and concluded her argument as to why the decision should be set aside.

The President looked at me and asked for my response. Getting to my feet I said, 'Mr President I will be brief, but could I first ask you to read from page 59 of your and Mrs Bateson's book on Industrial Tribunals.[2] I am prepared to allow my arguments to rest on what you both published in that book'. After pausing for a while and tapping his fingers on the desk he looked down and said, 'Mrs Bateson, I am afraid we've just been had.' The original decision was upheld.

Eugene in Transport House

Another notable case was when I was requested by a fellow trade union official to undertake a case for him. The case concerned a group of road haulage drivers who went on strike over conditions which were being imposed upon them. These drivers were subsequently dismissed. The union official concerned consulted one of our trade union solicitors who advised him against bringing a case. In view of this advice the Regional Secretary was reluctant to authorise legal funding. Without funding for legal representation my colleague turned in desperation to me. I gave my advice, which was contrary to that expressed by the solicitor, so he asked if I would take on the case. I made it clear that if I did so it would have to be on my terms with no interference from anyone. As I was my colleague's last hope he had no alternative but to agree.

I set about preparing the case, in the course of which I interviewed every driver who had been dismissed. I then researched the company's background and records. Unbeknown to many at the time there was a small publication called *Searchlight* which I believed would have valuable information. I enlisted the aid of a close friend, Jack Myers, to get me a copy from the library. Jack was a very determined character and I was confident that if there was one to be had he would find it.

The case opened before the President of the Industrial Tribunal, John Maguire. The defendants were represented by both senior and junior counsel who had been instructed by a firm of solicitors. Senior counsel was later elevated to the position of High Court Judge. The applicants were represented only by me. The applicants were none too pleased and who could blame them as their livelihoods were at stake.

In Industrial Tribunals the usual procedure is for the defendants to present their side first. Senior counsel in opening directed the President's attention to the St Edmundsbury Council case[3] claiming that arising out of the decision in that case the defendants had no case to answer. He further elaborated on various points of law. Listening to his submission, a senior official of the union was heard to remark to my colleague on whose behalf I was presenting the case, 'I told you so; he – meaning me – is out in the first round.' This was not much comfort to the unfortunate members who were depending on me salvaging something for them.

Looking over the top of his glasses, the President very sternly asked me to respond. I referred to Stock and Jones House of Lords ruling. In this case with Stock respondant and Frank Jones [Tipton] Ltd, House of Lords 13 Dec. 1977; 2 Feb. 1978,[4] it was stated that where a group of workers had been dismissed and the employer had reinstated some but not all of the workers then those who had not been re-employed were deemed to have been unfairly dismissed. In regard to the argument refusing to comply with a reasonable instruction I directed their attention to the 1976 Industrial Relations Orders.[5] In this it stated that where it might be deemed, in normal circumstances, that refusing to carry out a reasonable instruction was sufficient grounds for disciplinary action it also stated that where such an instruction requires the employee to breach a statutory regulation then the employee is quite entitled to refuse such an instruction or – to put it in very plain English – an employee cannot be sacked for refusing to break the law. I stated it would appear to me that the tribunal had a responsibility to test these arguments before arriving at a determination. At this point the President adjourned to consider the points made.

Turning to my sceptical union colleague, I said: 'Well the first round's over and I'm still standing.' On resumption the President declared that the applicants' representative was correct and the evidence would be heard. By this time Jack Myers had returned and proudly held up *Searchlight*. Jack had gone to the libraries. They did not have it. He then went to Marshall's, a large newspaper distributor, who did not have it either. Not to be outdone Jack trawled all the newsagents on his bicycle, finally finding a copy in a newsagent at Balmoral. The publication contained information which showed that the company had numerous convictions in Great Britain for traffic offences, almost all of which were for speeding. Part of our argument was that the drivers' schedules were so tight that they were compelled to break the speed limit; so this could be invaluable information.

The company's witness, who held a Certificate in Professional Competence, was a disaster under cross examination. His knowledge of European legislation was pathetically limited. When challenged on the company's speeding convictions he admitted that only by breaking the speed limit could they maintain their schedules. If he was bad, their next witness was even worse. He was employed as a driver and claimed he had never been on strike and that those on strike only did so because of threatening phone calls made to their homes. In cross examination I reminded him of the seriousness of what he was saying. I further asked if the police had been notified about these threatening phone calls to which he replied that they had. Probing further I asked what the police had done. He replied that they had done nothing. I then asked if he was aware that in a case of perjury the matter could be referred for prosecution. He insisted he was telling the truth.

I showed him a large photograph of the picket line and asked him to identify the person holding the notice which said 'Official Strike Transport Union'. When he failed to answer I said, 'Would you agree that it is you holding the placard and that you were lying when you said you never went on strike? In fact your evidence has been a tissue of lies from start to finish.'

The President took took the photograph from me, studied it for a minute or two and said it would be appropriate to adjourn for lunch. During the lunch break I telephoned Assistant Chief Constable Ramsey, whom I had met on previous occasions. I advised him of the evidence which had just been given by the defendant's witness and asked if he could check if any complaints had been made. Within 15 minutes he rang back and told me he had checked with both Glengormley and Newtownabbey and there was no record of any complaints having been made. I suggested that if it were possible I would like a witness from the police to give evidence as it was important; what had been said cast a slur on the police force. When we resumed after lunch a police officer was present.

The defendant's representative asked for an adjournment to allow them to speak with the applicant's representative. This was agreed for a short period to see if a settlement could be arrived at. When I was approached and asked what it would take to settle the case I suggested they negotiate directly with the applicant's trade union official as I was only the mouthpiece. They agreed to this and retired to a separate room. I stayed outside and did not participate. After a period they emerged and advised me that a settlement had been reached. The tribunal resumed; this was necessary in order to formally withdraw the application. The police officer was not now required to give evidence due to the settlement.

The agreement reached provided for the reinstatement of all of the dismissed drivers, compensation for loss of earnings, procedure agreement and a further meeting to be arranged with the trade union representative for the purpose of arranging pay roll deductions.

When leaving the tribunal both sides took the lift, except for me. I used the stairs. The company's financial advisor asked the trade union official, 'Where did you get that barrister?' When he replied, 'He's not a barrister, just an ordinary guy from the office next to me.' 'My God', he said, 'and he ran rings around our people and they cost thousands.'

I acted as a lay representative and panel member for 13½ years. As a panel member some of the decisions I made were controversial. The Catherine Dornan case[6] is one that springs to mind. Catherine was employed in a senior position at Belfast City Hall. A more senior post became vacant for which she applied and was unsuccessful. Her claim before the Industrial Tribunal was that she was the best qualified candidate due to her experience and her educational qualifications. Both the applicant and the defendants were represented by barristers instructed by solicitors.

During cross examination by Miss Dornan's barrister, Seamus Treacy (later to become a High Court Judge and 'Sir'), it was admitted that Miss Dornan had considerable experience in a management position albeit in a different type of work. Her educational qualifications were equally as good. But at the conclusion of the hearing by majority decision the tribunal found in favour of the defendants – the City Council. I was in the minority finding for Miss Dornan.

Now this is rather a hard one to get your head round. The majority view appears rather convoluted. They believed the real reason for Ms Dornan not getting the position had nothing to do with the merits of the two candidates, so she had not lost out on any of the normal grounds of religion, race or gender. It was that for some reason the City Council favoured the other candidate on grounds that were not based on the relative merits of the two candidates. Clearly the City Council was not going to advertise the grounds of its favouritism in public so the tribunal hearing was something of a 'phoney war'. As such it never got to the crux of the matter and so the real reasons for not appointing Miss Dornan were never put before the tribunal in a form in which the tribunal could come to a judgement on a point of law. Since it was never put forward as an argument by the defendants the tribunal was substituting their view for the view of a reasonable and fully informed tribunal.

The case subsequently went to the Court of Appeal[7] where the minority view was upheld. The case was sent back to the tribunal for further consideration. Once again there was disagreement. The other panel members argued for an amount which I believed did not represent the true value of the case. I argued for the maximum award which at that time was £10,000 plus some odd hundreds. The Chairperson agreed with me and finally the other panel members agreed resulting in a unanimous decision. The findings of this case have been quoted on many occasions when citing precedent.

I believe that during my time serving on tribunals I made a valuable contribution but the main benefit was gaining vast experience and knowledge which stood me in good stead over the years as I strove to represent my members to the best of my ability.

Becoming a full-time officer of a trade union is both a privilege and the opportunity to serve working people more effectively. But not everyone sees it that way. For some becoming a full-time official converts them from precarious employment to a salaried, pensionable job with a car and they too easily forget why they are there. For one thing the transition is not always easy.

As employees – or even as shop stewards in their place of employment – the rythym and discipline of the factory, as well as the camaraderie of their colleagues, imposes a pattern and a structure on their daily life. As a full-time official they largely set their own daily agenda and work pattern. They also move from having a massive amount of knowledge about the place they work and operate in as a shop steward to having to know a lot about many different industrial sectors, areas of law and regulations, to say nothing of the union's rules and procedures. They may well become officials for sectors of industry in which they have never worked. They are at the beck and call of their members. That was the reason I ended up having my phone number withheld because members would phone up at all hours to settle some argument on a detail they had been arguing about over a couple of pints. As a full-time official you really were thrown in at the deep end; there was little in the way of training or induction and 'burn out' was a constant risk – as I recount here some of my colleagues died in harness from heart attacks.

But there were also temptations. Union officials had influence and could be courted; they might be offered positions in which balance required a trade unionist to be appointed and such positions often brought extra money which was additional to their union salary. So they were exposed to the 'discreet charm of the bourgeoisie'[8] and could easily take on the sense of entitlement to a lifestyle that increasingly diverged from that of the members they represented. Perhaps the most pernicious effect of this on occasions was a lack of commitment to securing the best terms and conditions for their members. 'Keeping the lid on' things could be more comfortable and a lot less stressful than always striving to better the lot of their members.

Sad to say neither the union itself, nor some of its members, made much effort to check the inclination of the few who choose to rest on their laurels or of others to feather their own nests or indeed of some to work themselves into an early grave. Time and again in these recollections I have felt obliged to draw attention to the failure of the union to effectively look after its members. But perhaps even worse are the occasions when a few officials used their ascension from the ranks to promote their own interests.

I referred in Chapter 4 to the incident when the Regional Committee prevented the Regional Secretary from serving on a quango. It was a rare victory for the rank and file. Quangos are bodies which, while under the control of government, have a function which is to ensure that government undertakings are monitored in such a way as to give the impression of democratic accountability. The idea conveyed to the public was that the membership of the boards of a quango was a public administration position and as such they were advertised. They were much sought after positions in that they brought with them a handsome remuneration for one to two days' attendance per month at board meetings. Quite a number of these types of bodies were supposed to be representative of both sides of industry – that is employers and trade unions. Applicants were vetted and appointments were made at that time based on the recommendation of civil servants to the Westminster politicians sent by the government to administer Northern Ireland.

One might think that this would be a good thing and that men and women with first-hand experience from both sides of industry would be able to provide first-class guidance and advice to ministers. As such, some positions on quangos were reserved for representatives of the trade union movement but on the basis of nominations put forward by the Northern Ireland Committee of Congress. To my knowledge I cannot recall a single occasion when an ordinary rank and file member was appointed on the recommendation of NIC/ICTU – but I can recall being roundly abused for having once proposed a well-qualified lay member whose nomination, needless to say, got no further than being one of my less well received initiatives. In this way the top layers of the trade union movement were co-opted into the system. The fees they received for serving on public bodies were not paid to their unions but were added to their salaries so they were now serving two masters.

These positions looked as if they were strategically important and it should have mattered to working people that the trade union movement was effectively represented in decision making bodies and bodies with influence within government. They were also financially valuable prizes. As a result there was considerable interest at the top of the union movement as to who got what. Nominations were the subject of bargaining and deals between the top dogs in the unions. One particular senior official – held a position on the European Economic Committee, the Airport Authority, the BBC, LEDU and at least six other quangos. His income from the quangos must have far exceeded the already generous salary he earned as a union official.

And over the years little changed as would be demonstrated decades later when the Keith Moffatt affair surfaced. Moffatt became Chief

Executive of Translink in April 2003. His salary was reputed to be twice that of the prime minister, and in one year he was paid £374,000 compared to his predecessor's already generous package, which was believed to be £215,000. The full details of his and his predecessor's final year remuneration packages were revealed in answers to MLA John Dallat's written Assembly questions on 8 June 2007.[9]

Mr Moffatt resigned suddenly in unexplained circumstances towards the end of his third year in post. While the board of the Transport Holding Company expressed uncritical appreciation of his contribution to the development of public transport in Northern Ireland, his total remuneration did, however, excite some press comment. As one of the Transport Holding Company board members was the Assistant Secretary to the ICTU he was tackled about Moffatt's remuneration package by journalist Joe Oliver from the *Sunday Life*.[10]

As a trade unionist he could not defend the sums involved. Indeed he described the remuneration package as 'obscene'. But in doing so he was breaking ranks with the board of which he was a member. What happened next was to say the least bizarre but demonstrated perfectly the ambiguity of the Trade Union leaders' involvement with 'quangocracy'.

The Assistant Secretary's second term on the Transport Holding Company Board was due to end in 2008. As non-executive directors were alleged by then to be receiving around £14,000 a year it was a well-rewarded sinecure.[11]

When his term of office was coming to an end his name was put forward by the unions for this 'public service' reappointment. As he had successfully served since 2002 the last thing that could happen was that his re-appointment would be blocked on the grounds of unfitness. That would be both gratuitously insulting to him and a damning indictment of the whole system as his sacking would show that trade union members of quangos were not entitled to break ranks and be critical. But that is what happened. His nomination was rejected by the Minister,[12] on the grounds that he did not meet the criteria. So how had he been appointed on two previous occasions?

This understandably prompted an angry response from the Northern Ireland Committee of ICTU whose sense of entitlement was clearly outraged. A delegation was sent from Congress to Stormont. The conclusion: the said Assistant Secretary was later appointed to another board – Northern Ireland Water – which came under the control of the same Minister. I am not aware that it was ever revealed how he met the criteria for this board if he failed to meet the criteria for the other board.

So what were the criteria for getting picked for the board of a quango? In an effort to get to the bottom of what was going on I put my name forward for the board of the one industry of which I could claim unique, unrivalled knowledge and experience, which no-one in the Northern Ireland administration could either dispute or gainsay. In July 2008 I completed the appropriate application forms to be a member of the board of the Transport Holding Company, posted them off and waited to see what response I would get.

I was of course not hopeful. True, my background knowledge of public transport was unquestionable. True, I had actually driven buses for both Belfast Corporation and for Ulsterbus for 17 years including some of the worst years of attacks on buses. True, I had been the trade union official in charge of bus workers throughout 15 years of the Troubles and had negotiated every significant and insignificant change in the industry in that period. True, I had had meetings with almost every Secretary of State for Northern Ireland during the period when buses were burned and drivers murdered. True, I had successfully fought off attempts to privatise the undertaking by arguing the case against privatisation to the Mergers and Monopolies committee in London. But despite all this – or perhaps because of all this – I knew better than to be hopeful.

And I was not to be disappointed. No expense was spared in putting the board together. It seemed members could often be brought in from all sorts of locations outside of Northern Ireland. Perhaps my turning up expenses free on my bus pass would have lowered the tone of this prestigious body. I requested and received the interview notes and I received two marks at short-listing.

Perhaps the reason for my rejection lies in the fairly widespread perception of me as something of a maverick, or was I blacklisted for not showing enough respect to those in authority? But this is to flatter me. The stark truth is that working men and women no matter how experienced and well versed they were in any industry or sector of the economy were rarely if ever appointed to these positions. In my opinion, their expertise and their perspective on the issues were not valued and socially they are not going to be allowed to ride in the gravy train with their betters. The criteria were clearly designed to exclude working people. But as a smokescreen to obscure this statement of the obvious, a privileged few – like the nominees of ICTU who might not rock the boat – could have an exception made in their favour.

Of course this personal view is not the official position and would be disputed by any government. In order to ensure that appointments to public bodies were made in a fair and equitable manner the government had previously appointed Lord Nolan who was requested to inquire into standards in British Public life and subsequently put forward principles and proposals governing appointments to public office.[13] Those principles of selflessness, integrity, objectivity, accountability, openness and leadership were subsequently adopted. Who could disagree? But have we seen any change in the social mix of those appointed to public bodies?

I wrote to the Department for Regional Development via the Office of the Commissioner for Public Appointments challenging the assessment and received a reply which upgraded the markings but still turned me down on the basis that I did not meet the criteria. I again asked what part of the criteria I did not meet. On receipt of the response – which was to the effect that I did not own or run a business – I again wrote to the Commissioner's Office and received a reply to the effect that this was a new criterion which had been introduced. In response to a further query the Commissioner's office confirmed that the criterion was only applied by the Minister for Regional Development. I am sure the public would find it strange that a socialist minister – for so Sinn Féin describe themselves – would introduce a policy which would bar 100 per cent of working class people from positions of advice and influence. Logically, this too would have barred most if not all of ICTU's nominees because they had no more experience of running a business than I had.

You would be hard pressed to find adherence to the Nolan Principles in Northern Ireland if you take as an example Conor Murphy's criterion that you either had to own or run a business before being able to serve on the board of the Transport Holding Company, though of course no such criterion is applied to being a Minister and having charge of hundreds of millions of pounds of taxpayers' money. I would venture to say that that criterion, as well as breaching the Nolan Principles, also breaches the Equality Legislation in discriminating against the majority of the population. In fact it grants a virtual monopoly of this advisory role in our society to people all locked into the same group-think and not subject to the challenge of differing viewpoints.

It is also open to other abuses as demonstrated by the unethical behaviour of politicians in Great Britain which prompted the establishment of a committee to create a Ministerial Code to be based on the Nolan Principles.

The trade union movement has failed to be the guardian of high standards in the making of public appointments. It lets its members down when it allows some of the leaders to use their positions to advance their own positions but blocks rank and file membership from the possibility of making a greater contribution to the progress of society. And that this happens at all brings into question how our own leaders were appointed in the first place, and how the behaviour of a few who do not adhere to those high standards, is monitored and if needs be, challenged. I have already related examples of officials who really should never have been appointed and sorry to say there will be more tales of union incompetence as this story goes on.

But one example – the Marshall versus the Transport Union case[14] – probably tells you all you did not want to know about how too often the wrong people manage to populate the union hierarchy. This story, of one applicant who was not appointed, also provides insight into how some officials were appointed in a manner which is open to question.

Marshall, a female officer, sued the union before an Industrial Tribunal after she failed to obtain the position for which she applied. In the Tribunal she alleged that when she applied she was put under pressure to withdraw her application, which she refused to do. She further alleged that she was told she would not be getting the job anyway. At the hearing two serving officials were summonsed as witnesses for the applicant. Under cross examination they both stated that they had been visited by the Regional Secretary before the interviews for their positions, given a list of questions and answers, and told they would be getting the positions.

Marshall's barrister claimed the very same thing had happened in Marshall's case. The rest of the evidence was equally damning and needless to say Marshall won her case. The fall-out split the officers and staff in two which led to acrimony and bitterness. There were two sides: those who – for reasons best known to themselves – condemned the two officials who had refused to perjure themselves and those who supported their honesty.

Of course the losers in all of this are the members who – when the appointments are not made on ability – end up with incompetent officials of the kind who do not win improvements for their members even when they are shooting at an open goal.

11
Battling on other fronts: championing the 'General Workers'

The union was not called 'Transport and General Workers' for nothing.

 Most of the members did not work in transport and as a member of the Regional Committee I had had plenty of exposure to the issues which arose in other sectors. This stood me in good stead when I became a full-time official and was dispatched from time to time into battle on fronts other than transport.

In the late 1980s there was, as a result of government policy on imports and anti-trade union legislation, a sharp decline in trade union membership. The closed shop had been outlawed and recognition of trade unions by employers had become more difficult to achieve.

Restrictions on the import of carpet and linen from low-wage countries were being removed and these items were now being purchased by wholesalers at rates which could not be matched by factories in Great Britain and Northern Ireland. This in turn resulted in reduced production and job losses.

In their wisdom the management of the trade unions decided to appoint organisers to recruit unorganised workers, although it is difficult to understand why they had not been already organised. The Regional Secretary restructured the allocation of full-time officials' duties and appointed Albert Hewitt – an existing official – to organise duties. Why they chose Albert Hewitt I could never understand as that type of role was clearly not where his talents lay. Some of Hewitt's work had consisted of work previously performed by Billy Mann. Billy had serviced the membership of Courtaulds carpet factory in Donaghadee until the workers found out that he was a Catholic – after which things became unpleasant for him. I understand that a delegation

Central Office
Transport House
128 Theobald's Road
Holborn London
WC1X 8TN

from Courtaulds went to the Regional Secretary threatening to leave the union if he was not removed. To his credit the Regional Secretary refused. However, a short time later Billy Mann took early retirement with Albert Hewitt taking over. Other branches attached to the 11/105 branch which Hewitt took over were Spence Bryson Carpets in Bangor, Canadian Tec Tape, Pritchitt's Foods and Hide and Skin in Killyleagh.

At a later stage the Regional Secretary decided that I should take over responsibility for Hewitt's 11/105 branch. Given the problems within the bus industry which required almost daily attention, I felt this was an odd decision. I already had a membership of approximately 3,000 while other officers had a membership of less than 1,000. Nevertheless, like it or not, I had no say in the matter. One of the first decisions I made was that before I would take over I would commission a full audit of branch membership and finances. In order to complete this exercise I approached Ross Aiken who was the finance officer. Ross agreed to let me have the services of Audrey Ward, who was responsible for keeping Hewitt's register of membership, and Billy Hamilton a senior finance officer.

After obtaining permission from the various managers we made a tour of the factories, records were checked to ensure we had an accurate record of trade union membership. I instructed both Audrey and Billy that anyone who was not up to date with their payments was to be removed from the register. I was anxious to ensure that in a few months' time I would not be accused of losing members. This turned out to be a wise course of action as the audit established that what the branch held was in part a paper membership and in fact there were 800 fewer members than had been reported. Branch finances were also not in the best of health. Ross Aiken took a special delight in informing the Regional Secretary of the outcome.

Within a week of taking over 11/105 branch I received a call from the Donaghadee factory to the effect that the company was proposing to make 70 employees redundant. I contacted the senior shop steward and arranged for a meeting with the members. I also contacted the factory manager and personnel department for a meeting on the redundancy issue. The meeting with the membership was arranged for the following morning and timed to coincide with the end of the night shift and the start of the day shift. The meeting with management would follow. When I arrived I made a point of walking through the factory; in this way any worker could see and talk to me and I to them. When the meeting got underway there was a full turnout. I felt that this was the time to clear the air as to who I was. I pointed out that while I spoke with what many would consider a southern accent I was not a southerner but I said, 'I do come from Crossmaglen and I kick with what many of you would say is the "wrong foot"; nevertheless I am here to do a job and with your cooperation, together we will get it done.'

I then established the facts of the case, which were, that there had been no consultation, 70 employees had been selected for redundancy, there was no code of practice and quite frankly it was hard to believe that this was a union-organised factory. I then asked for those who would be accompanying me to the meeting with management to let me have their names. The senior shop steward spoke up and said, 'But we never meet with management, Albert just goes in, meets with them, then comes back and tells us what happened.' I replied, 'You must be joking!' On being assured that this was the case I said, 'That's about to change. Nominate a delegation to come with me.' They said, 'You know Sid Cormack has been brought over by management for this meeting, we call him Sid Vicious.' This was the name of a punk pop star of the time. I said, 'You nominate the delegation, you don't have to say anything if you don't want to, I will deal with the issues.'

Eventually we had a delegation and went upstairs to meet the senior managers. During the course of the introductions I made it clear that any future meetings would require the presence of the shop stewards and workers' representatives. 'No ifs and no buts', that was how it would be. Sid Cormack then outlined the company's reasons for the redundancies and reiterated that those selected had already been identified.

When he had concluded his summary of the company's position I directed him to the legislation and pointed out his and the company's failure to meet their obligations under the legislation. I then spelled out that complying with the legislation entailed a 60-day consultation period. During that period they must consider any representation made by the union, if the company rejected the union's arguments they must set out in writing their reasons. As the company had failed to follow the legislation I made it clear that I expected the redundancy notices to be withdrawn. If the redundancy notices were not withdrawn I also made it clear that I would immediately file for a protective order. I then lambasted them for their lack of procedures and reminded them that they had received a grant of £13.5 million from public funds for the purpose of underpinning existing jobs and creating new jobs. The grant contained a clawback clause which I would now put pressure on the government agency concerned to enforce. I pressed them to make their decision.

Perhaps the force of my argument and the robust way it was delivered took them by surprise. The managers had certainly never been spoken to like that before or at least not in a long time. The company asked for a short adjournment. Following a period of time, we reconvened; the managers asked for time to consult with their legal advisors.

Within two days we resumed the meeting, redundancy notices had now been withdrawn, agreement was reached for consultations to be held on the drafting of proper procedures which would then be jointly agreed. I had a further meeting with the workforce who were not only impressed but delighted with the outcome. I thought to myself now is the time to make the most of the goodwill towards the union that my robust approached had created so I said, 'Let us get this into perspective, we won a battle today because they underestimated our strength, unless you are all in the union things could be different next time.' The cry went up, 'You hear that boys, everybody get in the union.'

I then decided to push the boat out and what I said, although it overstated the position, got the reaction I needed if I was to continue to be effective in that role. I said, 'You know there is a lot more to do but unless the powers that be change their minds I may be moving on; you see I am a troubleshooter and was just sent here to clear up this problem.' As one they said, 'No way', I would be their choice and therefore not imposed upon them. Thereafter, when I visited the factory I always made a point of walking round the different departments and keeping in touch with everybody.

A letter from 3M in appreciation of Eugene's support

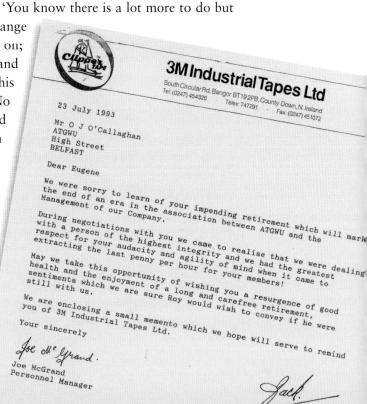

3M Industrial Tapes Ltd
South Circular Rd, Bangor BT19 2PB, County Down, N. Ireland
Tel: (0247) 454326   Telex: 747291   Fax: (0247) 451072

23 July 1993

Mr O J O'Callaghan
ATGWU
High Street
BELFAST

Dear Eugene

We were sorry to learn of your impending retirement which will mark the end of an era in the association between ATGWU and the Management of our Company.

During negotiations with you we came to realise that we were dealing with a person of the highest integrity and we had the greatest respect for your audacity and agility of mind when it came to extracting the last penny per hour for your members!

May we take this opportunity of wishing you a resurgence of good health and the enjoyment of a long and carefree retirement, sentiments which we are sure Roy would wish to convey if he were still with us.

We are enclosing a small memento which we hope will serve to remind you of 3M Industrial Tapes Ltd.

Your sincerely

Joe McGrand.
Joe McGrand
Personnel Manager

Enc

Jack.
J McCartney
Site Manager

Approximately two weeks after the initial meeting the personnel manager walked into my office in Transport House. He said, 'I am in trouble; I have been sacked and need your help.' He went on to say that he had been accused of passing on information to the unions. He said the senior managers had come in, cleared his desk and installed his replacement who had been flown over from England. I said, 'Look if I took your case they would claim that by doing so I was confirming their allegations.' I asked him to leave it with me as I would get someone to represent him.

I later contacted Richard Steele, law lecturer and an old friend. Richard agreed to handle the case as a favour to me. In discussions with the company a substantial settlement amount was agreed. One day Richard and I went into the Crawfordsburn Inn for lunch, the ex-personnel manager was at the bar having a drink. He had by then joined Denroy Plastics. He totally ignored us both despite having had his case successfully dealt with at no cost.

In further meetings with Courtaulds a new agreement was reached which embraced all aspects of the legislation. Time off on full pay was agreed for shop stewards to attend union courses and a raft of procedures were now in place to ensure the workforce was fully consulted.

For the record I can honestly say the question of my religion never became an issue; I was treated at all times with respect and had the full support of the workforce who were now 100 per cent organised. As a result of the new procedures and training most matters were being resolved without my involvement. Although this is how it should be, I still kept tabs on the situation and all agreements were passed to me for inspection and required the approval of the workforce. At the time of my retirement I was still in charge.

Spence Bryson

Spence Bryson Carpets was a small factory overseen by a very decent factory manager called Harry McConkey. It is true to say that a member of the Bryson family also participated in the running of the factory, which produced high quality carpets sold on the open market. Unlike the major producers, they did not own any retail outlets, which made it more difficult for them to compete.

My first visit to the factory was informal; the first person I met was the works study manager Freddy Burns. Freddy was a half-brother of one of the union officials, Howard Burns. I learned an awful lot from Freddie Burns. From the many visits that I made there I came to realise that there was no doubt that Freddy knew the game inside out.

Despite the company's best efforts they were finding it difficult to compete in a shrinking market, cheap imports were having a devastating effect. Freddy Burns and myself privately discussed how best to address the situation. The company operated a bonus system which operated up to a maximum of 100 per cent, anything above did not qualify which meant that wages could vary depending on production, e.g. if the machines broke down a delay in restarting them, or indeed a variety of other reasons, could affect the wage packets.

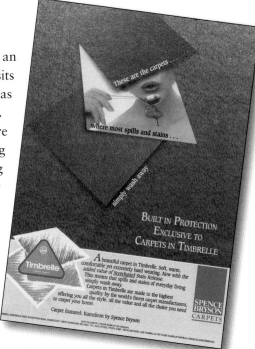

Freddy realised that by removing the ceiling on bonuses production could be increased and this would benefit both the company and the workers. However, he was convinced that the company would not buy the idea as they had an exaggerated concern about quality control. I put it to Freddy that if he could convince me and I was happy with what he said then I would put his case to the company. Freddy convinced me but was adamant that I would not be able to sell the idea. I then floated the idea of the production of a cheaper run carpet. Freddy's words were, 'Good luck to you mate.' I arranged a meeting with management and put forward the suggestions which Freddy and I had hatched. The company was totally opposed to them. 'Well', I said, 'what is the answer? Try it and if it fails what have we lost, don't try it and risk closure as the present system is not going to solve the problem.'

Freddy who was present supported the argument. I had also got Harry McConkey on board but Harry was reluctant to commit himself other than to say we could try it for a short period and if it does not work we could revert back. Jeremy Bryson finally agreed to take the proposal away and look at it. Approximately a week later we reconvened, this time the company had brought with them a high-flyer from Great Britain. Obviously they had undertaken some research into the idea and to Freddy's surprise they agreed to implement the proposal. I said, 'Hold on a minute, I need to meet the workers to convince them as we need their co-operation. I will also need Harry and Freddy present at the meeting with the workers to copper fasten the agreement.' This was accepted.

We scheduled a meeting at a time when the machinery was shut down to allow everyone to be present. I addressed the meeting and outlined all the facts emphasising what was at stake, there was no wriggle room, and if it did not work we were in trouble. For it to work everyone would need to make the effort. Freddy who had a reasonably good rapport with the workforce outlined how the scheme would benefit the workforce in terms of earnings – provided everyone played their part. He said it was up to the workforce and the ball was in their court. Harry McConkey confirmed the company would also play their part in trying to make the proposals work. It must be stressed that both sides were taking a gamble.

After the scheme was introduced production went up as did bonus payments. The cheaper carpet was selling well. If a machine stalled for a minor problem there was no waiting around for an engineer, where possible the production workers fixed it themselves. Although what had been achieved was remarkable, Freddy and I knew that it was only a temporary reprieve unless government policy on imports changed. Another problem was trying to compete with competitors who ran their own retail outlet.

Relationships between the union and the company were now very good. One day out of the blue I received a telephone call from Harry McConkey. It was about an issue which in the second decade of the twenty-first century is seldom out of the news – sexual harassment. Harry said he had a problem as one of 'your' members had pushed a canteen worker against the wall and she claimed that he tried to assault her, asking, 'What should I do?' I told him he should not have to ask, 'As you know what has to be done. Bring the man in and establish the facts, if he is guilty then dismiss him.' Harry asked, 'But what happens if I do that and there is a strike?' I told him, 'Let me worry about that, I will defend the person being harassed not the harasser.' I reminded him that we had put in place procedures for dealing with this sort of thing: 'If you do nothing and the lady sues, as she probably will, then you are in trouble; however, if you deal with it I believe you have nothing to fear.' Harry took my advice and the next call was that the workers were planning to hold a meeting which I arranged to attend.

As usual at a large meeting there were a few loud mouths saying what should and shouldn't be done. I said, 'Hold on a second, if it was your sister or your wife how would you feel? Let me be very clear, the man is lucky the police were not called.' I then spelt out the ramifications of what would entail if they walked out. The factory closes for good. I advised them to go back to their work while they still had it.

The woman in question did sue the company but lost the case as the company had procedures for dealing with matters of this kind and had implemented them and as a consequence dismissed the employee. Looking back over the 30 years that have elapsed since this incident, it is worth noting that we had all those years ago the knowledge and procedures needed to stamp out the shameful treatment of women in the workplace. Think how much further on as a society we might be if there had been the will to act on that knowledge and to unfailingly apply those procedures.

Afterwards things quietened down and the matter was never raised again. The company still struggled but managed to stay afloat for another few years, eventually closing by the time I retired.

Crepe Weavers

Crepe Weavers was situated on the Comber Road, Newtownards, employing around 150 workers. Although it was supposed to be organised by our union to my surprise I discovered we had only 20 members. I arranged a meeting with Francie Gilmore who was their spokesman. Francie was an affable type. When we met his first remarks were, 'We heard how you sorted out Donaghadee but you will have a problem here.' He went on to explain how they had been let down by the union. On one occasion they had been out on strike and when they contacted their official, he told them he was too busy and to contact him in a week or so if the dispute was not settled and he would see if he could come down.

I assured Francie that as far as I was concerned if they had a problem I would be there within 24 hours to deal with it. If I was on holiday or out of the country I would ensure that procedures would be in place for an official to attend. Francie was happy enough but said I would have to convince the rest of the workers. We arranged a meeting so that I could

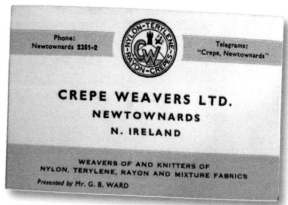

Phone:
Newtownards 2351-2

Telegrams:
"Crepe, Newtownards"

CREPE WEAVERS LTD.
NEWTOWNARDS
N. IRELAND

WEAVERS OF AND KNITTERS OF
NYLON, TERYLENE, RAYON AND MIXTURE FABRICS
Presented by Mr. G. B. WARD

address the workers. I did not try to defend what they had claimed to have happened in the past. All I could do was give them my word. I must have been convincing because everybody signed up to join the union. We elected shop stewards for the various departments and shifts. I made arrangements to meet the factory manager – a Mr McBride who turned out to be a reasonable guy, although the first time I met him he did try to give the impression of being a hardnosed manager.

A frequent source of problems in the factories was that managers were often ill-equipped to manage as they frequently did not have a full grasp of the laws and their obligations under the law to their workforce. I explained to Mr McBride what obligations the company had under the legislation and the problems they could face in the event of having to appear at an industrial tribunal without appropriate codes of practice or procedures or worse still having to appear before the courts to defend a compensation claim in the absence of a Health and Safety policy.

The message was well received and he realised I was not there to make life difficult for management but by co-operation and working together we would both benefit. Over the course of a number of meetings procedures were developed in draft form which covered all aspects of the relevant legislation including collective bargaining. Procedures that permitted trade union contributions to be directly deducted were put in place with a check-off system from wages and sent to Transport House. The draft procedures were sent to the Labour Relations Agency and approved. We agreed time off with pay for trade union duties and generally we got on very well.

Wage and bonus systems were negotiated and agreed. Francie Gilmore, the senior shop steward, went on a 10-day union course which helped him interpret and deal with the various strands of agreed procedures. If there were matters on which the steward and manager could not agree I would, as promised, meet with them within 24 hours to resolve the issue.

This did not happen on one occasion as I was on holidays and the colleague that I had asked to fill in for me was called on to resolve a bonus arrangement. At that time we had to arrange our own cover. When I returned to work I received a phone call from Francie Gilmore who wanted to know when I was coming down to resolve the bonus dispute. I asked if my colleague had not attended, Francie said, 'Yes, a very nice man.' When I asked what happened he said, 'Well he told us all about asbestos neurosis, how to breed canaries, how to race greyhounds in fact everything under the sun except the bonus. In the end McBride and myself surrendered, it was obvious we were not getting anywhere so we decided to put things on hold until you got back.'

I had a meeting arranged for the following day and at that meeting the issue was resolved to the satisfaction of both parties. It is a matter of record that the policies and procedures put in place were instrumental in avoiding disputes. Mr McBride whilst initially having reservations agreed it was the best way to do business. Instead of dealing with each department separately it simplified everything to have a collective agreement. Once an agreement was reached management could arrange their budgets confident that any agreements would be honoured. The fact that he was prepared to allow the union access to the order books and the company's financial position left no room for rumour as to the profitability of the company which in turn governed the workers' expectations.

Three months after I engaged with Crepe Weavers the union's financial officer, Ross Aiken, made a report to the Regional Committee advising it of an increase in members in my 11/105 branch of 800. A committee member voiced the opinion that the organiser must be doing a good job. Ross Aiken replied he did not recruit them, Eugene O'Callaghan put them on in the branch that the organiser left. The truth was that I did not have to go out of my way to recruit members. Workers were coming to me to join, members who had left the union were now rejoining. Around the same time I was requested by Francie Gilmore to speak to Down Linen Yarns, a new factory which was operating in Newtownards.

Down Linen Yarn

I visited this factory and spoke to the workforce. I outlined to them the benefits of union membership and held a question and answer session. Afterwards the workers agreed to join the union. After the membership was recruited elections were held for shop stewards who would act as worker representatives.

The following day I arranged to meet with the management. It turned out that this company was set up with a cancelled order of machinery which had originally been manufactured by Mackie's Engineering for export to Thailand. After the machines had been made the government refused to back the credit export deal which meant the machinery stayed at Mackie's. How Down Linen Yarns obtained it I never found out.

From the word go it was obvious that the company would have difficulty surviving, they were entering a declining market, producing yarn for local firms who themselves were finding it difficult. Government policy on imports was devastating the textile industry. Textiles and carpets were being imported at rock bottom prices, major wholesalers were beginning to set up production in the third world. Workers recruited in those countries were paid a few dollars a week and worked under appalling conditions. Although campaigned against by trade unions, the fair trade movement and other organisations, only recently have these conditions been fully exposed by the press and usually following some fearful accident costing many lives. Factories were built with total disregard for safety resulting in the death and injury of hundreds of workers. Compensation for injury was limited and seldom if ever paid.

How Down Linen Yarns expected to compete is beyond me. Nevertheless, they agreed to implement statutory regulations covering Health and Safety, codes of practice on disciplinary and other employment practices, etc. We also reached agreement for trade union recognition for wage bargaining. Normally they provided reasonably good employment but in the climate of the time I believed they were in an impossible position.

After a couple of months in operation they suffered their first major setback when over 20 workers contracted dermatitis. I visited the factory, held discussions with management following which we agreed to ask the Health and Safety Executive to conduct an investigation and establish the cause. Following an in-depth investigation, it was established that the outbreak was caused by an oil leak spraying from one of the machines, the spray was so fine it was invisible and took some time to detect. The spray only affected those workers who would be passing or in direct contact with that part of the machinery.

Once the reason had been discovered I contacted our solicitor Ken Young and arranged for him to meet and advise the workers as to their legal rights. Claims were submitted on behalf of all those affected and fortunately the company had had the foresight to take out insurance so the issues were straightforward. In due course an offer of settlement was made. Ken Young advised me and asked if I could get the workers to hold off on accepting the offer as he felt he could do better. My response was, 'Why keep a dog and bark yourself.' I arranged for Ken to address the affected workers and explain his analysis of the situation. All but one female employee agreed to allow the case to proceed as outlined by the union solicitor. This lady demanded her offer be accepted. We got this lady to sign a disclaimer to the effect that contrary to our advice she accepted the offer, the disclaimer also absolved the union from any further claims in the event of the remaining workers receiving a higher offer. Ken drew up the document which she signed. The remaining cases were later settled as Ken had suggested at a much higher rate.

After a short while the company contacted me and asked if I would come and talk to them. It soon became obvious the company was in trouble. They were not receiving new orders nor selling what they were producing and consequently holding large stocks of unsold products. It was only a matter of time and the only thing possible was to soften the blow for workers and make whatever arrangements we could. Not long afterwards the company closed with a loss of employment.

Pritchitt's Foods

An incident occurred in the vicinity of the Belfast City Hospital. The police ambushed a group of loyalist gunmen who were on a mission to bomb a nationalist target. When arrested the men were found to be in possession of guns and other items to be used for the purposes of terrorism. Three men were taken into custody and a fourth was reported to have escaped. On the Monday following this incident Albert Hewitt came into my office and advised me that the person who had allegedly escaped had not in fact escaped but had been apprehended by a different police patrol who were unaware that he had been allowed to escape as he was an informer. He went on to say that he had come to warn me as the man in question is 'your senior shop steward' in Pritchitt's. He told me to be careful and never give him a lift or travel in his car as the paramilitaries were after him. Hewitt said if you are with him you could be in danger of your life but did not elaborate any further.

Pritchitt's Foods was one of the factories for which I had been allocated responsibility when Albert Hewitt was appointed organiser. As I later found out the workforce was predominately Protestant. Albert, I am sure, would have had plenty of contacts who would pass this information on to him. Albert's son who worked in Pritchitt's Foods was also a part-time member of the UDR.

Never one to dodge an issue, I requested permission from the factory manager to hold a meeting with the workforce, initially on a 'get to know you' basis as I was anxious to put a face to the name and to get a general feel of the place. Within 48 hours the meeting was arranged. I cannot give his real name for legal reasons so for the purpose of this story I will simply refer to him as Sammy.

Sammy was present at the meeting, a small man, pleasant and amicable. He was very friendly and showed no animosity towards me; in fact, he pledged his full support and offered to be of whatever assistance he could. I had a frank open discussion on various aspects of the working relations at the factory. The wages were quite good, working relations reasonably good and they had a full order book. What appeared to be absent was any kind of formal agreement or codes of practice which would comply with the legislation.

I pointed out that all of these things were of paramount importance and would of necessity have to be addressed. I arranged to meet the factory manager, a man called Crawford Huey, which took place within a few days. Sammy, I and two other representatives met with Mr Huey and two other individuals. Mr Huey was a reasonable gentleman and the meeting was quite straightforward. He had no objections to my suggestions for the introduction of a formal agreement covering the terms and conditions of employment; he also thought it a good idea for written procedures. He suggested that I draft the agreement and when he had a copy he would run it by the Labour Relations Agency. Subject to agreement by the LRA he would bring it to the company for consideration.

Drafting the agreement was not a problem as by now I was getting well used to it. Much of the material could be taken from agreements which I had previously prepared for other companies. The agreement was duly prepared and sent to Mr Huey for consideration. I had inserted a clause in the disciplinary procedure whereby no shop steward or union representative would be disciplined without a full-time official being present. The LRA and management agreed with what had been drafted and we both signed, I on behalf of the union and Crawford Huey on behalf of the company.

In general, things ran very smoothly until one Sunday when Sammy was on overtime. During his lunch break he visited a local pub, on his return the foreman claimed he smelt of alcohol and dismissed him. Sammy rang me on the Monday morning; he said, 'There is no point appealing as I am guilty.' I said I would come down anyway. When I met Mr Huey I directed his attention to the clause in the agreement regarding disciplining shop stewards and pointed out that they were in breach of the agreement and if the agreement meant anything then we both had to honour it, otherwise it was not worth the paper it was written on. Mr Huey agreed, reinstating Sammy.

This was the beginning of a friendship as well as a period of good industrial relations. Each side kept their side of the bargain, even if on occasions, when we might have got it wrong, we would still honour what we had agreed to.

On one occasion Crawford Huey said to me, 'You know I was dreading you coming here as your reputation had preceded you. Now I am glad you came as I know I can depend on your word. Once an agreement is reached that is it.' Six months later I received a call from Crawford Huey telling me my shop steward had disappeared. I said 'Who? Sammy, where did he go?' Mr Huey said he did not know. Two men had come to the factory the previous night and cleared out his locker. He said he understood his house had also been cleared out and his wife and children were gone. You did not have to be a genius to work out what had happened.

I suggested to Crawford Huey that we let things settle for a while as eventually the workers will sort themselves out. This they did by electing a new shop steward and things went on as before. After a period of time I received a call which turned out to be from Sammy. He asked for my help claiming he had been abandoned by his handlers, had no money and could not get a job. I suggested that he leave it with me and ring me back the next day. I then put a call through to a contact in England explained the position and asked him to try and get Sammy work. I told him I would get Sammy to contact him directly. The next day when Sammy rang I advised him to go and talk to the official in central office. About a month later Sammy rang again, this time to thank me as he was now employed and things were working out. I said I was very glad and said, 'Now do me a favour and never ring me again, I don't want to get involved.' I never heard from him again.

As I said previously, Crawford Huey was a decent man. He would employ students in the holiday periods and would pay them the same wages as permanent employees. The story goes that it was a graduate that led to him losing his job. What the circumstances were I do not know other than the company terminated his employment. At that time I received a call from Mr Lawes junior. The Lawes were the owners of

Pritchett's Foods. Without going into detail, he advised me that Mr Huey was no longer 'in charge', as he put it. They wanted to arrive at a satisfactory settlement with him. Both the company and Mr Huey would appreciate it if I would agree to help them work out a settlement. I agreed to this and we all met at a hotel in Bangor. In a very short while an agreement was reached on a cash sum compensation with full pension rights guaranteed. Unfortunately, the poor man did not have long to enjoy it. He and his wife purchased a small dwelling; in the course of clearing it out the story goes that he was overcome by fumes from some old rubber he was burning. He was sitting resting and smoking his pipe when he died, which was very sad.

Ulster Print Works

This company was divided in two; they had a base in Newtownards and one in the Portadown area. Both produced and dyed textiles but because of the plentiful supply of water most of the dyeing was carried out at the Newtownnard's plant. But there seemed to be ongoing labour problems in this location

The Portadown plant had a different official who had a very friendly relationship with the owner. The Newtownards plant was in close proximity to other factories and the workers would meet and socialise often, exchanging comparisons on wages and conditions. When I took over, the workers, not unexpectedly, expected improvements. We held numerous meetings with the owner who made no bones about his right-wing views and membership of the Monday Club. To put it mildly, he was not an easy man to get along with. Every concession made had to be fought for, and disputes between the owner and the workers were a common feature. He could not understand why I would not make agreements without first consulting the workers or why he could not have the final say. Apparently this was how they operated in the other factory.

I spent endless hours at the factory resolving unofficial disputes when workers would just walk off their shift. There is no doubt we were making progress but not quickly enough to satisfy the workforce. Finally, they all walked out on strike and despite my best efforts I could not bridge the gap between workers' expectations and what management was prepared to concede. In a sheer act of defiance the owner decided to close the factory and move all the operations to his other factory. He advertised for workers at Portadown to cover the work which was being transferred.

I met with the owner and pointed out to him that this would not resolve the problem. He was obliged to offer the workers who were being made redundant the opportunity to transfer to that location, otherwise they could claim for not only redundancy but unfair dismissal. The case I presented was rejected out of hand.

The closure went ahead so I lodged a claim for all the production workers with the Industrial Tribunal claiming failure to consult, unfair dismissal and redundancy pay. All overtures for conciliation were rejected. When the case was held I outlined in considerable detail the background to the dispute which led to the closure. I then dealt with the failure to consult under the legislation, the rejection of the union proposal that the workers be offered the opportunity of redeployment at a time when the company were advertising for workers and the issue of redundancy arising therein, and the question of unfair dismissal. Several workers were called to give evidence and when asked by the Chair of the Tribunal if they would have been prepared to accept an offer of redeployment they all said they would. Under cross examination by the owner's solicitor as to how they expected to travel the distance, it was pointed out that they could get a small or large bus as it was not unusual for workers to travel together for work. A number of examples were put forward.

The Tribunal found for the workers awarding compensation of £1.4 million.[1] I personally, despite winning the case and securing substantial compensation for the workers, came in for severe criticism from the Regional Secretary who seemed to be more concerned about loss of union income from any loss of membership arising from the closure than he was about the rights of the workers. He conveniently was forgetting that I had recruited 800 members since taking over the branch and that those members had only joined because of the policy pursued which guaranteed them the right to be consulted and decide for themselves. After all, this is surely what democracy is about.

Canadian Tec Tape

Canadian Tec Tape was another factory which came within the responsibilities of 11/105 branch. I made a number of visits to this factory which was fairly well organised. Much of the credit can be attributed to Nevin Agnew who was the senior shop steward. Nevin was a good organiser and was backed up by a pretty effective group of shop stewards.

Arrangements were made for many of the shop stewards to attend the educational classes that we were running.

Although the stewards operated a well-run method for dealing with day-to-day problems, they had no idea how the union was structured or managed. This, I believed, was an important element in what the union was about. I stressed the importance of being part of the decision-making process through their collective strength rather than someone else making decisions on how the organisation should be run.

The factories for which I had taken over responsibility were now formed into a branch and brought together under the constitution as a unit. I convinced Nevin Agnew to put his name forward for nomination to the Irish Regional Committee. The branch endorsed his nomination and in the election that followed the branch which I had built up had sufficient numbers to get him elected.

Our candidate from the bus industry was also elected, which meant the membership for which I was responsible had two members on the Irish Executive Committee. I had also secured the election of Dickie Atwell from the bus industry to the General Executive Committee. Only two places were allocated to Ireland on the General Executive Committee which met in London and ran the union between biennial-delegate conferences. I conducted a strong campaign for Dickie Atwell who was duly elected to one of the positions. The members for whom I had responsibility were now well represented on two of the union's most powerful committees.

My first experience of dealing with the wage negotiations with Canadian Tec Tape was a new kind of experience for me. After submitting our claim in writing a meeting was arranged with local managers and a Canadian gentleman. On arrival, for what I had assumed was a negotiation meeting, the Canadian gentleman addressed me and said, 'This is what I am giving you, there will be no other offer, it's take it or leave it; my workers will not support any action and will take what I give them.'

I said that I would need some time to speak to the workers. A meeting was hastily arranged and held in the canteen. I laid out what was on the line and by a unanimous decision the workers decided to down tools and walk out. I returned to the board room and invited the Canadian gentleman to look out of the window. He was shocked by what he saw, the workers were pouring out of the factory on strike. 'Well now', I said,

'when you are ready to negotiate send for me, and, as they say in your country, "have a nice day."'

Nevin Agnew suggested to me that we should ring John Freeman, the Regional Secretary. From years of experience I knew better. John Freeman's peculiar genius lay not in getting the best outcome for the members but in never being personally wrong-footed. Getting the best result for the members in any situation was not just a matter of having the right words – choreography was also of paramount importance. So I said, 'No, get in the car and we will go and see him. If you let him know you are coming he will not be there'. I went on to say, 'Remember Nevin, you are now a member of the Irish Regional Committee which gives you leverage.' We duly arrived at Transport House unannounced. Nevin explained the situation to John Freeman. Freeman put his arm across Nevin's shoulder and turned to me saying, 'I hope you have declared the strike official.' You did have to know how to handle John!

The strike lasted about ten days with the members receiving full strike pay. When I met the company representatives the negotiations were handled by Roy Burns the factory manager and two other senior managers. A revised offer was tabled and accepted with a full resumption of work. In fact, I went on to establish a good relationship with those managers. Nevin Agnew was a good negotiator and handled disciplinary and all other matters. He, in fact, led the wage negotiations; I simply attended as back up.

Hide and Skin of Killyleagh

My first visit to Hide and Skin, Killyleagh, County Down, was following a telephone call which was to the effect that the current owners were proposing to sell the operations to a Czechoslovakian leather-producing company. When I arrived the first thing I observed was a large pile of raw animal hides stacked outside the factory. The smell was absolutely overpowering. How anyone could handle or work with the hides was beyond belief.

Having a pre-arranged meeting with the factory manager, Matt Durham, I was shown to his office. Even there the stench was awful. Matt, a reasonable enough man, brought me on a tour of the factory starting with those who were kitted-out to handle raw skins, to a display of items made from the finished product. On display was a selection of goods such as handbags and shoes and a variety of other items made from leather from the hides. Even on the tour I soon learned the importance of staying downwind of the manager to avoid the smell coming from his clothes.

There is no point glossing over the issues, conditions were not good and, as the saying goes, the wages were nothing to write home about. As the factory was one of the few employers left in the area the workers did not want to see the plant close, bad as it was. The financial state of the company, however, would likely lead to only one thing – closure. When politicians talk about getting people back to work claiming they are work-shy they obviously know nothing about the real lives of working people. There was certainly nothing work-shy about this group of workers in Killyleagh who were prepared to work in unbearable conditions.

On my return to Transport House I appraised the Regional Secretary of the situation. His suggestion was to bring the National Officer over from England as he was the official with overall responsibility for the industry throughout the UK. John Freeman's idea was to see if the National Officer could come up with any suggestions which would help. The necessary arrangements were put in place and on the morning of his visit I picked him up from the airport and brought him to Transport House, as was the custom, to meet John Freeman.

The English official was a very large ex-rugby league player, a very powerful man originally from Bradford. Having completed the formalities, we headed for Killyleagh. We were just approaching

Ballyhackamore when traffic was brought to an abrupt halt. After sitting for some time the National Officer asked what was wrong. I told him I did not know but to wait there and I would go and find out. By this time soldiers were taking up positions in doorways with rifles pointing in all directions. I made my way towards the front of the traffic where I asked a policeman what was happening. The policeman said there had been a fatal shooting; a prison officer had been shot in the head.[2]

I returned to the car informing the National Officer of the situation. He seemed to be in a state of shock asking what happens now. 'Well', I said, 'it's hard to tell. If the gunmen have left the area it could be all over – or if not all hell could break loose.' 'Can you turn this car around', he said. By now he was in a state of panic. As we in Belfast were well used to these situations I said, 'Hold on, if we wait a while the traffic will soon start moving again.' In a very stressful voice he said, 'Never mind the Hide and Skin let's get the hell out of here.' There was no doubt which hide and skin had top priority.

Eventually I managed to turn the car and headed back towards the city. 'Just go straight to the airport', he said, 'my wife warned me about coming here, do what you like with the factory I won't be back'.

Not very long afterwards we were notified that the company was being wound up. A meeting of the workers and politicians was held in a hall in Killyleagh. Workers were still trying to retain the factory but regretfully nothing could be done. I cannot say I achieved anything other than to see that all statutory requirements were met on both notice and redundancy payments.

With the sad exception of the Killyleagh leather goods factory, the factories for which I had inherited responsibility were all now well organised and seldom needed my input, unlike the bus industry, where each day brought its own problems. It is sad to have to relate that due to government policy on imports many of those factories have since closed, which is tragic for the communities in which they were situated because they provided a good source of much-needed employment.

12
Back to the buses:
pensions for all

It is a common misconception that trade unions only improve the conditions of their members by going on strike and inconveniencing the general public.

The powerlessness of the individual worker facing the management of a company makes it essential that workers come together in trade unions to try to even things up. The right to strike and withhold their labour is an essential part of the workers' rights. In recent years the public's faith in the legal framework regulating employment has been undermined by shocking disclosures in the workplace: zero hours contracts where workers have to be available to the employer but the employer is under no obligation to provide work; oppressively regulated work places; gang masters with trafficked workers and the acknowledgement by the authorities and indeed revealed by high-profile court cases that slavery actually exists in modern Britain. What more proof is needed that without a credible right to strike workers would be no better than slaves?

But workers do not take the decision to go on strike lightly. Many working class families have little by way of personal savings; often living from week to week, they need the pay packet that comes in at the end of each week or month to pay their bills. Strikes come with a great deal of financial pain and sacrifice for the workers and their families.

So in fact most of the improvements in pay and conditions come through negotiations. But some also come about by changes in the law which are automatically put into effect. Sometimes, however, the potential of the law to improve pay and conditions is not immediately obvious and has to be identified by the workers themselves and secured by legal processes. Two of the major advances that were secured on my watch came about in this way. One of them concerned pensions. The other concerned parity in terms and conditions for the Ulsterbus workers, which I will recount later.

Quite early in my period of office as a full-time official I thought the time had come to resurrect the issue of pensions. One indisputably good thing that can be said about the officials representing transport workers in Belfast was that they had negotiated the entry of bus workers into the Northern Ireland Local Government Officers Pension Scheme (NILGOS). Though as Belfast Corporation was part of local government and as the bus workers were Corporation employees it would have been almost impossible to deny them entry into the pension scheme.

The scheme was exactly the same in structure and applied the same benefits as the scheme which covered other local government employees. But whereas two local authority clerks or school teachers with exactly the same period of service and on the same pay scales throughout their careers could compare their pensions and would be surprised if they differed, this was not the case with bus drivers. Busmen's wages were based on a complicated mix of payments for different types of hours worked and combinations of hours worked. Therefore, the pension that each retired bus driver would receive on retirement would be dependent on his own *highly personal* working history. Men with the same number of years' service could have different pensions. It was this matter of highly personalised pensions for busmen that would be at the root of the issues covered in the final chapters – but it would be another quarter of a century before the problems that came with that became evident.

The scheme applied to all salaries, wages and payments in respect of employment and other payments or benefits specified in the contract of employment as well as any emoluments not paid on a fixed basis and additional to pay. The significance of these details will become of greater importance later and do not affect what I am going to relate here.

The only exclusion was non-statutory overtime. In other words pay, for the purpose of calculating pensions, included spread-over payments, penalty payments, weekend working and uniform allowances.[1] However, while establishing the total pay on which a busman's pension would be based was more complicated than was the case for other public employees, once pensionable pay was established calculating the pension was straightforward and similar to the calculation for other public employees. It worked like this: if your pay on which your pension would

be based was £12,000 and you had 30 years' service your pension was calculated as follows:

1/80 x £12,000 x 30 years = £4,500 per annum

There was also a lump sum payable on retirement. This was known as the Retirement Grant and was calculated as follows:

3/80 x £12,000 x 30 years = £13,500 lump sum[2]

For anyone retiring early due to ill health the number of years used in the calculations would be double the actual years worked to that point. The scheme later attracted an additional one-year average pay based on the highest of the last three years' completed service. This was known as 'death in service'.

The pension scheme was a good scheme. But it only applied to Citybus. It had not applied to UTA employees and was not extended to apply to Ulsterbus staff. This was an issue which had been raised by my predecessor without success. I decided a more robust approach was needed. The company's initial response was to the effect that they were not opposed to a pension scheme but would like the bus workers to buy into a private scheme.

I made it clear that the scheme we wanted for Ulsterbus was the same as Citybus, i.e. the NILGOSC scheme. At the end of the day the weight of argument prevailed and NILGOSC was agreed subject to 70 per cent of existing employees agreeing to join. All new employees would be obliged to join the scheme. Pension calculations would be based on the highest average weekly earnings as opposed to basic earnings over the last completed years of service. This was consistent with the arrangements in place at the time for Belfast Corporation employees already enrolled in NILGOSC.

The scheme was circulated and approved by over 90 per cent of employees and Ulsterbus employees were admitted to the scheme in 1978. Despite the fact that the Derry 11/3 branch was a separate union entity – at that stage I had been negotiating only for the 11/15 branch as the

Belfast men in 11/12 branch were already covered by the scheme – they were also included in the arrangements.

Having concluded this part of the agreement, I had to consider what the consequences would be for employees in the period *before* the scheme would come into effect. For example, what would happen in the case of an employee who died in the five years before the scheme was operational for them? As things stood if an employee died within this period the only benefit paid was a refund of what had been put in as opposed to the full benefits of the scheme. Further negotiations took place and an agreement was reached whereby in the interim period a bus driver who retired on ill health or died would be paid a week's pay (calculated on the basis of average earnings on the previous completed 13 weeks including weekend payments on top of duty hours) multiplied by years of service. This was in line with the overall scheme. For the record it would also include the provisions as contained in the pension's scheme:

> if a scheme employer agrees with bodies or persons representative of any description of employees the method of determining the whole or specified part of the pay of employees of that description during the period which the agreement applies, the pay of the employee is the amount so determined.

Ulsterbus

And also:

> A scheme employer must notify in writing every member affected by such an agreement.[3]

In short, pensions would have to be calculated on average contractual hours and since spread-overs and weekend working was part of the contract of employment they would be included in pension calculations. Again for the record: the agreement concerning employment was a two-part agreement between the company and the union. The pension agreement between NILGOSC, the company and the union was a tri-partite agreement.

The company would agree to an 11 per cent contribution towards the members' pensions. The employees would agree to a deduction from their wages of 5 per cent for manual workers and 6 per cent for white collar workers. It would be the company's responsibility to make the deductions from the wages and make payments of the full amount to NILGOSC. They would in turn be responsible for ensuring that the pension negotiated and agreed to on behalf of employees would be met in full. NILGOSC also agreed that in addition to the pension lump sum there would be a top-up of one year's average salary for death in service, and an additional year paid by the company. I believe these pension conditions were later ratified at a general meeting held at Transport House. At this meeting NILGOSC representatives, having affirmed the details of the scheme, upped the ante by increasing the one year's salary for death in service to two years.

Ulsterbus staff were now in the pension scheme and as the pension engagements could in principle be transfered to another pension provider, Irish Life, began an attempt to move in. One of our former shop stewards in Newry had invited Irish Life into the Newry depot where they held meetings. Employees were told that if they left NILGOSC and joined Irish Life they would get back what they had paid in – which was not exactly true. I got the company to deny Irish Life access to their premises, in addition to making it clear that they would not make or handle deductions on behalf of Irish Life, nor would they contribute. This was a great victory. At no cost in industrial action the Ulsterbus – former UTA – busmen obtained entitlement to a pension on the same terms as Citybus staff.

But the harsh laws of unintended consequences kicked in – unforeseen and dormant for nearly a quarter of a century. For ironically the workers did not receive all they were promised and – even worse – as an indirect consequence of this extension of the pension scheme to all employees and management's reaction to it – some of the busmen in Belfast who retired before the pension discrepancies came to light ended up with lower pensions than they otherwise would have done.

A 'Scooby' – an armoured JCB-like vehicle – deployed to get the 'Wheelbarrow' into position to try and remove/disrupt a suspected device from a double-decker bus

All this normal trade union activity continued against the backdrop of the Troubles as I was never able to forget even for a single day. The attacks on buses continued. In the years 1984 to 1992 the bus services sustained the following losses:[4]

	CITYBUS	ULSTERBUS	TOTAL
1984	31	16	47
1985	14	15	29
1986	11	18	29
1987	37	18	55
1988	32	17	49
1989	22	15	37
1990	19	12	31
1991	13	2	15
1992	7	9	16

In total, from the day when I was appointed as a full-time official in 1977 until my retirement on health grounds in 1992, some 874 buses were totally destroyed,[5] hundreds badly damaged, thousands of panes of glass smashed by stone throwers and God knows how many thousands of passengers injured by flying glass.

Each incident brought its own story and they were invariably stories of ordinary people hurt or traumatised. What I do know is that without public transport normal life at any level in Northern Ireland would not have been possible. The blood would cease flowing through the arteries and the patient would not have survived. It was against that background that I was determined to keep doing all that I could to protect the lives and improve the wages and working conditions of the brave men who risked so much just to make normal life possible.

13

A rare victory:
a privatisation thwarted

Shortly after Werner Heubeck's retirement in 1988
the Northern Ireland Office through Lord Young, the
Secretary of State for Trade and Industry, asked the
Monopolies and Mergers Commission to examine the
efficiency and costs of the services provided by
Ulsterbus and Citybus.

In my view, what these Conservative politicians and some within the
management of the bus companies really were seeking was the
privatisation of the bus industry. I believe that is the reason they referred
the matter to the Monopolies and Mergers Committee, asking that body
to draw up a report because if they had only wanted to look at costs and
efficiencies they could have brought in a team of consultants to carry out
that sort of exercise.

But privatisation was in the air. This was in the period when, in former
Conservative Prime Minister Harold Macmillan's memorable phrase,
Margaret Thatcher was 'selling off the family silver'. And of course as
history shows she not only sold it off but she sold it off cheap, as a result
of which many individuals made a financial killing on the sale of public
assets. So it was no surprise that at least some senior managers were
hoping to receive a lot of money from the project. There were worrying
precedents.

Yorkshire Ryder Bus Company had been previously privatised on a
workers' buy-out scheme under the terms of which managers – of which
there were few – got 51 per cent of the shares while the workers – of
which there were many – got 49 per cent.[1] You do not have to be a genius
in mathematics to appreciate what the outcome of these arrangements
would be. Management floated their shares and they were sold on the

stock market. The workers remained driving the buses. I was determined this would not happen in Northern Ireland. Following discussions with the General Secretary a meeting was arranged between me, the branch committees and the Unity Bank – a bank that is owned by the trade unions. By this time I had valued the company's assets, had a good idea of the company's income and expenditure, and had drawn up a business plan for the takeover of the company.

Our proposal would guarantee every employee from the cleaners to the general manager an equal number of shares. On the death or retirement of a shareholder the shares would have to be sold back into the company and could not be traded outside. In this way the workers would always have control. The plan was approved and as it also had the backing of the union, the bank undertook to put up the money. This was a fall-back position as it had always been and remained our intention to oppose privatisation.

Having already written to the Merger and Monopolies Commission, we were invited to a meeting in London. The opposition to privatisation was led by the Transport and General Workers' Union but unexpectedly other unions, albeit with a smaller stake in the industry, tagged along and attended the hearings in London. To believe that they had learned anything from the earlier Industrial Court case (recounted below in chapters 14 and 15) would be a mistake. The company management was also in attendance.

I outlined the case on behalf of my union, highlighting the difficult period we had been through, the number of vehicles lost, the injuries and deaths which had occurred in maintaining a service. I highlighted that the cost to the public purse had been kept to a minimum in comparison to other companies of similar size in Great Britain. I pointed out the good relations which existed between us and the company and the danger that these would deteriorate under privatisation. I argued that private operators would be more prone to intimidation and would be more likely to cough up protection money to paramilitaries which could be used to purchase guns and explosives. A worst case scenario would be that the paramilitaries could put up front men to buy into the company which would give them an undetectable way of laundering money from crime.

I set out my reasons for believing that it would inevitably lead to population polarisation on an even greater scale than Northern Ireland had up to that date experienced. The black taxis were an example of private ownership in the public transport sector which is only accountable to its owners; they only operated in their own areas. As schools, universities and colleges were located across Belfast what was being suggested was a disaster which could at its worst lead to civil war. I asked if they were prepared to risk that as if they went ahead with their proposals on privatisation then they would be held accountable.

The foregoing forms only a small part of the case I outlined. It would, I said, not benefit or make public transport any more efficient, nor reduce costs. In effect the opposite would be the case. Addressing the Mergers and Monopolies committee on behalf of the delegation, I outlined the history of Northern Ireland from its origins. As Englishmen they would not have been familiar with the construction or set up and as this was relevant to the issues at stake I hoped the Chairman would allow some latitude in order to familiarise themselves with the structures and governance of Northern Ireland. In this way I hoped they would have an understanding of the essential part which public transport played in Northern Ireland.

Taking each of the six counties which made up Northern Ireland, I homed in on the religious divide in each county over the years of conflict, the various structures and how they came to be. Catholic children were educated in Catholic schools, while Protestant children were educated in Protestant or state schools. The Catholic schools had been originally built to cater for the position as it stood at a given point in time, whereas over the years the Catholic population had grown and became more dispersed. Nevertheless they retained a strong belief in their faith and invested often at great cost in their children's education at a Catholic school. These schools depended on public transport to take the children to and from school which resulted in buses criss-crossing areas where it would be unwise for the children to walk. Protestant schools had a similar problem. The same criteria could be applied to those lucky enough to find employment outside what would be considered their area, thus public transport was essential.

There was the added advantage of using profitable routes to subsidise loss-making routes. A privatised, for-profit transport system would not maintain unprofitable and underused routes. Many of the rural communities would be left without any form of public transport. In some instances schools would become non-viable in the absence of public transport, further polarising an already divided community. These fears and forebodings that I had then are coming back to haunt Translink today as the shortsighted withdrawl of provision on some routes threatens a serious reduction in bus services to rural communities; as always it is the poorest who will suffer most from these policies.

I pointed out to the committee that hospitals which catered for all sections of the community were in some cases located at flash points and on the boundary lines between communities (e.g. the Mater and the Royal Victoria hospitals). They depended on public transport for their work forces, recruited from all sections of the community, to be able to get to work. For example, the Royal Victoria Hospital, the regional hospital located on the Falls Road in a nationalist area, was and is world renowned for the skill and expertise in the treatment of victims of bomb blast and gunshots. Public transport was vital to the staffing of this and other hospitals and to cater for families who wished to visit. Even those who had a private car were often reluctant to bring it into Belfast for fear of hijacking and possible loss of their vehicle.

By 1969 things had deteriorated, the Northern Ireland Civil Rights movement was established to campaign for one man, one vote and a fair allocation of public housing. It is easy for people to forget that in some cases property owners had up to five votes at election time, those who did not own a property had no vote. Gerrymandering, as it was called, gave the Unionist 30 per cent of the population 100 per cent control over Derry city. Housing was allocated to ensure the system remained as it was. That is not to say Derry was unique; the same could be said of other parts of Northern Ireland. The Civil Rights movement set out to confront these abuses. Marches were organised to highlight what was essentially a denial of human rights. Ian Paisley and others organised counter demonstrations. The reluctance of the civil authorities to deal with the impending crisis led to riots and attacks on public transport. No private company could have coped with what Northern Ireland's bus companies had to contend with nor could a private company have retained the loyalty of its employees as Ulsterbus had.

I stressed that it was not my intention to take sides or give a political lecture but it was essential to understand the background and the role that public transport played in helping to maintain as normal a situation as possible. When someone looked out their window in the morning, having listened to the early morning news broadcasts about the bombings and shootings which had taken place the previous evening, and saw a blue or red bus driving by with passengers on board they assumed things were back to nearly normal and they went out to work.

But bus workers paid a very heavy price to keep the service operating. To reiterate, bus workers had been murdered and many injured and traumatised, hundreds of buses had been totally destroyed thousands of windows broken. Yet through the busmen's commitment and courage, backed up by strong union representation, the service kept going.

In conclusion, I said that no one should be in any doubt, a privately operated service would not have prevailed for numerous reasons, falling revenue, loss of vehicles and above all an inability to hold the staff together. This in turn would have resulted in further polarisation as both sides retreated into their own areas and what would have been the outcome for schools and hospitals?

In the course of making my case I made it clear that any private company had the same potential to be controlled by the paramilitaries as the black taxies were believed to be controlled. I gave the committee an in-depth analysis of how the black taxies operated in west Belfast.

The position of black taxis has since been regularised but in those days they were operating in a regulatory vacuum. As has been well documented they were – at that time – operating illegally and providing additional revenue to the paramilitary coffers. If you wanted to operate a black taxi on the Falls Road you needed the approval and permission of the West Belfast Association. Worse still, since the government had no control over these taxis and was constantly putting out statements threatening action against them, which never materialised, most insurance companies refused to insure them; those which did offer insurance demanded prohibitive premiums.

Protestant paramilitaries soon learned how valuable these taxis were for raising and laundering money. The UDA organised black taxis for the Shankill Road, while the UVF took Rathcoole and the Shore Road. Indeed some of the black taxies were used to carry out assassinations and brutal murders, in particular the Shankill Butchers who were later convicted of the most horrendous crimes.

Shore Road taxis came right into the centre of Belfast using Bridge Street as a collection point. Shankill taxis used North Street, while the Falls taxis used Castle Street. All of these taxis operated inside what they classed as their area unlike the bus services which catered for all sections of the community. I again pointed out to the committee that children were transported to schools across the religious divide and from county to county. Saint Malachy's Grammar school taught pupils from Lisburn, Antrim and Carrickfergus; without public transport this would not be possible and a privatised system was a recipe for disaster. I did not pull any punches and painted a worst-case scenario which was, in the light of our experience, all too possible: that a privatised system would eventually lead to an escalation in violence requiring the drafting in of additional troops to assist the police with Northern Ireland becoming completely ungovernable, and in the worst case scenario perhaps require further partition – at great cost in terms of life and destruction.

When I was asked to quantify the amount of money being lost to the bus company by the black taxis I said that Mr Sam Thompson, the staff officer from Translink, was present and would be in a better position to give an accurate figure. Sam Thompson then outlined details of the estimated loss in revenue to Translink. The three routes which the black taxis operated, i.e. the Falls, Shankill and Shore Roads, were at one time the most profitable and while it would be impossible to be 100 per cent accurate the amounts lost to black taxis ran into hundreds of thousands of pounds. Responding to questions he confirmed that the company had tried to get the government to act but they were reluctant to do so. He then gave details of the number of school children requiring buses explaining the system used including the criteria for free travel. Children under 15 were entitled to free school transport if the distance was more than three miles, children over 15 were entitled to half fare irrespective of the distance covered. Under this arrangement Translink recouped the fare from the government. The ticketing equipment identified and verified the numbers availing of this arrangement. No private operator would operate this system. Sam Thompson confirmed that my analysis of the situation was basically correct.

There is a saying: 'if you can't convince them confuse them' – and make sure too that they know they would be held to account for their decision if they got it wrong. The one thing I can be sure of is that if we did not convince or confuse them we certainly alarmed them to the extent that the committee was not prepared to put themselves in the line of fire. The members of the Monopolies and Mergers Commission were not used to having to make decisions where many lives were potentially at risk if they made the wrong call. When walking down the street after the meeting, the chairman tapped me on the shoulder and said, 'You pressed all the right buttons today, I don't think you have anything to worry about.'

Not only did the Commission accept our argument that a privatised bus industry would totally lack the resilience to stand up to the pressures of Northern Ireland's deeply fractured and violent society but they also dismissed the argument that the public sector is less efficient than the private sector. As reported in the *Belfast Telegraph* and the *Irish News* on the 7 and 8 June 1989 and as an implicit tribute to the recently retired Werner Heubeck and an acknowledgement that an efficient organisation is dependent on having good managers and not on private ownership, the commission's main conclusion 'found an efficient low-cost, lean organisation with short chains of command, supported by loyal, hardworking and frequently courageous staff.'[2]

The decision from the Mergers and Monopolies Commission was a recommendation that it would not be in the interests of Northern Ireland to privatise public transport. The end result was that the fall-back plan, which was later described in a newspaper article as sheer genius in its simplicity, was not needed. In retrospect what was curious about the outcome was that much of the reporting tended to focus on what a sound, well-run enterprise Ulsterbus was. There was virtually no mention of the fact that this investigation had been an attempt at privatisation that had fallen at the first fence. Too many in government, in finance and in industry had too much of a stake in privatisation as the panacea for every economic and social problem to want to publicise the fact that the MMC was not recommending it for Northern Ireland's buses. It would be another 20 years before the public in Britain would come to appreciate that privatisation of basic monopolies is no silver bullet that will provide low cost services with improved levels of efficiency in all circumstances.

Ulsterbus map of principal services throughout Northern Ireland, 1989

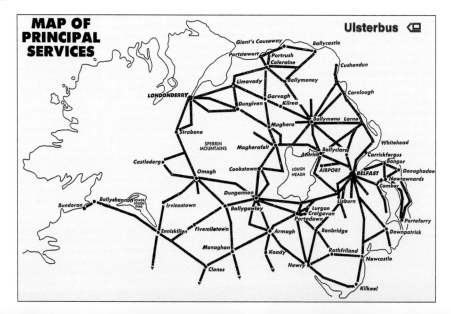

14
The Brandeis Brief:
part I

Did you ever hear tell of the Brandeis Brief? 'No?'

Well neither had I but it shaped the biggest, most complex battle for better terms and conditions for the busmen in the rural areas bringing them up to parity with their more fortunate colleagues in Belfast. And it did not inflict an hour of industrial action on the public or cost the workers an hour's loss of pay. What was it all about?

During the time I had served as a shop steward, on the Bus Council and the branch committee, I was concerned about the size of the difference in pay rates and conditions between Citybus and Ulsterbus despite both organisations doing what was practically the same type of work for the same employer. So it was clearly on my agenda when I became a full-time official.

By 1979 the rural busmen – although we had brought them into the NILGOSC pension scheme – were still nevertheless about £15 a week worse off than the men doing a similar job for Citybus. That seemed to me unfair and unjust. And there was no logic behind it because ten years earlier in 1969 the wages had been pretty much level pegging, with Ulsterbus even marginally ahead. The question was – how could we bring the rural men up to the Belfast men's level? There were formidable obstacles. First – as with the pensions issue – there was nothing to be gained by the Citybus workforce so how enthusiastically would they support industrial action? The company and the department would of course plead poverty and then stir up the press and public opinion with scares about higher fares and reduced services.

Another factor was the lack of support from senior union officials. No doubt they supported equal pay 'in principle'. But they considered that the case I made was 'hare-brained'. Moreover, government pay policy was at that time an additional complication. Although conceived as a measure of fairness and social justice for all sections of society, this placed limits on the scope for gains that could normally be secured from collective bargaining. But one potential major benefit to the strategy was that awards made by the Industrial Court were exempt from pay policy restrictions.

So how were we going to crack this particular nut? During the process of pursuing the educational policy we had had an in-depth look at the legislation, in particular section 44 of the Transport Act (Northern Ireland) 1967 and the 1947 Fair Wages Regulations.[1] Having convinced myself that that there were legal remedies to this problem of unequal pay for equal work and that a strong case could therefore be made for bringing Ulsterbus wages into line with Citybus, I decided to approach J.B. McCartney, as by this time we had become good friends, to seek his advice. I was only too well aware that I would only get one chance to make it happen; there would be no room for mistakes and there were a lot of obstacles to surmount.

Although convinced that I could establish a sustainable case, it would not be without its problems. The case would have to go to the Industrial Court whose president was R.W.B. McConnell a former Unionist government minister, who would, I felt, be leaned on heavily by the Northern Ireland Office (NIO). I knew I would require a person of substance to present the case, someone capable of commanding respect and at the same time, if necessary, be a match for McConnell.

So, one day I took the first step. I picked up the phone and called J.B. McCartney. He had been a tremendous asset to me in the past and I knew he was the man who could see us through this battle. So I set off eagerly at the prospect of a warm welcome for my plan as I rolled it out for him. But I was in for a rude awakening. We met at his office where I presented my arguments on the merits of the case. J.B. looked at me and said: 'You're talking balls.' But I pressed on with outlining my views on the issue and explained why I thought a claim to the Industrial Court would succeed. In short, he told me again and in no uncertain terms that I was talking rubbish. Far from being deterred I persisted with my arguments for some time. However, at the end of the meeting I had made no progress in convincing him. I left his office a sadly chastened man!

A few days, possibly a week, later I received a call from J.B. asking me if I would come back to see him and would I bring with me the research

I had done on the proposed case. I met with him some days after and when I arrived I found Richard Steele was also present. Richard was a colleague of J.B.'s but until now I had not met him. He subsequently became a tower of strength. J.B. looked at me and smiled conspiratorially, 'I had another look at your case, you may have something but we will need to take Richard on board to help us in preparing the case as it will require an awful lot of work.' And boy was he right! During the time we were assembling and putting together the case papers J.B. kept referring to the 'Brandeis Brief'. I had no idea what he was talking about so I decided it was better to ask the question and be stupid for a minute than remain silent and be stupid forever: 'What the hell is the Brandeis Brief?'

The Brandeis Brief – as it was explained to me – was a pioneering legal brief dating from 1908. The term was first used in the United States to refer to a case which relied more on a compilation of scientific information and social science than on legal citations. It is named after a then litigator and eventual Associate Supreme Court Justice, Louis Brandeis, who deployed it in his argument in the 1908 US Supreme Court case Muller v Oregon. The brief was submitted in support of a state law restricting the number of hours women were allowed to work. The Brandeis Brief consisted of more than a hundred pages, only two of which were devoted to legal argument. The rest of the document contained testimony by medics, social scientists, and male workers arguing that those long working hours had a negative effect on the 'health, safety, morals, and general welfare of women.' Brandeis's sister-in-law and legal reformer, Josephine Clara Goldmark[2] of the National Consumers League, helped compile the brief. Despite the fact that the scientific evidence detailed in the Brandeis Brief was later challenged and widely refuted, it was regarded as a pioneering attempt to combine law and social science. The Brandeis Brief changed the direction of the Supreme Court of the United States.

It became the model for future Supreme Court presentations in cases affecting the health or welfare of classes of individuals. This strategy of combining legal argument with scientific evidence was later successfully used in Brown v the Board of Education to demonstrate the harmful psychological effects of segregated education on African-American children. When Brandeis turned up in court it took a hand cart to bring in all the documentation he had researched for his case. So no matter what point of law was raised or what issue needed clarification, Brandeis was able to go to his hand cart where, rest assured, he had the information and his response prepared.

This was what J.B. was driving at. No matter what was thrown at us we must have the answer. We were going to be as thorough and comprehensive as Brandeis had been and if anyone was 'going to hell in a handcart' it certainly was not going to be the union. Stripped down to its bare bones our case was going to be: that across the industry employees doing the same work for public bodies were entitled to the same remuneration and conditions and that, as this was backed by law, it could be enforced by the Industrial Court. But there were several steps to negotiate.

The first step was persuading the Industrial Court that it should hear the case. The decision we wanted could only be made by the Industrial Court so the very first thing we had to do was to persuade the Court to allow the case to be heard. The second step would be to demonstrate to the Court that the Ulsterbus workers were employed under contracts with various public bodies and that therefore the Fair Wages Resolutions were relevant to the case. Thirdly, we had to show that there was one bus industry operating in Northern Ireland and therefore the terms which pertained in Belfast also applied in the rural areas for the same work. Finally, we had to persuade the Court that the work carried out by the Ulsterbus men was to all intents and purposes indistinguishable, for the purposes of determining levels of remuneration, from the work carried out by the men working for Citybus.

Once these points were established we would have succeeded in showing that it was not just a question of fairness, equity or goodwill, but that there was a compelling legal basis under which the application of the same remuneration could be enforced on the employer. It would then not be a matter of a finely balanced judgement by the Court. At this point the Court would have no option but to find in our favour. None of

this would be easy and we could not afford to fail to prove our case at any point along the way.

But the company was also in a difficult position. The company management knew as well as we did that the wages gap had opened in the course of the previous decade and that it would be difficult to defend the difference in pay because it was so recent and could not possibly reflect significant differences in the work performed by rural and urban drivers. Thus once we established the legal basis of our challenge the company would be defending the indefensible.

One might ask the legitimate question: how did this differential open up during the ten years when Eugene O'Callaghan was the main lay trade union representative of the bus workers? There is a simple and straightforward answer – 'one-man buses'. As I later had to explain to the Industrial Court, prior to the formation of Ulsterbus, when the Ulster Transport Authority (UTA) was in operation, the difference between Citybus and Ulsterbus – or Belfast Corporation and the UTA as they were then – was five pennies in Ulsterbus's favour. Negotiations were conducted directly with the company and they were conducted after negotiations were completed at national level.

At some point UTA made an approach to the unions for OMO – One Man Operation or 'one-man buses'. At first the unions flatly refused but as the company's case was based on serious financial difficulties after lengthy negotiations the unions agreed to OMO. Initially it applied to buses which would be used exclusively on school work. But the unions also had concerns about the future impact of one-man operations which seemed to be the way the industry across the rest of the UK was going to go. On the union side a longer-term strategic approach was needed. So it was agreed, in the event of a national agreement for additional payments affecting the wages of Belfast drivers because of the possible future introduction of OMO in Belfast, that the position taken by Belfast Corporation Transport would be taken into account by the UTA which would implement any associated payments.

However, before that could be done the Ulster Transport Authority was wound up and Ulsterbus took over. When the extension of OMO came up again Ulsterbus took a tough line threatening a run down in service, redundancy and job losses. The unions, faced with an unpalatable choice, were forced to accept what was on offer. Even so there were still redundancies.

In 1969 – that is about four years after the UTA and been converted into Ulsterbus – the Belfast Corporation Transport Department, as it was then still known, in its turn approached the unions about the introduction of one-man operations. In anticipation of an agreement they purchased £1.5 million worth of vehicles. On this occasion the unions flatly refused the introduction unless they received:

- written guarantees of no compulsory redundancy;
- compensation for those who requested voluntary redundancy;
- a 50 per cent share in the savings resulting in one-man operations to be distributed to employees; and
- an increase of 25 per cent on basic salary for operating OMO.

Agreement was reached with the Belfast Corporation Transport that guaranteed no compulsory redundancy. Those requesting voluntary redundancy would receive a lump sum payment and a pension based on their years of service in accordance with the Crombie Code.[3] It was agreed that 50 per cent of the savings would be distributed and ultimately 22.5 per cent on top of basic salary for operating OMO plus a ticket bonus on the number of tickets issued in excess of the norm.

This was very different from the outcome with Ulsterbus where no similar agreement had been reached. This Citybus agreement on OMO should have stimulated Ulsterbus to honour the pledge made by the UTA not that long ago. However, history records that Ulsterbus did not at this moment – when it might have considered itself called on to do so – honour or seek to honour the commitment given a few years earlier by the Ulster Transport Authority.

While in 1968 there was approximately a gap of 98p in average weekly earnings, this had risen to approximately £15.75 in 1979. There was no difference of opinion between the unions and the company about the cause of this gap. It was commonly acknowledged by both sides that this was due to the introduction of OMO. Nor was there now any difference between the two sides that moving to OMO should be paid for by 50 per cent of the savings going to the workers in higher wages. Wages in the economy grow as worker productivity increases. One-man buses represented a tremendous productivity gain since half the number of men were now moving the same number of passengers.

The arrangement in Citybus as we moved to one-man buses had ensured that 50 per cent of the savings to the company in reduced operating costs had gone to the workers in higher wages. Ulsterbus had moved at a different pace and at different times to one-man buses and their savings in this recent period were much smaller so the 50 per cent of the savings due to the Ulsterbus workforce brought them a much smaller fund from which to increase basic earnings.

In short the background to the dispute was that the Ulsterbus management had already spent most of any potential savings from OMO. By dispensing with bus conductors they obviously greatly reduced their wages bill. The other side of the coin was that with the disappearance of bus conductors the work load of the drivers had substantially increased. They now had to take in the fares and handle all the money; they became solely responsible for the safety and security of passengers and the maintenance of order on the buses. They were more isolated and vulnerable. In the case of any sort of trouble especially from drunk, rowdy or abusive passengers they were on their own with no back up. It was not disputed that they should receive a pay increase to be funded out of the savings and the industry-wide rule of thumb was that staff should receive 50 per cent of the gross savings. But Ulsterbus did not now have the money to give the workers their share – a share which management, in the days when it was still the UTA, had conceded the workforce would be entitled to if that were the outcome in Belfast.

However, that was their problem and a problem of their own creation. It was not ours and not one which should be solved by expecting rural bus crews to do the same work for less money than urban bus drivers. There is here a recurring theme: management often expect workers to bear the cost of management's mistakes.

Unlike the Citybus transition to one-man operations, for Ulsterbus there was no crock of gold in the form of productivity gains to pay a wage increase to Ulsterbus drivers. The company was forced to try to argue that the wage differences reflected a different and less arduous working regime while knowing full well that this was nonsense. I believe in reality we did the company a favour by taking this battle through the Industrial Court because once the Court decided in our favour the company had no choice but to comply and could not be accused by the political classes or the press of 'caving into union bullying' or any of the usual things people like that say about working people seeking to make an honest living. Therefore, we decided to go for it.

To begin with we had to collect all the information which established that the Ulsterbus workers were carrying out contracts for government bodies and that despite a multitude of contractual arrangements there was a de facto single bus industry operating in Northern Ireland. But we could not just assert to the Court that this was the case, we had to prove it. That meant we had to ask those government bodies which had contracts with Ulsterbus to submit to the Court written evidence of the contracts they had with Ulsterbus.

Letters were prepared for the Department of Manpower, service documents had to be obtained, analysed and cross-referenced. Contracts with the Education and Library Boards and contracts for the supply of buses to the Ministry of Defence were also obtained and analysed. We obtained references from the Labour Relations Agency. We worked out and compared cross channel undertakings. We researched and compared legislation and case histories. The list grew longer by the day. The amount of work undertaken by Richard Steele was colossal while J.B. stood over us like a schoolmaster making sure that nothing was missed. The 'i's were doted and the 't's crossed. Meetings of the Bus Council were convened and they were kept continually updated during this period of time.

The Industrial Court was set up to provide a means of managing disputes between employers and their work forces and it dated back to 1919.[4] It was presided over by a person with a legal background who was supported by someone from the trade union side and someone from the employers' side but obviously not directly connected with the case being considered. In our case the trade union representative was W. Wallace and the employers' was H.J. Selby. The President of the Industrial Court was, as has already been mentioned, the Right Hon. R.W.B. McConnell who had formerly been a Unionist MP at Stormont and the Minister of Home Affairs. The cynic might say that, after his fall from grace, he owed his position to his political connections but I make no such comment.[5] McConnell formed part of a nucleus within the Unionist Party which became convinced that O'Neill, although keenly aware of the need to broaden the base of provincial politics in Ulster, lacked the astuteness, familiarity with the grass roots of the party and the personal qualities necessary to carry this through.

Going to the Industrial Court was for us a high-risk strategy and a war on two fronts. We had to marshal our forces to take on the company's hostility to paying the workers more and to the complicated legal obstacles which were then in place due to the government's incomes policy. But we also faced the hostility of the other unions in the industry. You would think that other unions with members in the industry would want to join in the fray, if only to be seen to be championing the interests of their own members. Not a bit of it. Other unions were quick to make their views known and make comments to the effect that we were daft, we did not know what we were talking about, and that we had no chance. Indeed senior officials in my own union said the whole exercise was a waste of time and could never succeed.

The first hearing of the Court took place at 10:30am on 15 March 1979. On the morning of the hearing – perhaps surprisingly given their initial attitude to the case we had made – when we went to present our case we were met on arrival by the heads of all the other unions who had members in Ulsterbus: Bertie West of the GMB, D. Casey from Transport Salaried Staffs' Association (TSSA), John Luney from the Engineering Union, and Harry Cavan from the Association of Scientific, Technical and Managerial Staffs (ASTMS). These were the very same people who had previously poured scorn on the suggestion that we could establish a case, never mind win it. They had now arrived to establish a presence. They had come to realise that not only was there a train at the station but that it was about to leave. At the last minute they wanted to clamber aboard. Bertie West approached me and asked 'Eugene who is representing us?' I replied: 'Well, if you don't know why ask me? You said we had no case.'

He then asked J.B. McCartney, 'Will you represent us?' J.B. looked to me but quite frankly I would have said 'no' in view of what he had been saying about the need for a totally water-tight case. However, J.B. counselled me that it might be better to agree as the GMB, alone of the other unions, was a signatory to the platform agreement. The other unions represented other categories of workers in the workforce. Following further discussions between us, I reluctantly agreed, although it meant that the GMB was getting a free ride without contributing one iota of effort. But as we represented the same grades of workers any success we secured would be applied automatically to the GMB men so it was tactically sensible for us to have them inside our tent ... where they could do us no damage ... than outside our tent ... where they just might.

The President stated, 'The first thing we have to sort out is: what is the position with the different unions?' and he then asked Mr McCartney for whom did he appear? Mr McCartney replied, 'The TGWU and the GMB.'6

He then sought to establish who else was there and in what capacity. It quickly became evident that the other unions were less well prepared. Many of the documents they needed to provide the court with had only just been served or had not yet been served. That the other unions' representatives were less well prepared is evident from the transcript of the Court's proceedings.

Mr Luney said that he was from the Confederation of Shipbuilding and Engineering Union which represented the maintenance workers. He confirmed that they wished to go under the same headings as Mr McCartney. The President asked the Court Secretary what references the court held for Mr Luney. The Secretary replied: 'The Department, as far as I know, have received no documentation from the Confederation regarding a contract under the 1947 Resolution. Documents were received from the Amalgamated Transport and General Workers' Union and the General and Municipal Workers Union on that subject. They tendered documents from the Western Education and Library Board. So far as I know, we did not receive anything from the other unions on that subject. So far as I know, the 1946 Resolution document that we received referred only to those two unions as well.'

Mr Luney advised that he wrote to the Court on 1 February 1979 putting forward five points and enclosing a copy of a contract which was a copy of a letter from Mr Heubeck indicating that there was no formal contract but referred to commitments with certain departments. The Court Secretary advised that the only documents received were on behalf of the two unions.

The President said to Mr Luney: 'Mr Luney, the position so far as the Fair Wages Resolutions are concerned is that you have got to convince the two Departments, the Westminster one and the Northern Ireland one, that they would refer them to us and that the Fair Wages Resolutions are applicable. We cannot do anything until we receive the reference.' The President in similar vein explained the procedure to Mr Cavan of ASTMS: 'Mr Cavan, you have got to get the Labour Relations Agency to refer under Schedule 3 and you have got to get the two Departments to refer the Fair Wages Resolution. You have also to consider whether you want a reference from them under the Transport Act.'

He delivered the same message to Mr Casey of the Transport and Salaried Staffs Association and even to Werner Heubeck who was shrewdly trying to piggy back on the process to secure pay increases for some of his senior executives which he was currently prevented from doing because of incomes policy. But he too had failed to follow this procedure-based process rigorously.

What in fact had happened was that the other unions had had to move from total scepticism about what we were doing to having to move very fast to catch up. Documents were arriving at the last minute – and after it. I am glad to say that by jumping on our bandwagon they all subsequently secured improvements for their staff. This included Heubeck's senior executives.

I have absolutely no doubt that if it had not been for the preparatory work undertaken by J.B. McCartney, Richard Steele and myself the case would never have been heard and certainly would not have succeeded. There simply would have been no court hearing where senior trade union officials could argue their case. Of course in the absence of a court hearing who would ever have known that workers had missed an opportunity to substantially improve their pay and conditions? The unions and their leaders could have carried on complacently immune from the criticism that by lack of willingness to think outside the box their members were continually losing out. As it was – although we were never thanked for it – I take considerable satisfaction from having contributed to improved pay and conditions for the 218 workers in other grades which their own unions would never have secured for them if we had not taken the risk to our union's reputation of promoting this unique case.

But back to the court. The Industrial Court cannot just make it up as it goes along; it has to follow its own procedural rules. We had to establish that our claims fell within the jurisdiction of the Court and at no stage could we afford to fail on some technicality. J.B. navigated all these technical hazards successfully.

To satisfy himself that the unions had indeed passed all the tests they needed to in order to establish their right to 'their day in court' the President asked J.B. if he wished to bring claims under all three headings. To which Mr McCartney replied: 'Schedule 3, the two Fair Wages Resolutions and primarily section 44 of the Transport Act (Northern Ireland) 1967.'[7]

The President stated that the position was that schedule 3 had been referred to the court and asked if that was right. Mr McCartney said, 'Yes, by the Labour Relations Agency.' The President said he did not think the Fair Wages Resolutions had been referred. Mr McCartney replied, 'I don't know about the Department of Manpower Services but certainly they have been referred to the IMS as have the contracts regarding the Western Health and Social Services Boards. We also submitted confirmation regarding the supply of buses to the Ministry of Defence'. J.B. went on to point out that sub section (1) (*b*) of section 44 of the 1967 Act takes one to the Fair Wages resolution anyway. Further discussion took place under different headings of the claim.

Following further discussions, the President said that there was no reason why the unions should not co-operate with each other as it would not prejudice each other's case. He advised it would be a good thing if the unions got together and for all the unions to use any material there was jointly between themselves. In other words he was stating what should have been obvious to the other unions months ago – that we would have been well advised from the start to present a united front.

Mr McCartney stated that there were a number of single comparators and the Court might wish to hear them separately. The President said that it was up to him how he presented his case. However, there was no point going into the full detail at that time. The President advised him that he could make a few outline points, the transcript of which would be considered during the adjournment.

One of the building blocks in our case was establishing that there was such a thing as a bus passenger industry in Northern Ireland. So one of the first things Mr McCartney did was to outline the Ulsterbus operations covering Northern Ireland, the Republic of Ireland, the subsidiaries, excursions, parcel operations, tours and private hire throughout the British Isles. There was, he said, considerable overlap between the public scheduled situation and, as they call it in Britain, the coach operation. There were, he said, some 1,349 people in the grades classed as bus drivers, auxiliary staff, cleaners and miscellaneous grades who were covered by a memorandum agreement. Referring to documents submitted to the court he referred to 1,131 bus drivers and 218 other grades operating from a number of depots in Belfast and the larger country centres. The Transport Union represented 1,018 employees and the GMB the remainder. The other public transport companies comprised Citybus and the Londonderry and Lough Swilly Railway, which had its headquarters in Derry.

Having given further details of bus operations in Northern Ireland and establishing, as required by the legislation, that there was a road transport passenger industry, he turned his attention to how collective bargaining was conducted because the second building block in the argument concerned the way in which pay and conditions were determined across the industry through collective bargaining. He showed that in Britain there were, what were usually called, two central national bargaining organisations: the National Joint Industrial Council (NJIC) and the National Council for the Omnibus Industry (NCOI).

Mr McCartney referred the court to an ACAS report, Number 16. The Advisory, Conciliation and Arbitration Service, known as ACAS, was a Crown non-departmental public body of the government of the United Kingdom. Its purpose was to improve organisations and working life through the promotion and facilitation of strong industrial relations practice. It might do this in a number of ways such as arbitration or mediation, although the service was perhaps best known for its collective conciliation function – that is resolving disputes between groups of employees or workers. ACAS was an independent and impartial organisation that did not side with a particular party, but rather helped the parties to reach suitable resolutions in a dispute.

In particular McCartney referred to paragraphs 4.5, 4.6, 4.7, 4.8, and 4.9 of the ACAS report. In addressing these points he did not do so using legalistic-type language; rather he teased out and explained the various points in a manner which was easy to understand. In Great Britain most large towns and cities had their own municipal bus services and the National Joint Industrial Council set out the minimum terms for the industry within the municipal undertakings. The National Council for the Omnibus Industry looked after the rest of the industry. The terms and conditions of employment set out by both national negotiating bodies were similar and closely interrelated but had different implementation dates: the NJIC on 1st January annually and the NCOI on the 1st March annually.

After explaining other pieces of legislation he then turned directly to section 44 with some degree of intensity. Unlike Great Britain, Northern Ireland did not have a lot of different public authorities running bus services. 'The 1967 Transport Act applies of course to Northern Ireland but there is no district problem in either [a] or [b] of section 44(1). Subsection (1) requires that salaries, wages or other remuneration and conditions of employment of employees of the holders of road services licences shall be in accordance with paragraphs (a) or (b) of that subsection. The Act requires that the conditions of employment shall be no less favourable than those offered by an employer under the 1947 Stormont Fair Wages Resolution. If one examines the wording of paragraph (b) it is clear that the comparison is with a contractor who would otherwise have to comply, but there is no need to comply with it under section 44.' This he said led to the current problem about the non-reference of the Fair Wages Resolution.

'The evidence', he said, 'shows that Ulsterbus is paying less favourable remuneration but that argument was for another day.' He referred to documents submitted in relation to Ulsterbus, Citybus, Lough Swilly and the NJIC agreement. The NCIO agreement had yet to be submitted. The President suggested that the court adjourn until the parties could submit all the evidence and they had the parties before the court who had not got references. Mr McCartney said that if the Department of Manpower and the Ministry of Defence had not made references then pressure would have to be applied to them. He stated from the perspective of the TGWU and the GMB they were ready. The Court adjourned and reconvened on 9 May 1979.

Bristol RE No. 2223 destroyed 7 July 1990 in Wellington Place, just a short distance from Belfast City Hall
PAUL SAVAGE

15
The Brandeis Brief: part II
– the court resumes

When the hearing resumed Mr McCartney advised that
Messers O'Callaghan and Steele would deal with the
case for the Transport and General Workers' Union and
the General and Municipal.

He advised we would not be representing any of the other unions,
although they had been asked to represent the Confederation of
Shipbuilding and Engineering Unions including ASTMS. He said
unfortunately they had only been approached the previous Thursday
when everything should have been with the court for distribution. He said
that after consideration there was no way that they would have been
ready so he asked for those cases to be postponed.

This session got into the heart of the issues and became both detailed
and technical. At this point our emphasis was on proving that Citybus
set the standard for wages and conditions. There were lots of references
to other cases and decisions which might or should be regarded as
precedents for our case. Once again Mr McCartney addressed and
interpreted the various pieces of legislation taking the opportunity of
handing out maps showing the network of Ulsterbus services throughout
the British Isles. He went on to refer to a number of Central Arbitration
Committee Cases: the Shepherd Neame case 78/13; the Wigglesworth case
78/26 and the Normal Air-Garrett case 78/78. These rulings were to the
effect that a single comparator may set the general level. The clear
implication was that one company – in our case Citybus – could set the
standard for wages and conditions throughout Northern Ireland.
McCartney submitted that neither the context of the Acts nor the Fair
Wages Resolution required a contrary interpretation. He meticulously

addressed all of the issues, antecedence, case history, and interpretation of legislation. At this stage I was satisfied beyond doubt that we would win.

Richard Steele then referred to the documents showing the list of nine comparators; he also referred to the list of comparators provided by Ulsterbus which showed five of the same comparators. He advised that the main comparator was Citybus whose agreed rate was £74 plus £3 attendance allowance making a total of £77 for bus drivers for a 40-hour week. He identified four broad bands into which the workforce could be divided: namely Bus Diver, Charge Hand, Ancillary Drivers (shunters, car or van drivers and parcel attendants) and miscellaneous workers, which included cleaners, fuel issuers, parcel messengers and finally office cleaners. Ulsterbus had identical grades.

	ULSTERBUS	CITYBUS
DRIVER	£61.215	£74.00 + £3.00
CHARGEHAND	£54.22	£65.50
ANCILLARY	£52.25	£64.25
MISCELLANEOUS	£50.50	£62.36
OFFICE CLEANER	£44.55	£50.80

Mr Steele referred to the nationally negotiated rates: the National Joint Industrial Council and the National Council for the Omnibus Industry. He stressed that these were minimum rates, and it was £54.90 plus £6.86 shift allowance and an additional £15.90 for one-man operation buses which added up to a total of £77.66. The President requested clarification on the shift allowance asking if it referred to a particular shift or 'did everyone get it?' I was able to advise that anyone on shift work received a shift allowance which applied to anyone who was working outside normal factory hours – that is before 8:00am or after 5:00pm. The President asked if some categories of workers were excluded from it. I explained it was a round figure which had been been calculated and then factored into the overall wages bill so everyone benefitted to some degree from it.

It was generally acknowledged that the whole history of negotiation in the industry shows that constant reference had been made to the Citybus pay and conditions in the Ulsterbus negotiations. An agreement which was reached at a conciliation meeting with Mr Joe Scott on 5 February

Bill Morris, Richard Steele, J.B. McCartney and Eugene

1971 showed that not only was Citybus the direct level-setter for the reasons previously given but also the indirect effect of the NJIC. This is backed up by the CAC 78/131 James Lamont decision which took into account the nearest comparator. To summarise, what we were saying was: 'Ulsterbus follows Citybus because of the dates of implementation, therefore Citybus is the direct cost setter.'

I then came to my final submission, which was that Ulsterbus was in breach of section 44. In addition there was the issue of backdating any award. If we won and the rates of pay for Ulsterbus workers were to be brought into line with those of Citybus the question of whether the increases should be backdated would have to be addressed. It should be remembered that the Ulsterbus men had been underpaid for years. On the question of backdating Mr Steele presented the Court with a photocopy of a decision by the Northern Ireland Divisional Court. There Lord MacDermott had ruled – and his ruling was upheld by the Northern Ireland Appeal Court – that the Industrial Court has the power to back-date an award to the date on which the claim was substantially the same claim as the one before the court.

Mr Steele said we were claiming that there should be backdating by the authority which the Northern Ireland Court of Appeal provided and which of course was at the discretion of the Court. In the Londonderry

Corporation case there was backdating of some five years. We were also asking that because an award which was made up of pay itself would still have the inequity of the dates of application, the dates of future application should be 1 January as with Citybus with calculations based on basic hours.

Clarification was requested by the Court on the difference in consolidation by the two companies for the one-man operation. I explained that to begin one calculates the number of buses being converted to one-man operations and how much money this will save. Once they are converted the amount saved is divided in two so the resulting sum, which is 50 per cent of the expected savings, is divided by the total number of man-hours expected to be worked and then the basic rate of pay is increased by this saving per man-hour worked into a new consolidated rate.

At that time the extra money to be consolidated into the Citybus weekly basic rate amounted to £9.40. Due to the fact that Ulsterbus had so little left to convert it amounted to £1.44. Even the Citybus rate was by no means top of the range. As I pointed out, nationally the one-man operation had been revamped to guarantee, for 100 per cent conversion of the bus fleet to OMO, under the NJIC terms a minimum of £15.00. I also understood that agreement had been reached at NCOI level for a minimum of £11.44 for 100 per cent conversion rate.

It was clear that Werner Heubeck in making his contribution to the proceedings would – like his former commanding officer Rommel in North Africa – be intent on conducting a retreat but trying to inflict some damage while doing so. Much of his argument turned on the differences which he claimed existed between the working and operating conditions of Ulsterbus and Citybus drivers. I addressed the court and said,

> Mr Heubeck referred to the fact that whilst he considered there was some justification in the claim he did not readily accept that there was a claim for parity. Could I for the benefit of the Court advise you that the three main Ulsterbus depots are situated in Belfast and operate within the periphery of Belfast, and that the maximum mileage out of Belfast from any of those three depots is less than some of the mileage operated by Citybus. I am thinking of Ballyhenry and Roughfort which are operated by Citybus. But some destinations operated by Ulsterbus are shorter distances from the city centre – for example Belvoir is 4.1 miles.

Going to the city of Londonderry again Ulsterbus operate a city service which is similar to that which is operated in Belfast. In fact in quite a number of provincial towns we operate either a town or city service. In practice with regard to route distances in many cases there is little difference between the urban driving of Citybus and Ulsterbus drivers.

In Belfast the Citybus driver has the advantage that practically 80% of their passengers have already purchased their tickets and he is therefore only responsible for collecting 20% of the fares, nor does he operate an express parcel service like the Ulsterbus man.

The Ulsterbus man, whether in city service, town service or express service is responsible at all times not only for issuing tickets but also for the cancellation of tickets, the collection of cash, the carrying of parcels and the carrying of papers. He also operates a cross border service which is vastly different to the service which is operated by Belfast Citybus.

With the introduction of EEC legislation the European Parliament in all its wisdom, in possession of the best medical advice, was of the opinion that there was no necessity to apply the strictness of the EEC legislation to services which operate within a 50 kilometre radius like those in the city of Belfast.

The EEC legislation has been applied and will be applied rigidly to all of the services which operate in excess of 50 kilometres. I think the EEC legislation kills the argument, if Mr McCartney has not already done so, in relation to the overtime, because here again the EEC restricts the amount of overtime people outside the 50 kilometres, namely Ulsterbus staff, would be allowed to do.

Mr Heubeck referred to average hours. For the benefit of the court I should explain how average hours are arrived at. They are hours which are accumulated as a result of Saturday and Sunday working where there is an enhanced rate for Saturday and Sunday or where they are doing spread-over shifts or shifts of that nature. I would suggest that far from reducing the argument on behalf of the Ulsterbus employee it in fact improves the argument because his higher average hours is a result of being called on to do more Saturdays and Sundays when everyone else likes to have their weekend off.

With the debate over the heat was now on the President of the Court to lead us all towards an acceptable outcome. The President asked, 'Supposing we were to make an award – I don't know whether we will or not – there have been suggestions about how we should make it. If we go down the list and say bus drivers £x, chargehand £y, and shunter £z, alternatively should we allow an area of negotiation between the two parties?'

Mr Heubeck replied saying, in another attempt at possibly creating wriggle room, 'I would have thought that if you confined yourself to observing whether you can make an award in the case of drivers the unions and management would then take the spirit of the award and apply it to the other grades.'

Mr McCartney stated, 'I am sorry but the unions would not agree. In the history of this issue they have had too much of this business where agreements have been made and have not been implemented. An agreement in principle of 1971 has not been implemented. We ask the court to make the award and not leave it to the parties.' I then said, 'What we are suggesting is simply that it is a claim for parity with Citybus. If the court were to agree with the claim then I do not see any problem as it is a straight forward issue.' The President said, 'yes if the court agrees with the claim.'

In fact both sides were content that once the rate for drivers was agreed that the others could follow based on some binding formula such as the percentage those grades bore to the pay of drivers. Because government pay policy applied at that time it was important that the arrangements were based on a decision of the Court as that took the rates outside the rules and restrictions of pay policy. The President adjourned the hearing saying they would consider and come to a decision.

However, he then reconvened some weeks later because of what he described as 'a certain confusion.' There was, he said, a letter from Mr Heubeck which he thought the unions should see. It had only arrived that morning and he thought it would be helpful if Mr Heubeck elucidated further on what was in the letter.

This was the danger we had always feared – last minute confusion derailing the process. But if that was management's intention they had not reckoned on J.B. He rose magnificently to the occasion blocking off any danger that the court might be talked by Mr Heubeck into diversionary bye-ways which would have re-opened issues that had already been definitively dealt with. Mr McCartney said, 'With respect, Mr President, I am concerned at what you propose doing. I don't think you have the jurisdiction and may I address you on that point.' He stated,

'We are not concerned with section 3 at all, we are concerned with section 44 and the provisions of section 44. Could I draw your attention first of all to Hanks v Ace High Productions 1978 Industrial Case Reports 1155. That is a decision of the AET of July 1978 and could I also draw your attention, though it is not so directly on the point, to the Queen and the Industrial Tribunal, ex parte, Cotswold Collotype Company Limited. This is a decision of the Divisional Court in England on the 23rd and 24th November 1978.'

Mr McCartney said he would like to draw attention to the Hanks decision and to the very explicit limitations which the AET and Mr Justice Phillips in the chair drew there, 'Which I submit applies to this court in the absence of any legislation.' So he argued that there was consequently nothing left to consider other than the interpretation of the award.

The President felt that it would seem to revolve around the award and whether the Court had made a decision. Mr McCartney agreed. The President then asked if we were contending that the Court had already made a decision. Mr Mc Cartney said, 'You will have seen from the cases that even an oral decision is quite sufficient without having followed that up. In my submission your two letters constitute a decision that Ulsterbus must pay the basic rate for a 40-hour week and it remains therefore only for this court to say what the basic rate for a 40-hour week is. Mr Heubeck in his letter has very kindly spelled out that the basic rate is £74 plus £3.'

More wriggling by the President. He replied, 'Well if you take the letter of the 29th May the last paragraph is just the one sentence. "Any award of the court will take effect from the 1st January 1979." The word "any" surely means that no award has yet been made. It does not say "the award of the court."' Mr McCartney stated he appreciated that but he must submit that these two letters appear to constitute the decision of the Court and all that is left is for the formal award. In his opinion the *ex parte* case to which he referred made it clear that this was the submission of counsel and it appeared to have been accepted by the Lord Chief Justice. He went on:

> Now I submit that that is the common law, there is nothing in the Act and only section 3 [1] applies to this situation. There is nothing there other than a reference to an interpretation and then we are thrown to the regulations and the only regulation, regulation 8 has effect and that again is interpretation.

Mr Heubeck has made a request in his letter today but we would be prepared to waive the fact that it has not been carried out in the form laid down in section 8 in order that the court can give an interpretation of what the basic rate of a 40 hour week is.

'The only issue left', Mr McCartney submitted, 'is what is the basic rate in Citybus for a 40-hour week and that Mr Heubeck has spelt out in the letter he has sent to the court – it is £74 plus £3.' The President stated the court should hear from Mr Heubeck both on anything he might say by way of the legal position and to the extent of clearing up his letter so that issues might become clearer. 'We have indicated our decision and we do not intend to go back on it but we want to see how it can be effected so to be fair to both parties.' Mr McCartney said, 'So long as we are not taken as acquiescing in a view that the court has jurisdiction to open any further argument.'

It became rather tetchy, so much so that the President felt compelled to mutter, 'I think we – both parties – should concentrate on being as friendly as possible'. This would seem to be a curious way of putting it in the circumstances. But in the end there was no backtracking – J.B.'s alertness prevented that; the busmen were not going to be cheated out of this victory by a last minute fudge.

The subsequent award from the Industrial Court (Northern Ireland) was history making under section 44 of The Transport Act (Northern Ireland) 1967. After considering all the evidence presented by the parties the outcome was – with effect from 1 January 1979 – Ulsterbus drivers and other grades included in the reference should be paid the same basic rate per 40-hour week as though they are and had been employed by Citybus. This award in no way interfered with the current attendance allowance paid to bus drivers. Ulsterbus parcel attendants should equate to Citybus car/van drivers, and Ulsterbus parcel messengers to Citybus cleaner/fuel issuers.

This was a unique case in that it was the first and last brought under section 44. Its success was due to diligent research and preparation by Mr McCartney, Mr Steele and me. I have to say that if it were not for our persistence the case would never have seen the light of day. Ulsterbus employees received £1.4 million in back pay and an increase of £15.90 on basic rates.

As I mentioned earlier one group of beneficiaries of our action was management, whose incomes had been slipping behind comparators in

Great Britain. Because of pay policy catching up was not possible so Heubeck got them included by the court. So indirectly I was also responsible for pay increases for management! Well they are workers too though the ending of pay policy shortly afterwards meant that any benefits I had conferred on them were not long required. To his credit Heubeck asked that he be excluded from this 'open sesame' saying, 'I do believe in the principle that you look after your horse before you look after yourself.' How many of the often grossly overpaid chief executives of today would take that line?

Were there lessons to be learned from this case and if so were they learned? The answer to the first question is 'yes' but unfortunately the answer to the second question is 'no'. One such lesson which should have been learned was the benefit of having a close relationship with the universities. Unfortunately that relationship was not built upon. When one considers the amount of funding provided by the trade unions to the Labour Party and what they get in return, and then think what – for a fraction of that contribution – the return could be from the universities by way of expertise in research, education for officials and members, access to case histories and much more.

In this particular case with the academics' input we secured £1.4 million pounds in back pay plus the weekly increase in basic pay of £15.90 at little or no cost to the unions. Did the unions learn from this case to properly prepare the evidence or ensure that proper references were put before the courts? We very demonstrably made the case for an intelligent, active trade unionism based on careful research and analysis backed by the best expertise the universities and union research departments could provide. Did others learn that? I leave it to the reader to judge.

Following the success of the Ulsterbus case Mr McCartney, Mr Steele and I carried out some further research and concluded that a successful case could be made to the European Court for parity with the highest comparator in Europe, either Germany or France. This would of course entail making a number of trips back and forth to Brussels. The union would have had to finance those trips but unfortunately my approach to the Regional Secretary was rejected out of hand, and without this finance we were unable to proceed. We then ran into the buffers when the government repealed the legislation under which the case could be brought. Since then other cases have been successfully brought before the European courts on various aspects of the law in relation to the rights of workers.

I cannot say that we would have been successful but I do feel that we should have had the opportunity to try. It is as a result of the success of cases brought under European Law for the protection of workers' rights that the current government is pursuing such a high profile case for changes and derogation from, in particular, Human Rights legislation. At present there is a steady erosion of the protection afforded by the law to working people and their ability to defend their pay and conditions. If workers lose all the remaining protections they enjoy from membership of the European Union, or the United Kingdom having been a member of the EU, this process of the destruction of workers' rights will only accelerate.

Are the trade unions through the congress of trade unions and the international labour movement doing enough to highlight, educate and mobilise opposition to government arguments? Have they forgotten the lessons of the miners' strike when, in my opinion, they failed to come together in a single unit, but instead stood back and allowed the whole mining community to be bludgeoned into the ground and starved into defeat? They then covered their shame by blaming Arthur Scargill for not holding a ballot.

The miners did not receive support and solidarity they so badly needed. They were by and large abandoned to their fate. To cite but one high profile example: Frank Chapple, who became leader of the Electricians' union in 1966, and in 1985 went on to take a seat in the House of Lords, withheld support (I am reminded of the old quip, 'there is ermine and there is vermin'). When the safety inspectors in the mines deserted their comrades their reward was to be made redundant.

But think how different it could have been if the trade union had stood shoulder to shoulder with the miners. Of course coal as a major energy source did not have a long-term future. But would not an orderly run down of the coal industry have avoided the need to beat into submission the close-knit mining communities and paid the country's debt to the generations of brave men who, at enormous personal risk, had fuelled the industrial revolution and enabled the UK to come through two world wars?

By abandoning the miners the trade union movement set the pattern for abandoning those industries and communities exposed to technological and economic change. If there had been collective support and the miners had won would we still be suffering today from the legacy of Margaret Thatcher? Put simply, the trade union movement can do better in unity which gives strength: divided we fall. Furthermore, we will not progress or develop improved living standards if we continue in our failure through apathy.

But meanwhile 'back at the ranch', despite all of these problems we still were able to make progress on the terms and conditions of bus workers. In 1977 when I became the full-time official Citybus drivers were in receipt of £74 for a basic week of 40 hours. Ulsterbus drivers were paid £15 less. The Industrial Court case in 1979 benefitted Ulsterbus drivers to the tune of £15.90 per week bringing them level with their Citybus counterparts. When I retired in 1992 both Ulsterbus and Citybus basic rates for a driver working 38 hours a week was £180 with an attendance allowance of £9.25 per week giving a total of £189.25. In addition holidays were increased and qualified for a premium rate of £202 per week.

However, this does not tell the full story; due to the nature of bus work when one adds in the penalty payments for spread-over schedules, weekend working, etc., the average wage for a 43-hour week amounted to £212.93 without overtime. What we had achieved confirmed that we were far better off than when we depended on national negotiations.

These improvements were not achieved without a struggle; on one occasion labour was withdrawn on nine consecutive Fridays before a settlement was reached. The GMB instructed its members to cross the picket lines and work. Where have you heard that before? Thankfully, most men ignored these instructions and joined the Transport Union. In situations like these there are sometimes no winners but the union did put down a marker that we would not be pushed around.

16
Bus stop in cancer ward

At the beginning of 1992 I was diagnosed with colon cancer and was placed on the waiting list for surgery.

Before I went into hospital, I felt it would be prudent and appropriate to have a written document drawn up which would incorporate all and any agreements which existed between the unions and the company. This would be a complex task as bus work is different to what exists in any other industry. Different interpretations could be placed on aspects of an agreement which could in turn lead to disputes.

The company agreed with me and appointed the following representatives: Alan Mercer, Head of Human Resources, Alan Hamilton, Personnel Manager, and Bob Wilson, an Area Manager. As the union official I nominated my branch chairman and two Bus Council members to accompany me. The GMB nominated Robert Carson and Ernie Cooley as their representatives. Discussions took place over a long period of time. Documents and minutes of meetings were checked and finally a formal agreement was reached. The agreement was signed by my branch chairman and me on behalf of the TGWU, by Robert Carson and Ernie Cooley on behalf of the GMB, and by Ted Hesketh who was now Managing Director of Translink and Alan Mercer on behalf of the company. It was agreed that a copy would be provided to every employee.

The agreement became known as the 'bible' to which the company and employees would adhere. The agreement was signed on All Fools Day, 1 April 1992! On 16th November 1992 I went into hospital for surgery. I recall asking the surgeon what my chances were and his response: 'I won't know until I get in there.' This was a very difficult time for me. Following the operation I was recovering in the Intensive Care Unit of the Mater Infirmorum Hospital. I do not know exactly what the reasons were – I believe some emergency arose and the space was required – but I was moved to a side unit in a surgical ward. During the course of being moved the internal stitches gave way and I was rushed back to theatre where I could hear the doctors proffering differing opinions as to whether to open me up again or take a chance on it holding as the rupture was not as bad as at first thought. In the end they took a chance and sent me back to the ward.

I was not allowed food or liquids. After a day or so I became delirious and instead of showing signs of recovery was going downhill badly. I believe that if it had not been for the intervention of my daughter Patricia, who was a senior nurse in a different hospital, I would have died. She insisted on seeing the surgeon, going into the theatre to speak to him. I was not party to what was said but I was again taken back to theatre, the back of my neck was lanced and I had some sort of drip inserted. I can recall lying on the stretcher barely conscious with the blood flowing out of my neck where they were inserting the tube; a drip was then set up through which vitamins were fed directly into me.

After a few days I began to improve and was moved into the general ward. My daughter came to the hospital every day before and after her night shift at the Royal Victoria Hospital. She would assist me in getting washed in the morning and made sure I was well looked after, speaking to the ward sister and director of nursing. I do not believe I ever said how much I appreciated what she did at that time but when she reads this she will know I really did. When I recovered sufficiently I was allowed home.

On the approach to Christmas the bus shop stewards were having their annual Christmas get-together at the Chimney Corner Hotel. I received a phone call asking if I would be fit to attend, I said 'no' but my wife Patricia took the phone and said, 'He will be there.' She then turned to me and said, 'You're going whether you like it or not.' When I arrived at the hotel I was met by one of my shop stewards, Liam Hughes. Liam was a character; he had a glass of whiskey in one hand and a half pint of beer in the other. He said, 'O'Callaghan get this into you; if you're going to die you might as well die happy!' He meant no harm. Well, I drank it and a few more.

I was 64 in March 1993 and still on sick leave. Eddie Sheridan was taking care of my branches for me. As I would have had less than a year to go if I returned to work at this stage I asked for and was allowed to take early retirement. Bill Morris, who was the General Secretary of the

Bill Morris presenting
Eugene with the TGWU
gold star at a gala dinner
in the Chimney Corner
Hotel, 13 November 1993

union at that time and whose election I had strongly supported, flew in from London to my retirement function organised by shop stewards at the Chimney Corner Hotel, where he personally presented me with the union's highest honour – the TGWU gold star. 'Eugene O'Callaghan was the best regional secretary Ireland never had', he said. Well it was nice of him to say that and his generous sentiment let me go out on a high note. But it was the words of one of my shop steward colleagues, Liam Hughes, which touched me more deeply than any other awards or praise or honours could have done when he said, 'It should never be forgotten that it was Eugene O'Callaghan who got us up off our knees and gave us respect and credibility when it mattered most.'

I did go back very briefly to cover for Eddie during the summer while he took his annual leave. Now that is more than 25 years ago and I never looked back. The cancer never returned, thank God.

Sunday World,
14 November 1993

WHEEL ON THE TRIBUTES FOR THE BUSMEN'S HERO!

17
A busman's holiday

I took things easy for almost a year as might be
expected after what I had gone through. Although
I had not anticipated that my working life would be
ended so abruptly through a life-threatening illness,
I had expected to hang up my boots for good around
this time and to do so without any regrets.

I had done what I could for the union members for whom I was
responsible, and for the busmen in particular I felt a particular bond as
we had achieved so much together. But I knew that there was more to life
and there was my family as well as other interests to which I wanted to
devote more time.

I mentioned near the beginning of my story my dog, Toby, whose
memory exercised an enormous pull on me. Indeed, dogs have been an
abiding lifelong interest of mine and in fact through my enduring love of
dogs I had a very enjoyable social life.

Once I had well and truly married and settled down and years after my
return from England the longing for the sort of companionship that an
intelligent and well-trained dog can give returned – but maybe only
genuine dog lovers will understand what I mean. One day my wife and I
were in Gresham Street in Belfast when she spotted a pedigree Irish Terrier
pup for sale at £5 and wanted to get it for me as a birthday present. Out
of what little she had she haggled and bought me the pup for £4.50. We
brought the wee pup home but it wasn't very well due to diarrhoea and
dehydration. She nearly died. However we nursed her back to health and
named her Judy; the first of a long line of dogs called Judy.

Judy remained with us until she died at a ripe old age.

In a previous chapter I recounted the tragic story of poor Tommy
Killops who painted a picture of her for me and who had acquired one of
Judy's pups just two days before he was killed. We registered her show
name as 'Glenowen Patricia': Glen for Crossmaglen, Owen my own name
and Patricia for my wife. Judy became a champion dog, winning many
best of breeds, best in show and trophies such as The Challenge Bowl,
Saunders Cup and India Cup. Some of her pups were exported to
America, winning on some of the biggest stages in the world.

It was by chance that I switched to Kerry Blue Terriers. Patsy Kane, a
breeder who lived near me, bred Kerry Blues. I used to come across her
when out walking the dogs and she talked me into buying one, but
unfortunately it died. George, who was an was RUC man, then came to
my house with five Kerry Blue pups; he noticed me eying a small pup
whereupon he proceeded to tell me it was the runt, a rubbish dog and no
good. He then recommended another pup which he valued at £75. I said,
'I'll tell you what; you see that pup that is no good. I will give you £25
for it.' Whereupon he went into a bit of a rant. '£25 for a Kerry Blue', he
said, 'you must be joking.' 'Well', I replied, 'that is it I don't want any of
the rest but I will give you £25 for rubbish.' We finally struck a deal: we
would bring in my young son and whichever pup he picked I would pay
for. Damian, my son, picked up the runt saying this is the one whereupon
I paid George £25. I now owned Malfar Rock of Bawn who went on to
become an international champion. He won more best in shows than

most prize dogs win firsts. At home he was Shane – the first of many.

It was during this period that I made friends with a fellow exhibitor; it was at best a strange relationship as we both came from completely different walks of life, culturally, religiously and in every other way. He held a position in government which in normal circumstances would make it impossible for us to meet never mind establish a friendship. We remained good friends for over 25 years travelling throughout England and Ireland together showing our dogs. We socialised and visited each other's homes. When he went on holiday I would look after his dog and he would do the same for me. Never once did he ask about my background and I didn't ask about his. The friendship and our shared love of dogs crossed all boundaries. For security reasons I will make no mention of his name. The moral of this story is that we, the people of Ireland, can have our own culture and belief and would still be there for each other if it was not for the politicians who constantly stir things up.

Eugene and Judy. Judy's show name is Breath of Fresh Air and she is also a Green Star Champion

Recently, when many thought I was at death's door, my friend called and groomed and clipped my current Kerry Blue Terrier – another Judy. To him I say goodbye old friend and thank you for the friendship. If only others could learn from us – how we lived respecting each other's differences and by our deeds earning and keeping our respect for each other.

But despite rediscovering life outside the union and its battles it was not long before I was approached by Joe Cooper who asked me if I would join the Retired Members' Association (RMA). The Retired Members' Association was founded by Jack Jones, our union's former General Secretary. I had a great regard for Jack. He was one of the best, if not the best General Secretary we ever had. James Larkin Jones known as Jack was born in Garston, Liverpool. He was named after the Irish – but Liverpool-born – trade unionist, James Larkin. He left school when he was fourteen years old and joined his father as a Liverpool docker where he became a member of the Transport and General Workers' Union and was subsequently elected first as a shop steward and then as a delegate to the National Dock Workers' Group Committee.

Trade Unionism in the Seventies

JACK JONES ARCHIVE, MODERN RECORDS CENTRE, UNIVERSITY OF WARWICK (MSS. 126/JJ/X/59)

He was converted to socialism after reading *The Ragged-Trousered Philanthropists* which had a remarkable effect on his thinking. Jack organised protest meetings against fascists in Liverpool and was once beaten up by a group of blackshirts armed with knuckledusters. In 1936, at the start of the Spanish Civil War, he joined and served with the International Brigade. He was seriously wounded in the battle of Ebro in 1938 and returned to Britain where he became a full-time official of the TGWU. He played a key role in organising the workforce in the West Midlands car industry. He later became Assistant General Secretary of the union and a member of the Labour Party National Executive Committee.

Jack chaired the Labour party policy group on industrial democracy. In 1968 he was elected General Secretary of the union. Together with Hugh Scanlon of the Amalgamated Engineering Union he led the left-wing trade union opposition to the 1966–70 Labour government's industrial relations policy to introduce legislation which would have enforced a 28-day cooling-off period before strike action could be taken. He was chief economic spokesman for the Trades Union Congress and later one of the authors of the 'social contract' a Labour Party policy from the 1970s. In January 1977 a Gallup poll found that 54 per cent of people believed Jack to be the most powerful man in Britain, ahead of the Prime Minister.

In addition to increasing membership to more than two million Jack had a hotel built in Eastbourne for the benefit of ill or retired members who could stay there for two weeks free of charge. He also purchased another hotel in London where delegates attending meetings in London could stay at a reasonable cost. A further facility was established in Wales which again catered for those in retirement or ill health. In retirement Jones served as President of the National Pensioners' Convention – an organisation representing over 1,000 pensioner groups.

At the 2003 Labour party conference in Bournemouth, then aged 90, he received a special award in recognition of his services to the trade union movement. Jack Jones' last public act on 7 December 2008 was to unveil a memorial at New Haverport, 70 years after British battalion members returned to port after the International Brigade was withdrawn from Spain.

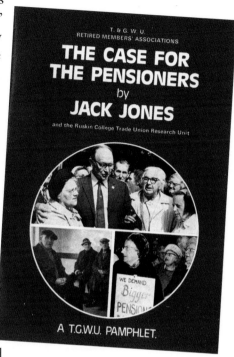

The Case for Pensioners
JACK JONES ARCHIVE, MODERN RECORDS CENTRE, UNIVERSITY OF WARWICK (625/7/11)

The Transport Union building in Liverpool has been refurbished and renamed Jack Jones House. Jack was consistently re-elected as President and was still actively working until his death. He lived at a care home in South London until his death on 21 April 2009 aged 96 years.

Part of the vision of Jack Jones was to see members looked after, not only in work but also in retirement. When he himself retired he was presented with a large sum of money collected by ordinary members who wanted to show their appreciation for the service he provided to them over the years. Instead of accepting the money Jack donated it to the founding of the Retired Members' Association. In addition to this he negotiated with the then General Secretary a sum of £100,000 annual subscription to be used to run the Association. The union would also provide an office in Transport House, London with a secretary to be paid from general funds. Telephones, postage and printing services would also be provided by the union. The organisation would be structured on the same lines as the union with an executive committee, regional committees and branches. Positions would be filled by elections.

Joe Cooper was a retired trade union official who had worked out of

Jack Jones

JACK JONES ARCHIVE,
MODERN RECORDS
CENTRE, UNIVERSITY OF
WARWICK (625/17/435)

an office a couple of doors down the corridor from me. In addition to his job Joe had a history of working for and representing the less well off. He had been President of Belfast and District Trades Council and had worked with, among others, Betty Sinclair. Anyone who knows anything about Belfast and the efforts made on behalf of the working class will have heard of Betty Sinclair. She championed the poor and worked tirelessly on behalf of the mill workers. Betty was born to a Church of Ireland family in the Ardoyne area of north Belfast. She became a mill worker and joined the Revolutionary Workers Group in 1932. In 1933 she was involved in the Outdoor Relief strike. She stood for the Communist Party in the 1945 Northern Ireland general election for Belfast Cormac winning 33 per cent of the votes cast. In 1947 she was appointed full-time secretary of the Belfast and District Trades Union Council and was their representative at the talks which founded the Northern Ireland Civil Rights Association.

I agreed to join the Retired Members' Association and before long I found myself working and organising meetings, writing letters and lobbying parliament on behalf of the elderly. We had many successful campaigns, under the leadership of Jack Jones.

When the government was proposing to increase VAT from 7.5 per cent to 12.5 per cent on gas and electricity we held a mass demonstration outside the Palace of Westminster, and lobbied members of the government. When Gordon Brown became Chancellor of the Exchequer he took up our cause and reduced the rate of VAT for households to 5 per cent which was as low as he could make it under EU rules and perhaps

176

surprisingly even subsequent Conservative governments have not dared to suggest raising it again so that is where it remains to this day. To the people of Northern Ireland, where we then paid more than the UK average for our gas and electricity, this meant a lot.

Due to his poor health Joe, although he remained secretary, passed an increasing amount of the workload on to me. We had established and maintained a good working relationship with our counterparts in the Republic of Ireland and Great Britain.

Another former official in our union for whom I had a lot of time was Matt Merrigan. Matt was Secretary Organiser of the retired members in the Republic. He was very involved in politics and at one time ran for a seat in the Dáil. Known for his catchphrase, 'Profits are wages that have not been distributed yet', he was also the author of a number of books. Unfortunately, Matt did not get the support he deserved from the powers that be who considered him a maverick. This could in part have been true as Matt was his own man: what you saw was what you got.

Michael O'Halloran was another leading light from among my fellow trade unionists. Under Irish legislation he was provided with an office and funding by the government of the Republic of Ireland to represent the interests of senior citizens. Indeed, he would be consulted when budget plans were being made. As he would tell you himself, free transport for pensioners came about as a result of a chance meeting between Dick Spring, who was then the leader of the Irish Labour Party, Michael and me. It was coming up to election time in the Republic so Dick Spring asked what we thought should be in the programme for government. I said, 'Free travel for pensioners.'[1] We discussed the issue and lo and behold it appeared in the programme.

When free travel was originally introduced citizens from Northern Ireland could only travel to a pre-determined point in the Republic but there was no free travel in Northern Ireland. Joe Cooper arranged for a delegation of retired members to meet with Peter Robinson as the Democratic Unionist Party (DUP) was sympathetic to the idea and he was in a position to do something about it. The meeting was held in the Adelaide Street offices of the Department for Regional Development. We outlined our case and received a sympathetic hearing, although Robinson was concerned about the costs which he estimated would amount to £9 million per annum. Gregory Campbell took over from Robinson for the next meeting, he was equally supportive but again referred to the cost. This time I was better prepared with information on the number of pensioners in Northern Ireland, the numbers likely to use public transport for cross-border trips, etc. I had estimated the cost at less than half the figure put forward by the civil service. Under DUP stewardship free travel was introduced for pensioners within Northern Ireland. Since then all sorts of organisations have claimed credit, but credit where credit is due: it was the DUP who moved on the case that we presented.

The story does not end there. Sadly Joe Cooper died and for a while no-one knew exactly what to do. He had influence in Transport House and was able to demand the services of a typist, free postage and an office. Tommy McClinton and Jim Campbell approached me and asked if I would take over. I was reluctant as I felt it was time I took things easy. They persuaded me to take over for six months which would give them time to find someone. Jim Campbell volunteered to act as an assistant secretary. Those six months extended to 17 years during which time we had many successes in progressing programmes for the benefit of senior citizens.

Pensioners' group to campaign for free travel all over UK

ROADS YET TO TRAVEL

THE man who shamed the NIO into finally granting free travel throughout Ireland for all senior citizens declared last night: "This is only the beginning."

The formal announcement that OAPs would be entitled to travel free of charge on buses and trains on both sides of the border was made last week by Secretary of State Peter Hain.

But — as Sunday Life revealed last November — Government ministers in the province were originally OPPOSED to any immediate proposals to harmonise arrangements for pensioners in Northern Ireland and the Republic.

That was clearly shown in documents obtained by pensioners' champion Eugene O'Callaghan **(left)** under the Freedom of Information Act (FoIA).

The all-Ireland free travel scheme was initially mooted by Mary Coughlan, the Irish Minister for Social and Family Affairs, at an intergovernmental meeting in September 2004.

She told John Spellar, then Minister for the Department of Regional Development, that it was a key objective in the Republic's Programme for Government.

But as the FoIA documents embarrassingly revealed, Mr Spellar was far from enthusiastic.

He cautioned that "due to budgetary constraints and pressures for concessionary fares from other groups within Northern Ireland, there would be difficulties in DRD entering into such an arrangement".

Other documents relating directly to the discussions were withheld by the DRD on the grounds that they related to the development of "Government policy, which has not yet been finalised".

Mr O'Callaghan — secretary of the TGWU's retired members association — told Sunday Life: "We could never understand why direct rule ministers kept putting off something that would benefit all pensioners.

"And, while I'm delighted Mr Hain has finally taken the plunge, this is only the beginning.

"We will be seeking an early meeting with him to discuss extending the scheme for all pensioners in Northern Ireland to Britain.

"After all, we are citizens of the United Kingdom and senior citizens should have the right to free travel anywhere in the UK."

SCHEME: Peter Hain announced the free travel plan with Irish Foreign Affairs Minister Dermot Ahern

SPELLAR RAILED AGAINST OAP FREE TRAVEL PLANS

FLASHBACK: Our story

Our first policy decision was to raise funding to enable us to provide educational classes. Primarily these classes were to explain the intricacies of the various benefit schemes and how to access benefits to which pensioners were entitled. Classes on how to stay healthy were also given with dieticians and fitness experts being engaged. Cross-border seminars were held in Dundalk with the union providing travel expenses and meals. Jack Jones had published a book which covered pensions, sickness benefit, disability benefits, etc, and he travelled over and participated. On a weekly basis an advice centre was held in Transport House. Postage and the services of a typist were provided by the union.

We affiliated to the National Committee and sent a delegate to national meetings in London. We also sent delegates to the Pensioners' Parliament's annual meetings. Fares and overnight accommodation were negotiated and paid for by the union. Within a short period we restructured and organised ourselves as a campaigning organisation.

I wrote to John Spellar MP, who was a Northern Ireland Minister, and also to the Taoiseach in Dublin requesting that free travel be extended to

Sunday Life,
2 July 2006

cover journeys in the Republic as opposed to pre-designated points. At a meeting held in Stormont, Mary Coughlin, the Minister with responsibility for transport in the Republic of Ireland, proposed that our suggestion be adopted. John Spellar turned it down on the grounds that it was unaffordable. Mary Coughlin offered to pay for the scheme but the offer was declined.

On receipt of this information I contacted the Northern Ireland Office and requested copies of the minutes of the meeting under the Freedom of Information Act. When I received the minutes they confirmed what I already knew. I approached Joe Oliver, a journalist who wrote articles for the *Sunday Life* newspaper, and told him the story and showed him the

Eugene with Thomas Boyle, a former Ulsterbus driver, who queried his pension, highlighting the bigger pensions issue

minutes. Joe wrote and published an article which showed the NIO in a very bad light for denying old age pensioners the benefit of free travel throughout the island of Ireland. As a result of the pressure we put on the NIO they did an about turn and agreed that the scheme would be implemented.

The *Sunday Life* arranged for me to be taken by taxi to Stormont to have some photographs taken, they then published an article which highlighted what I had achieved through bloody-minded persistence. As usual, since then, when referring to the benefits of free travel for senior citizens, the 'butcher, the baker and the candlestick maker' all claim credit, hoping to gain from something they played little or no part in achieving. Then again, what difference does it make who gets the credit? It is the benefit that counts and there is no doubt that senior citizens have benefitted from free travel.

There was, however, another part of the story which has not yet been told. I again wrote to the Taoiseach asking for free travel to be extended as part of a package deal for expatriates who would come back to Ireland on holiday. In my letter I pointed out the potential benefit to tourism. Spain and other European countries had the benefit of sunny weather and beaches but free travel might be a draw for Ireland. The Taoiseach was quite receptive but later wrote back to say that there was a problem. The

European Union had expressed the view that it would have to be extended to all European countries otherwise it would be seen as discriminatory; this view killed the idea.

Now that free travel had been extended to citizens throughout Northern Ireland, Translink moved quickly to have the free travel provisions in their agreement, which had been negotiated with the trade unions for retired employees, transferred to the Northern Ireland Office. This would benefit them financially as the NIO would now accept responsibility for the cost. When ex-employees used the senior citizen pass issued by Translink it would register for a payment which would be made out of the public purse. Previously Translink got no return.

I wrote to both Translink and the Northern Ireland Office regarding the matter but received no satisfactory answer. My concern was that in the event of a future elected government deciding to withdraw the free travel concession from senior citizens ex-employees would lose out on what had been negotiated and agreed. With this in mind I embarked on a course of legal action using an ex-bus driver, Thomas Boyle, for the purposes of a test case. Before the case was heard the company gave a written assurance that in the event of the government or any successor government withdrawing concessionary free travel then retired employees would have all pre-existing rights of free travel reinstated.[2]

Eugene held a union card from 1956 until his death in 2018. This was originally with the TGWU and subsequently with Unite, which was formed by the merger of the TGWU and Amicus in 2007

I have, in view of my age, given copies of this written agreement to Margaret Stephens, TSSA representative, and Liam Hughes for safekeeping and future reference if required. A copy was also given to Davey McMurray of the Unite union.

At present we hear almost daily calls for the removal of pensioners' concessionary travel in order to save money. In fact only 55 per cent of those over 60 used the pass to which they are entitled to take even one train or bus journey in 2016/17. Those who begrudge the pensioners their free travel never stop to ask how many extra trains Northern Ireland Railways has run to cope with free rail travel for pensioners or how many extra buses Citybus and Ulsterbus have run. If they did they would realise that there is almost no extra cost – only additional benefits. Of course no-one knows how much pensioners would contribute to the income of the bus and train companies in the absence of free travel but it is clear that without free travel for pensioners, either

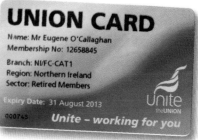

UNION CARD
Name: Mr Eugene O'Callaghan
Membership No: 12658845
Branch: NI/FC-CAT1
Region: Northern Ireland
Sector: Retired Members
Expiry Date: 31 August 2013
000745   Unite – working for you
Unite
theUNION

fares would be higher or services reduced. The free travel for pensioners provides over a sixth Translink's receipts from ticket sales. Indeed, very little is ever said about the overall economic and social benefits of keeping pensioners active and involved in society or the benefits to the environment in reducing reliance on car journeys. The £32m which the pensioners save gives them more money to spend on other things and in this way support local shops and businesses.[3]

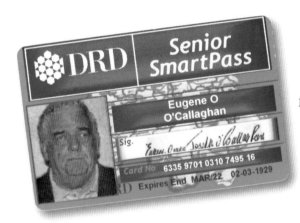

Eugene's Senior Smartpass allowed him, as a pensioner, free travel on train and bus both north and south of the border

18
Pensions again:
back to haunt me

If I thought that once I had succeeded in securing for
the Ulsterbus staff, who had manned the country buses
for years, the full public sector pension rights already
enjoyed by the Belfast Corporation Transport/Citybus
employees that would be a matter done and dusted for
all time I could not have been more wrong. This was an
issue that would haunt me during all my long years as
secretary of the Retired Members' Association. And as
I write these lines I still regard it as unfinished business.

This case might appear complicated but the issues, as I hope will become
clear, were relatively straightforward and simple:

1   Retired bus drivers and others were receiving pensions based on
    significantly less than their full pay. This was in breach of the
    pension scheme agreement.
2   Union officials were aware of this in the late 1990s and took no
    decisive action to rectify the situation. I only became aware of
    how early officials knew of this as a result of a Freedom of
    Information request in around 2005.
3   NILGOS, who were responsible for paying the pensions,
    became aware of the situation and drew it to the attention of
    the employer – Translink. But NILGOS had a legal duty to
    inform the pensioners as well and they neglected to do this.
4   Translink's remedy – once NILGOS had drawn it to their
    attention, thus requiring them to take action – gave the current
    workforce their entitlement on retirement but did not give to

those already retired the full pensions commensurate with the contributions which the employees and the employer would have made if the agreement had been honoured in full.

5   On becoming aware that the employer was not honouring its agreement with the unions, union officials not only took no action for a few years on this denial of their full pension rights to those who had already retired but initially resisted pressure from their members to do something about it.

6   By the time the union eventually came around to supporting the case the passage of time had significantly weakened the pensioners' bargaining position and the union on their behalf agreed to a poor compromise.

7   The employing organisation is Translink which is responsible to the Northern Ireland Transport Holding Company (NITHC) and ultimately the minister.[1]

I should make it very clear that there is no suggestion that any individual in Translink's management personally benefitted from what was going on. But the employing organisation in practice benefitted from reducing the cost of its share of funding pensions. That is to say as an organisation it reduced its costs or retained for other purposes funds which it was contractually committed to giving to NILGOS to invest on behalf of its employees. However, those MLAs with whom the matter was raised, the people to whom ministers and public officials are accountable, failed in their duty to critically examine what they were being told let alone investigate or challenge the conduct of a publicly-owned company. Nobody seemed to think it was worth asking if anything improper had occurred or if a wrong had been done to the workforce.

As mentioned above, pensions were to be based on all payments with the only exclusion being non-statutory overtime. Given the anti-social hours bus drivers had to work their wages were not simply an annual salary paid for turning up every day but were made up of a number of different payments and, according to the agreement, all these payments had to be taken into account in calculating pension entitlements. This was both logical and just since all these payments were part of the pay packet of every bus driver and a significant part at that. It was entirely to be expected that deductions would be made from these contributions to overall pay and paid into the pension fund. That was the theory; that was the agreement; but that was not the practice.

All this came back to bite me some time around 2002. Like everything else in this story it all seemed to happen by chance. As luck would have it I happened to be in Transport House one morning while a meeting of the Bus Council was being held. I was approached by an ex-shop steward colleague of mine. He told me, 'Eugene we are going up here to vote on an offer from the company to increase the pension entitlements from 38 hours to 43 hours, I thought our pensions should be paid on average hours. Is that not right?' I answered 'that is correct.' I approached the official in charge of the bus branches and suggested that he should have a re-think on the matter before recommending it as what he was about to do was wrong. He became angry and thumped a letter from Alan Mercer, Head of Human Resources at Translink, telling me to read it saying, 'He knows more than you.'

I said, 'Alan Mercer only joined the company in 1992. He was not even there when the pension was introduced. I was. In fact, I negotiated it. What you are doing is wrong.' Sad to say he totally ignored me and went ahead and signed the agreement. Little did I know at that time that I would be embarking on a journey which would last from that day to this.

The pensions issue was raised at a meeting between the company and the unions on 9 September 2002. Further discussions took place on the pensions issue after which the following offer was made by the company. From the 1 October 2002 pensionable pay would be based on an average duty pay of 43 hours plus £200 uniform allowance. It had previously been based on 38 hours basic. The notice was signed by Translink, and the ATGWU and GMB unions. It went on to say that the benefit would take effect one year after 1 October 2002. All previous pensionable service would be treated as if contributions have been paid at no additional cost to the employee. It was indisputably a good outcome for bus drivers still in service, for the employer was going to pay into the fund the contributions which the workers should have been paying during the previous 20 or so years.

But when the minutes of the consultative meeting dated 30 April 2002 became available they revealed that employees already retired would not benefit from the changes which had been forced on the company as a result of what an actuaries' enquiry had revealed. No effort was made by the then union officials to address the implications for all employees – past as well as present – of the change which had been introduced. While attempts were made to right the wrong that had been done to employees still in service no attempt was made to right the wrong done to those who had – in the recent past – already retired.

What left a particularly bitter taste in this was that the people who lost out were the men who had driven the buses during the worst years of the Troubles – men whose last 20 years of public service had coincided with the burning of a thousand buses and the murder of a dozen and more colleagues but who had nevertheless doggedly carried on to the end of their careers. In my view it was the punishing of men who had been the quiet heroes of those troubled years that was so cruel.

Around that time I was approached by Thomas Boyle who had a query regarding the basis on which his pension was paid. I asked him to provide me with a copy of his actual pension payments and a copy of his former contract of employment, which he did. On checking his documents it became evident that his pension payments were calculated incorrectly. Payments were based on 38 hours as opposed to average hours as per the agreement. At Mr Boyle's request I telephoned staff at NILGOS and made enquiries. I was informed that their actuaries were concerned that pensions were being paid on salaries which were thousands of pounds below what employees were earning. I drafted a letter for Mr Boyle which he sent to NILGOS regarding his pension. The reply stated that his lump sum and pension were calculated on figures supplied by Ulsterbus on form LG515 dated 19 October 1992 which they had accepted in good faith. The letter went on to say that should Ulsterbus wish to revise the final figures which had been sent to them they would be glad to review Mr Boyle's entitlements and pay any arrears that would be due.

Mr Boyle now found himself in a difficult position. The union, of which he was a member and had served faithfully as a shop steward, committee member and Bus Council representative, had let him down and seemed not prepared to attempt to rectify matters. The union did not want to know since it had accepted the company's decision not to include retired members when addressing the pension shortfall.

When I discussed his situation with Tom his financial position led me to believe he would qualify for legal aid and I made a point of ringing an old friend who had been the union's solicitor for many years. Although he was now retired he agreed to meet me. During the course of our discussion he advised me that the union's new legal representative, who had taken over his position, had just engaged the services of a young solicitor, who, he was told, was very good on labour law. All three of us met at John Long's fish restaurant and as a result of our conversation he agreed, subject to Mr Boyle's receiving legal aid, to take the case.

I arranged for Tom Boyle, Leo Flanagan from Derry and myself to meet the solicitor. At that meeting I outlined the details of the case backed up with documentation. An agreement was reached that Mr Boyle would apply for legal aid and his situation would be used as a test case. To say the legal system is ponderous would be putting it mildly. First the application and proof of entitlement had to be made; next we needed a barrister to say there was a reliable case. After that there was a meeting with a junior barrister who thought we should get a senior barrister and so it went on. We followed the torturous process and legal aid was obtained.

A further meeting was to be held with counsel. Tom Boyle and I met with a senior barrister and the solicitor at the Law Courts but, to my surprise, the union official was also present. As it was he who, on the union's behalf, had entered into the agreement with Translink which allowed them to exclude those who – like Tom Boyle – had retired prior to 2002 from the pension upgrade, his presence there was, at best, clothed with a certain ambiguity. Tom, in defending his rights, had been placed in the position of having to challenge an injustice to recently retired employees by their former employer but, to complicate matters, there was no denying that it was an injustice with which the union had gone along, and which on the scale of things could easily have been prevented by standing up for its retired members who were still union members and entitled to expect the union to defend their interests. To compound matters further if the union had collectively failed its retired members it was this union official on whose watch this had happened.

As events were to show throughout the history of this case the union's position would be conflicted between protecting the interest of its members and protecting itself and some of its officials from reputational damage. In the end this was not a tightrope that it walked with skill or success. The glaring ambiguity in the union's position very quickly became evident. It was not long before a very heated argument developed over the merits of the case. It was I suppose inevitable that the official at the centre of the row would want to defend himself though whether he recognised then or ever that he had not protected the best interests of his members I do not know. Certainly nothing he said helped matters.

With the value of hindsight I would say that at that stage we should have walked out. I had however a choice to make: whether to present and articulate the arguments on Tom Boyle's behalf and hope that the undoubted merits of the case would register or see the prospects of justice wither in the face of union indifference.

The Irish region of the union at that time was having internal problems and this may, in part at least, explain even if it does not justify, the lack of clear union leadership on this issue. The Regional Secretary and the Deputy Regional Secretary had been stood down by the General Secretary. I do not intend to comment here on the reasons but the fallout did lead to disruption. An officer was parachuted in from central office to run the region on a temporary basis which did not improve matters. To say that there were divisions in the Irish region would be putting it mildly. I believe the reverberations of this fallout continue to this day.

We waited for some considerable time on counsel's opinion. In sheer frustration I wrote to our solicitor on a number of occasions. He responded by sending me a reply with a copy of a letter he had sent to counsel threatening to withdraw his application for an opinion. Finally, after a year we received counsel's opinion which was not exactly crystal clear so much so that I immediately wrote to the solicitor asking for clarification.

Counsel's opinion claimed that Mr Boyle was put on notice of the pension shortfall when he retired in 1992. This was absurd because it was only true in the sense that in 1992, on his retirement, Tom, like every other retiree, would have been told what his pension would be. But unless he had made a calculation of what it should have been he would not have known that there was a shortfall. As I have stressed: drivers' pay was made up of many more components than most employees' pay and this would be reflected in their pension. Tom, like many other bus drivers, would not have felt that he needed to understand the intricacies of the scheme. He would have trusted the honesty of the system by which the pensions were administered and would not have imagined he was being short-changed until it came to light in 2002.

Counsel's reply showed that he simply did not understand the issues at stake: 'Mr Boyle did not make pension payments in respect of the additional hours.' He thus missed the point entirely. Mr Boyle certainly had not been paying contributions on the additional hours but he should have been, he thought he was, and the fact that he was not was because his employer had not been deducting in respect of them. But the NILGOS pension arrangements were quite clear as they state: 'contributions are deducted from your pay which includes all regular and recurring payments such as shift allowances, contractual overtime and other entitlements e.g. free accommodation or meals etc.'[2]

If there was any evidence available to the company which was not made available to anyone else that deductions were not being made then this would be a clear breach of the agreement and therefore a breach of contract by the company. The pension arrangements were not 'owned' by the employer and administered as some sort of charitable payment paid as a voluntary act of generosity to former servants. They were based on agreements between equal partners in which the pensioners were entitled to have access to the same information as their former employer, a point which counsel failed to pick up. The points highlighted are just a few of the concerns I had in regard to how Tom's case was being processed.

Accompanied by Mr Boyle I made numerous visits to his solicitors' offices where I explained and interpreted the agreements on both the contract of employment and the NILGOS pension scheme. Sad to say when we assumed the solicitor we were dealing with was getting to grips with the issues on our next visit we would find ourselves dealing with a different solicitor. As a result of this I was informed on one occasion when explaining the spread-over arrangements that 'I might as well be talking about spreading jam for all they knew about it.' I emphasised the importance of getting disclosure of information, this request was responded to by telling me how difficult it was to get a response from Translink. I pointed out that there were ways and means whereby they could be compelled to provide the information.

In frustration I had written to NILGOS on 8 September 2005 under the Freedom of Information Act requesting information pertinent to Mr Boyle's case.

I had already written to the chairman of the Assembly's DRD Committee seeking his assistance. There was very little response to that request. On the other hand the response from NILGOS contained a mine of information. For one thing it confirmed the company's statement to the unions at the meeting on 9 September 2002 which was referred to earlier. In this they had stated that they had not seen the actuaries' report and did not know what was in it, and, that in consequence, Translink's offer to the unions was not based on the actuaries' report but on other information which had been coming in over the previous four or more years. But what was the other information?

Translink had been engaged in correspondence with NILGOS, as far back as 22 December 1998. Significantly, in a letter dated 28 January 1999[3] the company stated that not only were bus drivers required to work 41.5 hours but that in practice the average duty hours were 43 hours per week. Therefore they expressly conceded that the basic hours were well in excess of 38 on which they were actually basing the pension.

In a responding letter NILGOS stated that contractual hours are required to be counted for superannuation calculations pursuant to local government regulations. This would mean that Ulsterbus would have to pay superannuation on the duty hours, thus increasing pensionable pay. NILGOS indicated that the additional cost on the pension fund would have to be met by Translink, and asked if Translink's staff wish to instruct the fund's actuary to calculate the estimated cost.

NILGOS staff subsequently wrote to the actuaries on 8 March 1999 providing information on average duty hours totalling 43 hours which should be pensionable. They provided an analysis of the additional cost to the pension fund based on 41.5 hours and 43 hours respectively in their letter of 19 April 1999. Translink staff were sent a copy of the actuaries' report by NILGOS on 22 April 1999. It seems possible if not likely that the company was aware of the substance of the actuaries' investigation even if the relevant officer had not read the report itself. It might have been expected that Translink would want to see the actuaries' report if only to challenge it as it clearly had cost implications for the company. And the company itself should want to be satisfied that it was correct before being seen to be acting on its conclusions.

In a letter to me dated 4 January 2006 NILGOS[4] stated that their actuaries' reply dated 19 April 1999 said that past services costs were quoted at a time when the scheme was in surplus and employer contributions were reduced to 4.6 per cent. These costs were no longer correct and would have to be recalculated at current values if past services were to be funded. In information provided to me by NILGOS the overall scheme was in deficit as at 31 March 2007 by £396 million.

NILGOS are obliged to notify the employees of both the actuarial valuation and the funding position. The actuaries' report to NILGOS staff is dated 19 April 1999 (Ref. NILGOS/5978). I also received a copy of the minutes of a meeting between Translink and NILGOS staff held in Templeton House on 2 April 2002: 'Translink advised that at some date in the future pensionable pay for bus drivers would have to be increased from 38 hours to 43.'[5]

It was also explained that the change would have to apply to everyone from the same date. In other words they could not arbitrarily decide to backdate for those who retire within 12 months of the date of change. Either backdating must apply to all or start from some future date. The start date should be notified in due course.

I also consulted Norman Campbell, who had been the pension's officer for Translink, on 22 January 2004. Norman confirmed that the method for calculating pension entitlements had been changed. He claimed he had been instructed by the company to make the changes. He claimed he went to his managing directors and complained. He was told to get on with his work. I asked if he was prepared to put this in writing and he replied he would go to court and swear it.[6] It will also be remembered that in sworn evidence to the Industrial Court in 1979 Mr Heubeck gave the average hours in Ulsterbus as 46 so that even 43 hours was still well below average.

For further evidence in support of Mr Boyle's case I turned to the circular of 15 April by G.D. Cheatley, Chief Executive of the Northern Ireland Transport Holding Company:

> The present staff pension scheme is being wound up and the assets transferred to NILGOS together with related services, with effect from 1st June all existing staff in our present pension scheme become members of the NILGOS scheme. You are invited to become a member of the scheme with effect from 1st June 1985.

On page two of his circular he states,

> Pensionable pay is the total of all wages and other payments made in respect of your contract of employment. Any emoluments which are not on a fixed basis and are additional to your pay eg performance related pay etc are averaged over three years or such favourable period of not less than three but not more than five years and are added to pensionable pay.

Alan Mercer was not working for the company when the unilateral and secret decision was made by management to calculate pension contributions on fewer hours than the agreement with the unions provided for. But he inherited the problem and it clearly placed him in a difficult position as he had to act as required by the law and as a loyal servant of the company when the company's past behaviour had been less than exemplary. It was indisputably a difficult role. But it is hardly surprising that the trail of paper I unearthed substantiated beyond reasonable doubt that company was less than frank with the employees' representatives about what they knew. By this measure he became involved in the smoke screen – if I may so characterise the company's efforts to obscure the extent of the wrong which had been done to all employees and which would not be rectified for those retired during the 20 or so years when the pensions were based on contributions levied on 38 hours and not on average contractual hours. To my knowledge, neither he nor anyone else ever offered any explanation for excluding the recently retired – and by definition the most exposed to unrecoverable loss – from the settlement.

It could be said that the solution offered cut the Gordian knot. All those retiring from now on received an unsolicited gift. The deductions from hours worked in excess of 38 over the previous couple of decades which were not deducted from their wages – and which in consequence they had been free to spend – were credited to their pension contributions. It was a one-off, clean cut, administratively-straightforward solution and for the employer arguably more expensive than it needed to have been. But there was a price exacted and it was paid by those who had retired before 2002. To make matters even more glaringly unjust the people who lost out were overwhelmingly the most pension poor of those who had worked on the buses.

Why was it that the poorest were the ones least well-served by the company's solution to the problem? In a previous chapter, 'Pensions for all' (Chapter 12), I described how we succeeded in bringing the rural workforce into the pension scheme. So the majority of those affected by the pension shortfall were the Ulsterbus drivers who only came into the pension scheme from 1978. These men at best had only enough years of contributions to give them a mere percentage of a working lifetime's pension. Tom Boyle was a case in point – he had 15 years of contributions. Thus the people with the lowest incomes – and who had driven buses during the worst years of the Troubles – were the ones who were asked to pay the price.

Translink might consider that at an overall level they had made amends. But they had a duty to all their employees past and present. But more difficult to understand was the attitude of the union. Trade unions exist to ensure that working people are treated justly. The union did not have to agree to a deal that singled out its poorest members for unfavourable treatment.

By comparison, was NILGOS beyond reproach? Well, perhaps not entirely. The pension scheme states quite clearly: 'All salary, wages, fees and other payments in respect of the employment with the exception of non-contractual overtime shall be classed as pensionable pay'. Since spread-over payments and weekend workings are contractual work covered by the agreement they qualified for inclusion in calculating pensions' contributions and thus feeding into the pensions that would eventually be paid.[7]

The regulations go on to state that if an employer agrees with bodies or persons, representatives or any description of employees the method of determining the whole or part of the pay of an employee of that description during the period which the agreement applies the employer must notify in writing every member affected by such an agreement.

When exactly did NILGOS discover that the regulations were not being adhered to? Why did they not notify the employees as required? The letters and communications seemed to me to indicate that when they sent in their actuaries to investigate they believed something was not quite right; letters going back to 1998 show that they were in discussions with the company at that time.

The Deputy Secretary should have been fully aware of his responsibility to inform the members and the union. The question is: why did he leave it to Translink to remedy these discrepancies which had crept into the administration of the scheme instead of discharging NILGOS's responsibility of keeping the members of the pension scheme and the union which had negotiated it informed as he was required by law to do?

NILGOS were supposed to administer the pension fund in an independent way in the interests of the employer and the employees. They had a written agreement with the union. But instead of treating the union as an equal partner with the employer it appears that they chose to give Translink the opportunity of unilaterally remedying the failings of the system. So they did not honour their obligation to inform and thereby protect the employees and also placed the union at a disadvantage compared to Translink in coming to an equitable solution. The union was, therefore, always placed in the position of having to 'play catch up' – and as we have already seen it was not very well equipped to play that role. But if NILGOS as the honest broker and disinterested party had early on convened a conference of unions and employer, my union would not have been placed in the position of having to 'play catch up' and an amicable and fair solution might have been arrived at.

By arrangement Tom Boyle and I had a further meeting with Mr Boyle's solicitors. On Mr Boyle's behalf I presented to them the documentation and evidence I had secured under the Freedom of Information Act. I again voiced my concern at the inordinate delay in progressing the case. I stated the importance of having the writ served on Translink thereby ensuring that the case would not be statute barred. I was informed that a protective writ had been served. One would have thought that as an interested party Tom Boyle would have been informed of the serving of the writ. But strange to say neither I nor Tom had been so informed.

By now further changes to those alluded to earlier had occurred in the union. The Regional and Deputy Regional Secretary, who had been stood down by the General Secretary, were reinstated by the newly elected General Secretary. I mention this here only because it had a bearing on the case as it resulted in changes of personnel in the union and in due course in the way in which the union managed its legal services and representation and opened the way for the union to take over the case for compensation for the retired bus drivers.

Initially this was all quite positive. I met the recently re-instated official by chance in the union's offices. He asked me how the case was progressing. I explained the difficulties we were experiencing and the never-ending delays. He asked if I would like the union to take over the case. I replied I would be delighted subject to Regional Committee approval. Regional Committee approval would mean financial backing. We agreed that I would go and see the union's solicitors and present them with the evidence and if they recommended that there was a case he would take the matter to the Regional Committee and recommend support.

A meeting was arranged with a legal representative from the union's solicitors. I was accompanied to the meeting by Tom Boyle. At that meeting I explained in considerable detail the full ramifications of the case and brought him through the various stages of agreements with the company. I detailed the various meetings held with Tom's solicitors, the delays experienced and the lack of progress. For his part the solicitor questioned me at length on aspects of the case. He concluded by saying he would need time to study all the paperwork with which I had presented him. I advised him he would also need access to the case file held by the Tom Boyle's solicitors. A short time later I met the same solicitor at a trade union conference. He took me to one side and again quizzed me on various aspects of the case. He requested and received a copy of the case file from the solicitors concerned for the purpose of advising the union if the case was worthy of support.

Following receipt of the case file, I was required to attend the offices of the union's solicitors on a number of occasions to interpret and explain how the agreement worked, e.g. spread-over hours; clock-on, clock-off times; guaranteed day; guaranteed week; weekend penalty payments and the pension scheme; how everything worked in the different clauses and, additionally, explain all of the correspondence I had received through the Freedom of Information Act. I was impressed that at last someone was taking matters seriously and making an effort to analyse the content of the information I had supplied.

In a letter dated 16 June 2006 I received a copy of the solicitor's letter to Eugene McGlone. In that letter reflecting on the practical difficulties experienced by Tom Boyle's solicitors he noted that experts and barristers had been working on limited legal fees and had taken a considerable time to return to their instructing solicitors. By way of example, he cited a senior counsel being asked to provide advice on the merits of an extremely complicated matter that constituted approximately 800 pages of documents and correspondence at a fixed fee in the region of £250.

His letter then went on to summarise the issues in dispute. In dealing with the facts of the case he referred to the part I played as follows:

> I must say that without the efforts of Mr O'Callaghan this matter would not have proceeded to its present position. Mr Boyle would not have had the documentation available to him to argue against the position presently adopted by the employer. I have no doubt that the matter would have reached an unsatisfactory conclusion some time ago. Documentation obtained under the Freedom of Information Act between NILGOS and the employer which goes to support the previous course of dealings between the employer and employee and further shows that the employer had expressed concerns to NILGOS that calculations being used were in fact

incorrect, consideration does need to be given as to what duty of care was owed by NILGOS to the employee and whether NILGOS should be made a party to the proceedings. There is a considerable amount of evidence and documentation which would be too fulsome for me to go through at the present time. I would, however, think that the case has merit and that it should proceed at all haste. I think the course of action needed is for an immediate taking of statements and then a conference with counsel, but not one subject to legal aid rates. At this stage a report can be given to the Regional Committee.

I should say that a protective writ has been issued as concerns exist in regard to limitations. I cannot establish from the file when the writ was issued, although it is clearly almost twelve months ago and as such urgency is required.[8]

The letter was presented to the Regional Committee who thus unanimously endorsed his recommendation for union support. So at long last the union was doing what the union was supposed to do and standing up for its members. Was I right to believe we had turned a corner and would see this through to a successful outcome?

19
Hopes dashed

Eugene at the Ulster
Folk and Transport
Museum, 2015

I and a handful of retired members had managed to
convert the union's seeming indifference towards the
retired members' claims to active support, and I have
no doubt that the union's conversion was a genuine one
and represented a commitment to do something for the
retired members. But how would the union deliver?

If for one minute, I had assumed that a union officer would take over the preparation of the evidence needed, I was badly mistaken. Although not employed by the union, having retired over a decade earlier, the burden was placed on my shoulders. While the union funded the legal cost involved in building our case no officer of the union took on the day-to-day responsibility for ensuring that the case was pursued with the full backing of the energy and resources of the union.

Many of those involved had given a lifetime of service to the union. If they were not now forgotten, it appeared to me that they were certainly no longer a priority. The principles established by Jack Jones of looking after members in retirement did not seem to apply with full effect in the Northern Ireland part of Irish Region. Jack Jones always recognised that the strength of the union came from the community. It was from communities that membership originated and from which unions derived their strength. But at this point there seemed to be reluctance amongst some union officials to commit time and energy to helping these retired members when they needed it most.

It seems likely that if I had died or sat back and done nothing the case would have faded out of existence. Not the best example of solidarity with a group of trade unionists who through their efforts kept transport operating throughout the darkest days of the Troubles. Their bravery and contribution have been treated respectfully by journalists and historians and in television documentaries such as 'Buses on the Frontline'.

As awareness of the case I was pursuing became known, telephone enquiries to Amicus House (which had become the union's offices following the merger of the Transport and General Workers' Union with Amicus to form Unite the Union) from members and retired members in relation to their pension were responded to with, 'I know nothing about it. You would have to talk to Eugene O'Callaghan as he is the only one who knows anything about it.' The only support I got was a typist when available to type letters, postage and of course the support of the retired members' committee. So although by now in my eighties the next few years placed a considerable burden on my shoulders.

There were four priorities: to be able to prove that Translink had withheld pensions; to quantify the reduction suffered by each pensioner; to find out how many pensioners were affected; and to make sure those who were representing us had a mastery of the case including the process for pursuing it.

Those retired members who knew of the case were calling and phoning to find out what their position was; I was required to attend the offices of the union's solicitors so many times that I lost count. I also visited the Law Courts for the purpose of interpreting the pension scheme and platform agreement. I would like to put on record my appreciation of the help I received from Anne Kinder. Her attention to detail was exceptional. I was able to assist her by my knowledge of those key parts of the story and links to key witnesses such as Norman Campbell and also Liam Hughes, an ex-negotiator who was now a depot controller with Translink.

I contacted Norman and arranged for him to attend the offices of union's solicitors with me, a statement was taken, typed up and copies sent to both Norman and me to verify that the facts were as stated. Paragraph 5–6 of his statement reads as follows:

> Having been instructed to change the pension arrangements in 1983 I aired my concerns on a number of occasions … . I was concerned that employees were losing out on their pensions which were rightfully theirs.

He went on to say:

> There is no doubt in my mind that there was express and intentional concealment on the part 3 of the defendant regarding their employees' pension entitlements. It was obvious to me that the subsequent scheme introducing a flat rate was done with the intention to reduce costs to the defendants at the expense of their employees.

The affidavit was signed and lodged in the court on behalf of the applicants.[1]

What Norman Campbell's statement indicated to me was that Translink had unilaterally and in breach of their legally binding agreement with the unions changed the pension arrangements. This was despite negotiating an interim arrangement to be put in place for the first five years in which it was written into the agreement that average hours would be the basis for calculations when an employee's employment was terminated on medical grounds before the full pension arrangements would come into effect.

Other sworn evidence supported this position. Liam Hughes, who as a member of the negotiation committee was fully involved in the meetings leading up to the introduction of the pension scheme, also gave a signed statement. He explained how meetings were held with shop stewards and members to explain to them the intricacies of the pension scheme and how the proposed scheme would be based on a calculation of the highest average weekly earnings over the previous three years. No other formula was ever agreed. 'Mr O'Callaghan', he said:

> undertook a tour of the depots, ran education classes to deal with queries. Application forms were subsequently sent out to each employee by Ulsterbus on behalf of NILGOS. There was a 90% response from employees who wished to join the scheme. NILGOS also sent out a booklet setting out details of the scheme.[2]

He stated that at no time thereafter was he made aware of any alteration in the calculation of pensions. In fact, as regards average hours, this is the basis on which pensions are calculated for management which included himself as a depot manager. Liam Hughes' statement was lodged with the courts on behalf of the applicant.[3] Not only did Liam Hughes provide a signed statement but he was able to turn up documents which substantiated his statement.

There was then the matter of quantifying the amount of the pension's shortfall. It was necessary for the court to have this work completed by a professional actuary or accountant. A firm of actuaries was engaged to undertake this work. The report they produced amazed me. They estimated Mr Boyle's losses at some £28,453. The section from their report reads as follows: 'Based on a revised pensionable pay at retirement of £13,476 the gross inclusive interest in line with Bank of England base rate is £28,456, if allowance is made for taxation of pension at 10 per cent the loss inclusive of interest reduces to £25,185.'[4] Our solicitors and I agreed that we should ask the actuaries to re-look at the figures.

The next report using the same criteria was more bizarre; the loss now estimated was given as under £5,000. At this stage I decided to work out the figures myself. I spent some time with Norman Campbell discussing how Translink worked out the figures. Then relying on my own knowledge I set about working out Mr Boyle's losses between what he had been paid and what he should have been paid. When I arrived at a sum I asked my son, Joseph who has a degree in mathematics, to check my figures.

He checked with the Treasury for inflation rates over the years as the pension was index-linked. He also checked the bank base rate on a year-by-year basis to establish what the money, which had been excluded from the busmen's pension fund, would have earned if it had been invested as it should have been. My daughter Sarah, who holds a master's degree in economics, double-checked our calculations. We all agreed a shortfall in Tom Boyle's pension which was just short of £10,000. It should be remembered that because of Tom's relatively short period in the pension scheme many of the other retired drivers with longer periods of pensionable service woud have suffered significantly greater losses.

I passed these calculations to our solicitors who hired an accountant to verify them. The accountant produced his report which showed a slight difference of a couple of hundred pounds from our figures. I was prepared to accept his conclusion.

The case was beginning to seem overwhelming and the potential payment which would result would be well into the millions of pounds as the amounts withheld from those who had retired before 2002 was very considerable in relation to the very modest pensions those Ulsterbus men, who had only been allowed to join the scheme 20 years ago, were actually receiving.

Earlier in this book I said that what made the union effective was not just its numbers or its unity but how intelligently its leaders used the hand that they had to play in each situation. And I had bemoaned the fact that the union all too often installed some officers who, in my view, were not up to the job or when it installed good people it did not always give them the support they needed. There were special difficulties in our region of the TGWU. There was not a strong central oversight of the main issues with which the union was involved. Each industrial sector was only as good as its full-time officer. This was aggravated by divisions within the region over the critical period of this dispute as officials were successively 'stood down', introduced from outside the region or re-instated. Consequently no one in a key position assumed responsibility for driving the pensioners' case forward. But as we gathered the evidence to support the legal action in what we had come to know as the 'Thomas Boyle Affair' it became overwhelmingly evident that the union had an extraordinarily strong case. So what went wrong?

From the very first news of the pension problem, I regret to say that in my opinion, the union became part of the problem. It had been sadly compromised because, as the minutes of the Consultative Committee of 29 January 1998 demonstrated, the trade union officials had more than four years' advance notice of the shortfall. That was plenty of time to think of a strategy for dealing with the issue and it did look as if that was beginning to happen. At the 1998 meeting the Transport Union official stated that he had written to NILGOS regarding the make-up of pension pay. He asked Translink's personnel officer, to put in writing the company's understanding of the NILGOS criteria for the payment of an ill-health pension. The GMB official at the next meeting held on 10 June 1998 stated that he was putting down a marker regarding the issue of pensionable pay. The union could and should have sorted the issue there and then. Translink had been caught in a legally and morally difficult position.

By the meeting of 5 May 1999 the existing Transport Union official had been replaced. The GMB official claimed that the unions had received legal advice which was to the effect that the company should be paying pensions based on average pay. What these minutes to me demonstrate was that the then union officials, having obtained legal advice, had alerted themselves to the problem, had knowledge of what was going on but, for reasons which remain unclear, their successors did not pursue the matter as they might have been expected to do.

So it appears the unions were aware what had been going on by the end of the 1990s. But insofar as I am aware they did not tell anyone else. None of the rest of us knew as much as they knew until many years later – and that only by accident as a result of a Freedom of Information Act request. If the members had known then what had been going on the pressure from them for sorting this out would have been irresistible.

Procedurally the prosecution of the case was to turn on whether writs had been served in a timely way and the scope that any failures to do so might enable the company to seek escape routes not on the strength of their case but on procedural grounds.

There were grounds for concern: even though the union had taken up the case and the union solicitors understood the issues they would not be able to easily recover all the ground lost by their predecessors. I am referring to the difficulties experienced by the current solicitors in getting the former representatives to sign an affidavit to the effect that the writ taken out in 2005, which I believe may have been funded by legal aid,[5] had been served. It turned out that this writ had not been served. I believe that no writ was served until 2008, when the union solicitor stated in his letter of 9 November 2006 that he was having problems with the Law Society. This indicates that he had brought the matter to their attention.

Not surprisingly Translink now changed tack and put forward a defence based on the time factor. I pointed out that we accepted that union officials became aware of the pension shortfall in 1998 and failed to pursue the matter but our case was that, nevertheless, neither Mr Boyle nor the other applicants had become aware until 2002 and had immediately thereafter lodged their claim and the case would, therefore, fall within the statute of limitations.

What had started out as a battle for justice to right a wrong that had indisputably been done to a group of pensioners would turn into a battle of nerves over the technicality of whether writs had been served in a timely way and on the probability of the judge coming down on one side or the other of the argument. Our advantage was slipping away. The sad thing was that expectation had been built up and those like Tom Boyle who had fallen into bad health were, with the passage of time, wondering if they would ever receive justice. The old saying 'justice delayed is justice denied' was eventually proved to be correct in the case of Tom Boyle who died on 29 January 2009. His wife Mary predeceased him. But the campaign continued; those who remained served the writs to claim on behalf of their estate.

Neither side could be entirely sure how it would go in court. If the court would hear the case the cost to the losing side would be considerable and the losing side would then in all probability be Translink. But if the judge decided it was out of time the union would get nothing for its members and have to pay Translink's costs. Translink changed tack again. If they offered the union something it would make it much harder for the union to assume the risk of going to court and all the costs of losing in court. Put in those terms the battle was now lost.

On Monday, 8 October 2012, along with Liam Hughes and Norman Campbell, I was involved in discussions at the Law Courts with senior counsel who at the same time was having discussions with counsel for the defendants. The company had made an offer of £2,000 to Ulsterbus employees but no offer to pay Citybus employees. This was of course far short of what we believed the men – or increasingly their widows – were entitled to. But how would the union react?

I, too, was in a personally difficult position. The union had taken over the case which meant that it had control of all the decisions regarding the funding of the case and accepting or rejecting any offer that was made. But while the union now controlled the money and the decision making, they did not deploy any full-time officer to take charge of the direction of the case and do all the information gathering needed to fight an effective case to its conclusion. So should I walk away and leave them to it or soldier on knowing that it was others who would henceforth be 'calling the shots'? Walking away meant abandoning colleagues who had braved the difficulties of providing a public service at a time of danger: it was not an option. But I knew that my scope for influencing the outcome in favour of the retired members had been narrowed to the point of disappearing.

Not that you would think this from the letter to me from the union's solicitor that stated that they were pleased where the case stood: 'As you know previous solicitors and counsel say they were extremely grateful to you for your advice and assistance which was crucial to the development of the case. Your input has been invaluable; [...] has asked me to convey to you that you have his personal assurance authorised by the Regional Secretary that you will be fundamentally involved in any negotiations that may occur in future between the parties.'[6]

In our discussion with counsel I made it clear that the offer of 8 October 2012 of £2,000 to some of the workers was totally unacceptable. It was put to me, 'Well what would you accept?' My response was that it was not up to me to accept or reject; that is a matter for the applicant's senior counsel. 'Ah yes but we know if you recommend it then it will be accepted, if you reject it then it will be turned down.' The next question was, 'What would you recommend?'

I replied that Thomas Boyle could be used as the lowest denominator due to his 15-year length of service (a shorter period of service than most of the busmen affected by the pensions issue) and the fact that he had since died. If his case was thought to be worth almost £10,000 then if they agreed £10,000 for everyone I would support it. Both legal teams had further discussions and counsel returned with a further offer that Citybus employees would now be included in the offer of £2,000 but the applicants would have to pay their own costs. The extent to which things had already slipped beyond my capacity to influence events quickly became obvious from what happened next.

The union's counsel outlined the danger that if the offer was rejected and we proceeded to a hearing the judge might throw the case out due to the time factor. If that happened then the offer would be off the table. He turned to me and said, 'You know the other side blame you for holding up agreement; I have a problem in that I don't know who my clients are, is it the union, or is it the applicants?'[7] This was a very serious question. If his clients were the applicants would he seek to amend the writ and enjoin the unions on the grounds of negligence and a failure to provide a duty of care in failing to follow legal advice given in 1998? In principle at this stage it was the union who was the client on behalf of the applicants – the retired union members – but was there again a divergence of interest between the union and its retired members? There was no straightforward answer to that question.

Senior counsel left me for a short period and when he returned he advised that he had been in telephone contact with the union's solicitors; a suggestion was made that the applicants should pay the costs out of their award. I was now having pressure put on me to acquiesce in what I regarded as a sell-out settlement based on a lack of principles such as I had never seen in my years as a trade union member. This was a further nail hammered in the coffin of the hopes of retired members. I flatly rejected that suggestion as it was contrary to the whole ethos and constitution of the union. I pointed out that in the 58 years of my membership I could not recall a single incident where a member supported by the union, win or lose, had to contribute to the costs of his case.

In practice I was no longer involved in any way in the union versus Translink dispute. That had in effect been settled on terms which allowed Translink off the hook financially as well as protected from the damage their corporate reputation might suffer from exposure in court and in the media for what had been done to workers' pensions.

Those who are beaten in a conflict often end up fighting among themselves. What happened next was an argument around whether the union should deduct from the £2,000, which Translink was offering to each worker, the legal costs incurred in promoting the union case.

For the record I had nothing to gain from the outcome. Although I had previously worked for Ulsterbus, I was not entitled to pension benefit as they had no pension scheme until after I had left the company and negotiated one for bus workers in my role as their union official. In fact I would get not one penny piece as I neither asked for nor received any payment or expenses. Any expenses I incurred in pursuing this case I paid out of my own pocket. Before we left the Law Courts I realised that I was now placed in a difficult position. I had provided the expert advice, documentation and got the witnesses to come forward and, as had been acknowledged by the union's solicitors, without my input the case would never have seen the light of day. But this most recent further turn of events placed me in an even more difficult position. If I encouraged the claimants to refuse the offer and the case was thrown out then despite everything I had done I would be blamed. I therefore had a decision to make: should I support the offer of £2,000, provided no expenses were taken out of it, or to take the chance of supporting court action and risk everything, no matter how unsatisfactory I found it, which had been secured for the retired busmen.

As far as the union was concerned all that remained to be done was to put the offer to the men and let them decide to accept the offer or to fight on without union support. But as far as I was concerned even within the narrow issue of the Translink offer there were the rights and wrongs of obliging the pensioners to make a sizeable contribution to the union's legal costs. To me this was no minor matter but a major issue of principle. I contended that the union never required members to pay their legal fees in a case taken by the union. Of course in most legal cases the union won and the other side would pay the union's legal costs. But where it lost the union paid and not the member it was representing. So we had something of a battle over that. The Regional Secretary initially agreed with me that there would be no deduction for legal fees but the union seemed to change its mind.

The upshot was that the deduction for legal fees was reduced from £500 per member to £200 per member so something was achieved. But a principle is a principle and I would battle on on that point, and because I did so another twist was added to the story. Surprisingly, this was an issue on which it appears I actually won my point. The union would later make clear that there had not been any deduction made by the union from the settlement offered to members, but where £48,000 of the settlement offered by Translink went to remains a mystery.[8] The one thing that is certain is that it did not find its way into the retired members' bank accounts.

Eventually a meeting of the pensioners was called to have the proposed settlement put to them. They were summoned to the meeting by a letter dated 15 March 2013 from the union solicitors. The applicants were advised that in light of further negotiations the defendants, Translink, had been persuaded to make an improved offer in respect of settling the case. This offer would mean each applicant would receive a lump sum of £1,800 in full final settlement, and 'you will appreciate that this is an enhanced offer; Unite have considered the offer and are prepared to endorse the proposal'. The letter went on to say:

> If you disagree with the proposals Unite will no longer be able to support the case which in effect means you would be liable to pay all legal costs in respect of the hearing as Unite will no longer indemnify you in that regard. [The union solicitors] would therefore have to apply to come off record and you would have to get another solicitor to deal with the case. Due to the fact that the trial dates are only a number of weeks away please return the enclosed form before Thursday 25th March 2013.[9]

You will have often heard the phrase 'having a gun put to your head'? Well, this was it, either sign up or go your own way. What happened was in fact not an improved offer. It was exactly the same offer except that the amount of costs to be deducted from the award had reduced from £120,000 to £48,200, i.e. from £500 per applicant to £200 per applicant.

When the pensioners' meeting got under way, the representative from the union's solicitors was in control. The person who was supposed to be in charge of the Irish region was reduced to the role of bystander. Their presentation of the case was certainly intended to take advantage of whatever goodwill the retired members felt towards me as they said that I had convinced them to take the case. When they were appointed to their present job with the union I again had convinced them to support the case to its current position where the company had made a final offer. If this wasn't being 'damned with faint praise' it certainly felt like it. The union solicitor said it had been achieved despite two previous barristers declining to support it. Of course what they failed to address were the reasons other barristers were reluctant, the main reason being the time factor. They also did not mention that the writ taken out in 2005 had not been served until 2008 and conveniently made no reference to the letter recommendeding support and which outlined the reasons why barristers were reluctant to take the case, which at that time had been prepared and progressed on legal aid.

Their concluding remarks referred to the fact the agreement was on the basis that the union would not support any other claims; there would also be a confidentiality clause to prevent further discussion on the matter.[10]

By the time it was my turn to address the meeting I had assessed the situation in which the pensioners and I found ourselves. Most of those present had no idea as to why they were being offered money for what they thought was nothing. It was not and still has not been explained to them in detail. Some wanted and needed the money. I could have swayed the decision by setting out in explicit detail the facts. I could have exposed what had happened or I could accept what was now being put to the busmen.

Had I chosen to challenge the position put forward by the union the meeting would have ended in chaos. It had already been made clear that if the men did not accept the offer the union would no longer support them and without union financial backing they could go nowhere and possibly lose what little they had gained. If that were to happen no doubt I would be blamed for losing the £1,800 offer. I had been around too long to fall into that trap. Sickening as it was I agreed that they should take the offer as it was as good as it was going to get, although in my mind they had, as I said, been shafted.

One of the participants asked if he would now get his pension upgraded, pointing out that a fellow worker whose pension was now based on a 43-hour week was receiving £100 per month more than him. This really showed up the lack of understanding of the complexities of the issues. The union leadership had made it perfectly clear that this was a non-starter.

Margaret Callaghan was the only woman present and was there representing her deceased husband Hugh. Hugh had also been underpaid in his pension. She was told that her case could not be processed due to the fact that it was out of time. If ever confirmation was needed that was it. These unfortunate members were relying on representatives who should have been doing their utmost to protect their interests.

In my opinion this day was a sad one for the union. In 1998/2000 it had faced an open goal. Translink by its own actions had placed itself in a vulnerable position. Thomas Boyle should have received something of the order of £10,000 but he was by no means one of the potentially biggest gainers in this dispute. I have always argued that the trade unions needed to be smarter than management; because if we were not the workers would pay a price for poor leadership. This dispute demonstrated just how big a price workers might end up paying if we allowed ourselves to be led by those who, however well they meant, were outmanoeuvred by management.

If you had lost your wallet but later, when you recovered it, you discovered that it now contained only one of the ten £10 notes it held when you lost it you might be relieved to get your wallet back but you would not regard that as a victory – now would you?

20
It's not all over

I took my leave of the meeting. I had pushed the
possibilities of getting justice for these men as far as
I possibly could within the structures of the union.

That it had been necessary to mount a campaign at all arose solely
because, as we saw in an earlier chapter, the union and some of its agents
had failed to look after the interests of its members. That was and remains
my firm conclusion but it is a conclusion which, as a proud lifelong
member of the union, I profoundly regret having had to come to.

Then with the intervention of the union officers and their legal team
there had been a period when it looked as if the union was going to make
up for its initial shortcomings. But it was wrong-footed by the errors or
the incompetence of those who had mismanaged the earlier stages of the
legal processes. What had looked like a sure legal victory had got bogged
down. The shortcomings of the preparations for the legal case had placed
the union on the defensive. Torn between its duty to its members – and in
particular the need to make up to them for its previous inaction – and the
possible risks and costs of continuing the campaign it made terms with
the company. But even then it was in a powerful position to counter any
dissent and enforce its views on members.

But if the union had decided to cave in I had not. Half a loaf may be
better than no bread but in this dispute, in my opinon, the union had
secured well less than 20 per cent of what I believed the men were entitled
to. One simple fact that would not go away: for years the men had not
had pension contributions deducted from their wages nor contributed by
their employers for five hours or more work per week. Their pensions
and their widows' pension since the day they had retired until the day
they died had been less and would continue to be less than that to which
they were legally entitled. They would now never get what they were
entitled to; instead they were each given £1,800 to settle.

There were two major matters which needed to be addressed. The most obvious one was the actions of Translink which required investigation, and if the original pension agreement had not been implemented as it should have, they should be compelled to make good the losses the men suffered. Secondly, the union needed to put its own house in order. It needed to apologise to its members for letting them down; it needs to ensure for the future that its officials are competent, well supported and fully accountable. In this case, I believe someone needs to show what happened to the money deducted from the payments made by Translink to the union members. But as readers will have realised for themselves when they get to the end of this chapter there is a third issue: the deafening silence from those institutions and agencies which are supposed to hold those in power to account – the media and the elected representatives of the people.

If the union had lost its battle there remained other avenues through which the issue could be aired. The pensioners were all former public employees as Translink was and is a publicly-owned company. I was surprised to find that this nugget of general knowledge appeared to be a secret concealed from those who walk the corridors of Stormont.

After much consideration I decided that I would make a submission to the Minister responsible for public transport. I wrote to him on 30 April 2013 outlining the details of the case, after all some of his constituents were among those involved. I drew attention to the court proceedings and costs to date which had come from the public purse. I suggested that it was in the public interest that the case should be investigated by the Assembly Finance Committee. I also directed his attention to the Waterford Crystal v the Republic of Ireland court case[1] which in its ruling states, 'At a minimum it requires the introduction of measures to protect benefit schemes.' Under different schemes in the UK following the Rollins Case article (3) Employees Insolvency Act 1984[2] member states must take steps to ensure that guaranteed payments of employees' outstanding claims resulting from contract or contract related payments are made.

As the Northern Ireland Assembly is in fact responsible for public transport employees one would imagine that its members would want an investigation into Translink. I am afraid if you believe that you are labouring under an illusion – at least that is my conclusion after raising this issue. This was the Minister's reply: 'This is an issue for Translink as the employer and not one I can comment on.'[3] Imagine a minister in

Westminster being allowed to get away with such a supine answer. Committees of MPs at Westminster have on numerous recent occasions summoned and grilled directors of private sector companies and here in Northern Ireland a minister was disclaiming responsibility for a publically-owned company. After all, what was he there for except to be accountable and defend the public interest?

I responded in a strongly-worded letter dated 28 May 2013. I reminded him that Translink was a public undertaking supported by millions of taxpayers' money and that it was incomprehensible that he should say that he could not comment and then go on to say that he was aware of the ongoing court case involving Translink.[4] This last point was in any case irrelevant as at the time of replying the case had been settled out of court and could not be considered sub judice. It is inconceivable that his officials would have left him unaware of that. Once again, I wrote to the Minister but sad to say I was wasting my time; it seemed he had little intention of doing anything.

I then embarked on a campaign to try and get the media interested. As a result of meetings with Paddy Rooney, Joe McGivern and Margaret Callaghan articles were printed in the *Sunday Life* and *Newry Reporter*. I also went on the Nolan Show.

John Dallat MLA, the SDLP transport spokesperson at the time, rang the Nolan Show to pledge his full support for the busmen. I contacted him directly and arranged to meet with him at Stormont. At that meeting I was accompanied by Margaret Callaghan, Joe McGivern and Paddy Rooney. I outlined the facts of the case backed up with documentary evidence. He asked if we would leave the documents with him. My experience over the years has taught me one thing; you should never surrender your evidence as in all probability you will never see it again. Therefore, I declined his request. Instead I made him an offer that if he would arrange for me to meet with the Finance Committee I would present the case for him. After another period of delay, I rang him to check what was happening. Finally, it was agreed that we could have the meeting with the Finance Committee at Stormont.

On arrival we discovered the meeting was not with the Finance Committee but with Jimmy Spratt, Chairman of the committee, and Mr Lynch of Sinn Féin. What position Mr Lynch held we were never told. Sad to say the whole exercise was a disaster from the word go. They did not even arrange an office or meeting room; instead we met at a table in the corner of the bar.

The MLAs showed little interest in what we had to say. This surprised me. Almost certainly some of the men and women involved would be their constituents. And the issues did require detailed understanding so I was expecting that they would submit me and my colleagues to lengthy questioning. In fact, nothing of the sort happened. When I asked a series of questions I was told that they had no power to investigate Translink finances and did not have the authority to question them. I put it to them, was it not inconceivable that despite the millions of public money pumped into Translink that they are answerable to no-one? Even if that were true, in my naivety I would have expected the elected representatives of the people would have wanted to query why they had no right to question Translink's conduct.

MLA Spratt turned sideways and said something like, 'I'm telling you Translink is a private company and as such are not answerable to us.' It was not hard to read the signals; although an elected representative of the people, my colleagues and I were given a very clear impression of an individual unwilling to intervene on behalf of the busmen or even take an interest in their case. This meant there was no point trying to impress on him the merits of our case so I folded my papers and participated no further in the few remaining minutes of the meeting, muttering to myself 'God help us if this is the calibre of people who represent us.'

On the way out we met John Dallat who had failed to show. We left him in no doubt as to our feelings while he tried to excuse himself for missing the meeting. Margaret Callaghan said, 'My God, what a waste of time, to think I travelled from Derry to meet those people. They are useless.'

John Dallat's now apparently semi-detached attitude was all the more disappointing after his initial high profile and completely voluntary intervention via the Nolan Show. Perhaps if he had been there to manage the meeting which he had arranged we might have got further. I do not doubt his good intentions but as someone else said in another context 'it is bloody brains that are required not bleeding hearts.' To me his enthusiasm drooped like a withering flower at the first sign of resistance from the powers that be.

This was unfortunate as we had high hopes for his involvement. Margaret Callaghan was determined to seek justice on behalf of her late husband Hugh. By arrangement she and her daughter came to my home with a photocopier. They took copies of some of the documentation I had accumulated. We also discussed various ways in which she could progress her case within her limited budget and these included writing to John Dallat giving him again the benefit of the doubt.

His response was troubling as it showed, in our view, the degree to which even a long-serving and experienced elected representative was ill-equipped and even diffident when it came to defending his constituents or holding those with power to account. I would not want to be thought of as singling John out for criticism; he clearly meant well and he had at least taken an interest in the welfare of his fellow citizens who were suffering from injustice. But, in my view, it is revealing how little power and understanding sometimes our elected representatives have of how to go about defending and promoting the interests of the people who elected them.

It is true that nobody in this story – Translink, NILGOS, the unions (though latterly they did try and did in the end secure something) – had covered themselves in glory: whether in identifying the issue in a timely manner, rectifying it immediately or seemingly willingly, or ensuring the full benefit of the original agreement was passed on to all the busmen and their widows. To me all these missed opportunities were compounded by politicians failing to hold those companies in the receipt of large sums of public money to account over this pensions issue.

After I had seen John Dallat's correspondence with Margaret Callaghan, dated 2 June 2014,[5] which claimed Translink was a private company, I wrote to the Minister for Regional Development on 2 December 2014 for clarification on this matter, requesting the following information under the Freedom of Information Act:

1　The date on which privatisation took place.
2　The date legislation was introduced by either the Northern Ireland Assembly or the Westminster Parliament to enable privatisation.
3　The date the proposals to privatise Translink were put to the public for consultation.
4　The amount of public money given to Translink since privatisation.
5　The names of the current owners of Translink.
6　The nature of the involvement – if any – of the Department with the present owners.

Having failed to get a response I again wrote to the Minister on the 7 January 2015 putting him on notice that should he fail to respond I would make an application to the Information Commissioner for an enforcement order. By return of post I received a reply to the effect that Translink had not been privatised and it was therefore not appropriate to answer the questions raised in detail.

John Dallat was re-elected to the Assembly in 2017 and should be well placed to pursue this issue; I have no reason to believe he will not do so, in fact I hope that he will lift the baton again. The facts are known; the injustice adds to the hardship of working families in their declining years; the status of Translink has not changed. It is owned by all of us and our public representatives have an obligation to ensure that it is run in the public interest. There is sworn evidence that a management decision was made that deprived former employees of part of their pensions. That is no minor matter. It would be a scandal if it happened in a private company. How much more appropriate is it that a publicly-owned company whose board includes ministerial appointees should be investigated when questions arise which cry out for answers?

Not only has there been an injury done to our employees. Although many of the facts are known, the fact that it has never been investigated is itself a scandal. How did this happen? Why have lessons not been learned so that it cannot happen again?

As I mentioned earlier, recently committees of the House of Commons have been investigating the shortcomings of private companies – the failure to pay the minimum wage or the collapse of a company leading to the loss of pensions. What is to stop the Northern Ireland Assembly carrying out an equally thorough in-depth investigation into what happened to the Translink pensions? That in my view is the best hope of the workers and they should lobby their MLAs to secure such a public inquiry.

Translink did pay £2,000 to each worker covered by the agreement. However, I understand that each worker received £1,800. How was the difference accounted for? I wrote to the union but it did not reply. I wrote to the Certification Officer who is responsible for ensuring that unions abide by their own rules and procedures. The Certification Officer wrote to the union on my behalf and the union was categorical that it had not deducted legal costs from the payments to the members. To quote the words of the letter from the Assistant Certification Officer:

You will note that the Union has denied there was any claw back or deduction of costs from settlements, that no meeting took place to make such decisions about legal costs cover and has further denied that there was ever any change to the terms of provision of legal assistance to the plaintiffs in these cases.[6]

Of course it is good to have it confirmed that the union honourably stuck to its tradition of not passing on the legal costs to its members. But it still leaves the question more unanswered than ever: what happened to the £48,000 not paid to the busmen?

If this pension issue had happened to all the teachers in Northern Ireland or all the civil servants or any other grade of public employees would there not have been a public outcry and pressure for redress? If all the disadvantaged busmen had been Catholics or if they had all been Protestants would there not have been champions in plenty to raise a clamour about injustice, discrimination and lack of respect? But they were just working men with no religious or political badge exclusive to them. Such injustices as they might suffer did not seem to count.

The road to securing justice and holding power accountable remains open. Public opinion is always and rightly angered by the arrogance of power which plays casually and carelessly with the lives and happiness of ordinary people and seldom considers the human cost of its actions. And when public opinion is roused and political remedies are available then justice can be secured.

My passion for social justice burns as strongly as ever even though age takes its toll on energy and health. But I believe I have assembled enough evidence for others – younger and more energetic than I now am – to fight this battle, to win it, and to see justice prevail.

A lot of the former employees of Translink/Ulsterbus owe him (Eugene) a great debt, as do I.

MARGARET CALLAGHAN
A busman's widow

Epilogue

The Da died on 16 April 2018 with my mother, my sister and myself at his bedside.

In November 2009 he underwent coronary artery bypass surgery, unfortunately complications from this procedure and old age led to declining health culminating in a significant respiratory crisis in September 2016. At that time the doctors advised us that we would be lucky if he survived for four months. The hospital discharge letter stated: 'There is nothing more we can do, best let this man go home to his family.' At home round the clock care was provided by our family; among other things continuous oxygen was required and at night a non-invasive ventilator.

Throughout this difficult time, black humour had us laughing through the tears. During good periods, usually in the middle of the night, the Da

Carrying Eugene's coffin are sons Eugene in front, Pat in the middle with grandson Christopher O'Callaghan at the back. On the other side of the coffin not shown are sons Damian, Joseph and Ciaran. Following the coffin are Eugene's wife, Patsy, daughters Anne in the middle, and Patricia

LEO MURRAY

217

would tell outrageous tales of his early life and characters in Crossmaglen. The Da had a wicked sense of humour and was a wonderful storyteller and mimic, which may not come across in the serious parts of this book. These tales alone would have warranted a second book and we unsuccessfully encouraged him to write them down. Former bus workers, union colleagues and what we called 'doggie men' frequently visited and there were many anecdotes of working life during the Troubles.

He had a razor-sharp analytical mind and an incredible memory but was a firm believer in maintaining records; it was a matter of regret for him that the records of all the cases he worked on as a union official were not retained when Transport House was closed, but, who knows, they may still be there. They would be a very important aspect of our recent history.

However, the Da knew he was on borrowed time and thought it was very important to place on record the injustice he felt was done to the former busmen who were deprived of their full pensions. This was an issue that haunted him and even though he was in declining health he still battled for compensation on their behalf and regarded it as unfinished business. The day before his death he dictated a letter on behalf of a former colleague who had spoken to him about his pension. It is, therefore, no surprise that a large portion of his memoirs relates to the pensions issue. As the Da said, 'This narrative is not about guilty men or scapegoats but rather an attempt to right a wrong.'

As a family we were overwhelmed at both the wake and funeral by the number of people who spoke about the debt they owed him for all the help and advice he had provided at difficult times in their lives; sorting out problems, not just employment-related but with benefit claims, wills, planning permission, re-homing dogs and loans. We received many letters, cards and emails in a similar vein, one letter in particular stands out; it said: 'Your father has not ceased to be. He manifests now in another form and will live forever through his genes, his words and his actions'. I loved that and it is easy to see how it is true.

In the preface to his book the Da writes, 'I would like to think that in my journey through life I have helped make a difference.' From the words of comfort our family received after his death I can safely say he did.

PATRICIA O'CALLAGHAN

ENDNOTES

PREFACE

1   Reprised by Larkin from French philosopher, Pierre-Joseph Proudhon's
    original.

INTRODUCTION

1   Andrew Boyd, *Have the Trade Unions Failed the North?* (Cork, 1984),
    p. 73.
2   To distinguish them from trade unionists, the usual convention is adopted
    here of referring to supporters of the Union with Britain with a capital 'U',
    whether members of the Unionist Party or not. Similarly, to distinguish them
    from the mass of labour, activists in trade unions, trades councils, or Labour
    political groups are referred to as 'Labour' or 'Labourites'.
3   John W. Boyle, *The Irish Labor Movement in the Nineteenth Century*
    (Washington DC, 1988), p. 126.
4   Emmet O'Connor, *Big Jim Larkin: Hero or Wrecker?* (Dublin, 2015), p. 5.
5   See Ken Coates and Tony Topham, *The History of the Transport and
    General Workers' Union* (Oxford, 1991); Andrew Murray, *The T and G
    Story: A History of the Transport and General Workers Union, 1922–
    2007* (London, 2008). For a personal take on the union in Ireland, see Matt
    Merrigan, *Eagle or Cuckoo? The Story of the ATGWU in Ireland* (Dublin,
    1989). The title reflected Merrigan's consciousness of the rivalling
    perceptions of the union as a workers' champion or a British cuckoo in the
    nest of Irish Labour.
6   Charles McCarthy, *Trade Unions in Ireland, 1894–1960* (Dublin, 1977),
    p. 597; John McIlroy, Nina Fishman, and Alan Campbell, *The High Tide of
    British Trade Unionism: Trade Unions and Industrial Politics, 1964–79*
    (Monmouth, 2007), p. 120.
7   Denis P. Barritt and Charles F. Carter, *The Northern Ireland Problem:
    A Study in Group Relations* (Oxford, 1962), p. 141.
8   Central Statistics Office, *Regional Trends* (London, 2000), p. 85.
9   See 'John Freeman: a life on the left', *Saothar*, 24 (1999), p. 138.
10 Kieran A. Kennedy, Thomas Giblin and Deirdre McHugh, *The Economic
    Development of Ireland in the Twentieth Century* (London, 1988),
    pp 107–09.
11 McCarthy, *Trade Unions in Ireland*, p. 597; McIlroy, Fishman, and
    Campbell, *The High Tide of British Trade Unionism*, p. 120.
12 Boyd, *Have the Trade Unions Failed The North?*, pp 49–51.
13 Cited in 'John Freeman: a life on the left', p. 129.
14 Emmet O'Connor, *A Labour History of Ireland, 1824–2000* (Dublin, 2011),
    pp 216, 267–75.
15 Paddy Devlin, *Straight Left: An Autobiography* (Belfast, 1993), pp 133–4;
    Aaron Edwards, *A History of the Northern Ireland Labour Party:
    Democratic Socialism and Sectarianism* (Manchester, 2009), pp 171,
    208–09. I am obliged to Douglas McIldoon, former general secretary of the
    NILP, for his recollections on the party during these years.

16 Boyd, *Have the Trade Unions Failed The North?*, p. 53.
17 Terry Cradden, 'The Tories and employment law in Northern Ireland: seeing unions in a different light?', *Industrial Relations Journal*, 24:1 (1993), pp 59–70.
18 Brian Tipping and Patricia McCorry, *Industrial Relations in Northern Ireland: The LRA Survey* (Belfast, 1988), p. 174; Boyd Black, 'Industrial relations under competition', *Review of Employment Topics*, 1 (1993), p. 28.
19 Black, 'Industrial relations under competition', p. 23.
20 Edwards, *A History of the Northern Ireland Labour Party*, pp 162–3; Robert Fisk, *The Point of No Return: The Strike Which Broke the British in Ulster* (London, 1975), pp 116–17.
21 Northern Ireland Information Service, 1979, cited in Liam O'Dowd, Bill Rolston, and Mike Tomlinson, *Northern Ireland: Between Civil Rights and Civil War* (London, 1980), p. 69.
22 Paddy Devlin, *The Fall of the NI Executive* (Belfast, 1975), pp 74–7; Devlin, *Straight Left*, p. 173; Boyd, *Have the Trade Unions Failed the North?*, p. 76; Fisk, *The Point of No Return*, pp 116–17.
23 Boyd, *Have the Trade Unions Failed the North?*, pp 75–8.
24 ICTU, *Political Policy in Northern Ireland* (Dublin, 1972), p. 1.
25 Public Record Office of Northern Ireland, UTAOU, COM 76/30; Cabinet minutes, 17 Nov. 1943, CAB 4/563/3; Terence Gerard Cradden, 'Trade unionism and socialism in Northern Ireland, 1939–53' (PhD, Queen's University, Belfast, 1988), pp 154, 210, 432–3; D.W. Bleakley, 'The Northern Ireland trade union movement', *Journal of the Statistical and Social Inquiry Society of Ireland* (1954), p. 160.
26 Terry Cradden, 'Billy Blease: from McClure Street to the House of Lords', *Saothar*, 19 (1994), pp 153–4; for the strike see Fisk, *The Point of No Return*, and Don Anderson, *Fourteen May Days: The Inside Story of the Loyalist Strike of 1974* (Dublin, 1994).
27 Barry Desmond, *Finally and in Conclusion: A Political memoir* (Dublin, 2000), p. 136; Francis Devine, *Organising History: A Centenary of SIPTU, 1909–2009* (Dublin, 2009), pp 517–18.
28 Michael Gallagher, *The Irish Labour Party in Transition, 1957–82* (Manchester, 1982), pp 138–9.
29 *Irish Times*, 4 Dec. 1972; ICTU, *Report*, 1975, pp 626–7.
30 Boyd, *Have the Trade Unions Failed the North?*, pp 79–82.
31 Paddy Logue, *Them and Us: A Socialist Response to 'Work is the Key'* (Dublin, 1994), pp 91–2.
32 Merrigan, *Eagle or Cuckoo?*, pp 236–8.
33 O'Dowd, Rolston, and Tomlinson, *Northern Ireland*, pp 82–3.
34 Vincent McCormack and Inez McCormack, ' "Equalizing advantages: lessening discrimination": reviewing Northern Ireland's fair employment laws', *Review of Employment Topics*, 2 (1994), p. 43.
35 Merrigan, *Eagle or Cuckoo?*, pp 250–51; Terry Cradden, 'Trade unionism, social justice, and religious discrimination in Northern Ireland', *Industrial and Labor Relations Review*, 46:3 (1993), p. 486.
36 Trade Unionists for Irish Unity and Independence, *Opposing Discrimination in Northern Ireland* (Dublin, 1988).
37 Cradden, 'Trade unionism, social justice, and religious discrimination in Northern Ireland', pp 480–96.

38 Terry Cradden, 'The trade union movement in Northern Ireland', in Donal Nevin (ed.), *Trade Union Century* (Cork, 1994), pp 66–84.

39 Michael Collins, *Buses Under Fire: Northern Ireland's Buses in the Troubles* (Newtownards, 2006), pp 100–03.

CHAPTER 2

1 www.legislation.gov.uk/apni/1967/37/contents, accessed 30 July 2018.

2 Incidentally, as Emmet Larkin also notes above (Introduction), the GMB holds the dubious honour of being the first union in Northern Ireland to have an award made against it for religious discrimination arising out of its failure to take on a Catholic who would have broken the Protestant monopoly in its local staff.

CHAPTER 4

1 See Merrigan, *Eagle or Cuckoo?*, pp 136–8.

2 Quango – a quasi-autonomous non-governmental organisation.

CHAPTER 6

1 There is some variance in the time given for the explosion at Oxford Street Bus Station, for example, the BBC say 3:02pm (www.bbc.co.uk/history/events/bloody_friday_belfast), whereas a Northern Ireland Office newssheet from the time gives it as 2:48pm (http://cain.ulst.ac.uk/events/bfriday/nio/nio72.htm).

2 McKitterick, Kelters, Feeney, Thornton and McVea (eds), *Lost Lives: The stories of the men, women and children who died as a result of the Northern Ireland Troubles* (Edinburgh, 1999), p. 232.

3 *Lost Lives*, p. 232.

4 Ibid.

5 Ibid.

6 Ibid., pp 229–31. In *Lost Lives* Jackie is referred to as Robert Gibson. His son, also called Robert, said of the attack: 'I would quote the American playwright who said there is no flag large enough to cover the shame of killing innocent people. It doesn't matter what the flag is, it was a shameful act.', www.bbc.co.uk/history/events/bloody_friday_belfast, accessed 21 Sep. 2018.

7 Ibid., p. 232.

8 *Lost Lives*, pp 84–5; see also http://cain.ulst.ac.uk/sutton/chron/1971.html, accessed 1 Oct. 2018.

9 Judgement of the Supreme Court given on 8 Feb. 2017, www.supremecourt.uk/cases/docs/uksc-2014-0180-judgment.pdf, accessed 21 Sep. 2018.

10 *Lost Lives*, p. 260.

11 Ibid., p. 142, see also *Daily Mirror*, Wed. 17 May 1972.

12 *Lost Lives*, p. 336.

13 A money order by which social security payments were made at that time to those entitled to them.

14 See Devlin, *Straight Left*.

15 *Lost Lives*, pp 446–59.

CHAPTER 7

1 Ibid., pp 532–3.
2 Ibid., p. 533.
3 Ibid., pp 720–21.
4 Martin Dillon, *God and the Gun: the Church and Irish Terrorism*, (London, 1997), p. 28.

CHAPTER 8

1 *Buses Under Fire: Northern Ireland's Buses in the Troubles* by Michael Collins (Newtownards, 2006).
2 Interview with Werner Heubeck by Ruth Graham, 2 Jan. 2002.
3 Ibid.

CHAPTER 9

1 Mike Morrissey lectured in the Department of Social Administration and Policy in the University of Ulster, Jordanstown.
2 Letter from Prof. D.S. Greer, Faculty of Law, Queen's University Belfast, 9 July 1985.

CHAPTER 10

1 Case no. 1/85FTC, heard on 21 Aug. 1985, decision on 23 Sep. 1985.
2 *Industrial Tribunals in Northern Ireland: a Practical Guide* by Phyllis Bateson and John McKee (Belfast, 1981).
3 (1980) ICR 513 (1980) IRLR 459.
4 www.uniset.ca/other/cs4/19781WLR231.html, accessed 30 July 2018.
5 www.legislation.gov.uk/nisi/1976/2147/pdfs/uksi_19762147_en.pdf, accessed 30 July 2018.
6 Case no. 1605/87SD, heard 22/23 Sep. 1988, decision 01 Nov. 1988.
7 Dornan v Belfast City Council (9 March 1990) EOR31A, www.xperthr.co.uk/law-reports/prima-facie-case-shifts-evidential-burden-to-employer/65146/, accessed on 1 Oct. 2018.
8 'The Discreet Charm of the Bourgeoisie', the title of a 1972 film directed by Luis Buñuel and written by Jean-Claude Carrière.
9 *Hansard*, NI Assembly, AQW 240/07, http://aims.niassembly.gov.uk/questions/printquestionsummary.aspx?docid=3 024, accessed 28 June 2018.
10 *Sunday Life*, 10 Dec. 2016.
11 Ibid.
12 Minister for Regional Development, 14 May 2007–04 May 2011, http://aims.niassembly.gov.uk/mlas/details.aspx?&aff=11729&per=80&cid=7, accessed 30 July 2018.
13 https://assets.publishing.service.gov.uk/government/uploads/system/uploads/attachment_data/file/336840/1stInquiry_Summary.pdf, accessed 30 July 2018.
14 www.irishtimes.com/news/award-for-sexual-discrimination-1.151662, accessed 1 Oct. 2018.

CHAPTER 11

1 Case No. 1/85 FTC, heard 21 Aug. 1985, decision 23 Sep. 1985.
2 It has not been possible to date the event exactly. The individual who died was possibly William Burns, prison officer, 30 December 1980, *Lost Lives*, p. 844; or William McConnell, assistant governor, 6 March 1984, ibid., p. 979.

CHAPTER 12

1 Spread-over payments were payments which recognised that bus drivers'
   working day could consist of two periods of work separated by several hours
   in which they would not be needed to drive buses but they would not be
   entirely free to do exactly what they pleased.
2 'Proposed Transfer of Ulsterbus Staff to NILGOS', dated 17 Feb. 1984.
3 Ibid.
4 Information drawn from *Buses Under Fire*, pp 165–79.
5 Ibid.

CHAPTER 13

1 http://archive.commercialmotor.com/article/12th-january-1989/24/power-to-
   the, accessed 17 July 2018.
2 For example see: https://hansard.parliament.uk/Commons/1989-06-
   08/debates/80cc73ce-e6fb-4f51-a81b-263cda298a0a/Buses?highlight=merger
   s%20monopolies%20ulsterbus#contribution-edff7cc5-0260-436c-b6f0-
   e59f8a4228ec, accessed 01 Oct. 2018.

CHAPTER 14

1 This was a resolution of the Northern Ireland House of Commons that
   applied to government contracts and required any contractor applying for a
   government contract to 'pay rates of wages and observe hours and
   conditions of labour not less favourable than those established for the trade
   or industry where the work is carried out'.
2 www.britannica.com/biography/Josephine-Clara-Goldmark, accessed
   18 July 2019.
3 The Crombie Code was not law but was used in regulations regarding
   redundancies in the public sector. Compensation payments under the
   Crombie Code are more generous than normal redundancy payments.
   For example see 'Statutory compensation for redundancy (Crombie code):
   compilation of a general code of …', TNA, T 48/621
   (https://discovery.nationalarchives.gov.uk/details/r/C10777006); also
   Superannuation (Northern Ireland) Order 1973, *Hansard*, HL debate, 3 May
   1973, vol. 342, (cols 222–3), https://api.parliament.uk/historic-
   hansard/lords/1973/may/03/superannuation-northern-ireland-order;
   Grant-Aided Colleges (Scotland), *Hansard*, HC debate, 20 Oct, 1981,
   vol. 10, (cols 274–5), https://api.parliament.uk/historic-
   hansard/commons/1981/oct/20/grant-aided-colleges-scotland#S6CV0010P0_
   19811020_HOC_465; and
   www.margaretthatcher.org/PREM19/1984/PREM19-1322.pdf.
4 https://www.industrialcourt.gov.uk/.
5 Obituary in www.telegraph.co.uk/news/obituaries/1372511/Lord-
   McConnell.html, accessed 17 July 2018.
6 From here on the quotations in chapters 14 and 15 are taken from the
   typescript of the hearings of the Industrial Court as taken from the
   shorthand notes of Miss M.I. Ferguson.
7 Section 44 – (1) The salaries, wages or other remuneration paid by the
   holder of a road service licence or an operator's licence to any person
   employed by him in connection with the use of motor vehicles to carry
   passengers or goods for reward, and the conditions of the employment of
   that person, shall –

(a) be in accordance with any decision for the time being in force of a joint industrial council or similar body representing a substantial number of the holders of road service licences or, as the case may be, operators' licences and of the persons employed by them in connection with the use of motor vehicles to carry passengers or goods for reward, being a decision relating to the remuneration and conditions of employment of a person so employed in the same capacity by the holder of a road service licence or, as the case may be, an operator's licence;

(b) where there is not in force a decision of the kind referred to in paragraph (a), not less favourable to that person than the remuneration which would be payable, and the conditions which would have to be observed, by a contractor complying with the requirements of any resolution passed by the House of Commons for the time being in force and applicable to contracts with departments of the Government of Northern Ireland.

(2) Any holder of a road service licence or an operator's licence, or any person employed by the holder of such a licence in connection with the use of motor vehicles to carry passengers or goods for reward, or any organisation representative of holders of such licences or of the persons so employed by them, may make representations to the Ministry to the effect that the remuneration paid to, or the conditions of employment of any person so employed by any such holder are not in accordance with the requirements of subsection (1), and if the matter in dispute is not otherwise disposed of the Ministry of Health and Social Services shall refer it to the Industrial Court for Settlement.

CHAPTER 17

1 Under Article 5 of the Transport Order (NI) 1977 pensioners were able to obtain half-price fares. Free travel for over 65-year-olds only came in 2001 and for over 60-year-olds in 2008.

2 Letter from Translink to Thomas Boyle, 18 Sep. 2003.

3 'Concessionary Fares – expenditure and usage statistics 2016/17', Department of Infrastructure, 11 Aug. 2017.

CHAPTER 18

1 The NITHC was established under Section 47 of the Transport Act (Northern Ireland) 1967. Under this legislation the NITHC shall consist of a chairman and not more than eight other directors all of whom shall be members thereof and shall be appointed by the Minister.

The chairman and other directors of the Holding Company shall be appointed from among persons who appear to the Minister to have had wide experience of, and to have shown capacity in, transport, industrial, commercial or financial matters or to have other adequate or suitable experience, and the Minister in appointing them shall have regard to the desirability of including among them persons who are directors of, or concerned in the management of, the subsidiaries of the Holding Company.

2 These are the Regulations that relate to the period:

The Local Government (Superannuation) Regulations (Northern Ireland) 1962.

The Local Government (Superannuation) Regulations (Northern Ireland) 1981.

The Local Government (Superannuation) Regulations (Northern Ireland) 1992.

The Local Government (Superannuation) Regulations (Northern Ireland) 2000.

3 Letter from NILGOS to Translink dated 22 Dec. 1998 in reply to a letter from Translink dated 16 Dec. 1998.
4 Letter from NILGOS to Eugene O'Callaghan, 4 Jan. 2006.
5 Letter from Translink to NILGOS dated 14 Oct. 2002 outlining new arrangements.
6 Signed affidavit by Norman Campbell to the High Court 2005, no. 23713, dated 5 June 2008.
7 NILGOS, although a highly professional organisation, was by no means infallible. In response to a letter from me seeking disclosure of information NILGOS revealed that it had placed $6.6m in Lehman Brothers immediately prior to that company being declared bankrupt, none of which would be recovered. Letter from NILGOS dated 11 Feb. 2014.
8 Letter to Eugene McGlone, copied to Eugene O'Callaghan by the union's solicitors dated 16 June 2006.

CHAPTER 19

1 Signed affidavit by Norman Campbell, 2005, no. 23713, dated 5 June 2008.
2 Signed affidavit by Liam Hughes, 2005, no. 23713. The affidavits have the same reference number.
3 Ibid.
4 Actuary report forwarded by Tom Boyle's solicitors, 7 Mar. 2005, ref: CMC/MBT/103058.
5 Letter to Eugene O'Callaghan dated 9 Nov. 2006, ref. AM/GDCK/Boyle.
6 Letter to Eugene O'Callaghan dated 5 Nov. 2010, ref. AK/SD/100619. Copied to the Regional Secretary, Unite the Union.
7 Letter from Eugene O'Callaghan dated 12 Oct. 2012, copied to Unite officers.
8 Letter dated 13 June 2017 from Unite the Union to the Northern Ireland Certification Office.
9 Letter from the union's solicitors dated 15 Mar. 2013, ref. AK/CMCG/ Bleeks & ors.
10 Ibid.

CHAPTER 20

1 See: www.rte.ie/news/2013/0425/385516-waterford-crystal/ and www.irishtimes.com/news/crime-and-law/court-rules-in-favour-of-waterford-crystal-workers-1.1372378, accessed 20 Dec. 2018.
2 Judgement R. v Rollins [appellant], 2010 UKSC 39.
3 Letter from Minister for Regional Development to Eugene O'Callaghan, dated 20 May 2013, ref. DRD/COR/520/2013.
4 Ibid., dated 29 July 2013, ref. DRD/COR/797/2013.
5 Email to Margaret Callaghan dated 2 June 2014.
6 Letter from the Assistant Certification Officer to Eugene O'Callaghan, 25 July 2017.

INDEX